The Girl
in the
Green Sweater

Praise for *The Girl in the Green Sweater*

"[A] gripping memoir. Lively prose deftly describes the smell, the pitch dark, the cold, the rats, and the harrowing fear of being discovered by Nazis. Through it all, Ignacy Chiger's ever-present sense of humor kept his family strong. Captures both tragic events and beautiful images that continue to haunt the author after more than sixty years."

—*Kirkus Reviews*

"This often unimaginable survival story should not be missed."

—*Port Washington News* (Port Washington, New York)

"*The Girl in the Green Sweater* is a haunting survival story you will not soon forget. Krystyna Chiger's memoir about her harrowing childhood in Lvov, Poland, during the Holocaust is a straightforward account of her family's witness to the incredible sadism, suffering, and cruelty heaped upon the Jews of Lvov under the Russians and then Hitler. Throughout Chiger's story, time and again, we are vividly reminded that we humans—even as very young and frightened children—are capable of enduring, and surviving, much, much more than we know."

—Karen Tintori, author of *Unto the Daughters: The Legacy of an Honor Killing in a Sicilian-American Family* and *Trapped: The 1909 Cherry Mine Disaster*

"Krystyna Chiger provides keen insight into her escape as a child from the Lvov ghetto, and her family's breathtaking survival for over a year   *e Girl in*
the Green S   parents,

who kept their family intact and able to survive the unimaginable. An important addition to Holocaust literature that vividly describes a harrowing childhood faced with enormous strength and courage."

—Michael Bart, author of *Until Our Last Breath: A Holocaust Story of Love and Partisan Resistance*

"Despite the substantial number of Holocaust memoirs that have been published, *The Girl in the Green Sweater* manages to touch us in an unexpected way, revealing highs and lows in man's capacity for evil, as well his capacity to love life and other human beings. Through the eyes of the child that Krystyna Chiger was in Lvov, Poland, in 1939 we see the whole moral universe."

—Naomi Ragen, author of *The Saturday Wife* and *The Covenant*

"Told from a precocious child's point of view, Chiger chronicles long, dark hours spent in silence with her younger brother, Pawel. Chiger's seven-year-old cypher possesses a self-awareness that springs from her inner and outer turmoil, capturing well the despair and terror of a life in hiding. With a powerful story and a keen voice, Chiger's Holocaust survivor's tale is a worthy and memorable addition to the canon." —*Publishers Weekly*

The Girl
in the
Green Sweater

A Life in
Holocaust's Shadow

KRYSTYNA CHIGER

with Daniel Paisner

ST. MARTIN'S GRIFFIN
New York

HOUNSLOW LIBRARIES

HOU

C0000 002 465 607

Askews	18-Nov-2009
940.5318	£10.99

by Kristine Keren. All rights reserved. Printed in the United States of America.

For information, address St. Martin's Press, 175 Fifth Avenue, New York, N.Y. 10010.

www.stmartins.com

Design by Kathryn Parise

The Library of Congress has catalogued the hardcover edition as follows:

Chiger, Krystyna, 1935–

The girl in the green sweater : a life in Holocaust's shadow / Krystyna Chiger with Daniel Paisner.—1st ed.

p. cm.

ISBN 978-0-312-37656-7

1. Chiger, Krystyna, 1935– 2. Jews—Ukraine—L'viv—Biography. 3. Holocaust, Jewish (1939–1945)—Ukraine—L'viv—Personal narratives. 4. Jewish children in the Holocaust—Ukraine—L'viv—Biography. 5. L'viv (Ukraine)—Biography. I. Paisner, Daniel. II. Title.

DS135.U43C533 2008

940.53'18092—dc22

[B] 2008022521

ISBN 978-0-312-37657-4 (trade paperback)

First St. Martin's Griffin Edition: October 2009

10 9 8 7 6 5 4 3 2 1

This book is dedicated to my parents, Paulina and Ignacy Chiger . . .
may their memories be for a blessing. . . .

Contents

Acknowledgments

It is not an easy thing, to tell the story of a difficult life. I have been fortunate to have many talented professionals help me to tell mine. At St. Martin's Press, Nichole Argyres has been a very thorough, very talented, and very enthusiastic editor. Her assistant, Kylah McNeill, has also been very helpful. I appreciate all of their assistance and their many kindnesses, and that of their many fine colleagues at the publishing house. Most of all, I am grateful that they have chosen to help me share my story.

I would also like to thank John Silbersack, my literary agent at Trident Media Group, for believing in this project and strongly supporting it.

Also, I am extremely grateful to my collaborator, Dan Paisner, for his passion, his patience, and his understanding. We spent many long hours together working on this book, going over some very emotional, very painful material, and his encouragement was very important. I do not think I could have told this story so well without his help.

Together, Dan and I would like to thank Rabbi Lee Friedlander, of the Reconstructionist Synagogue of the North Shore in Plandome, New York, for his careful reading of the manuscript and his many insightful comments.

Personally, I am grateful to my family—to my husband, Marian, for his constant love and support, as well as to our children, Doron and Roger, and their spouses, Michele and Jennifer, for their incredible encouragement. I also wish to thank my two grandsons, Jonathan and Daniel, for their genuine interest in my childhood stories, and for asking endless questions and waiting for answers which to them seemed always unbelievable. It is through the telling and retelling of my family's struggle that I have been able to keep these memories alive. This is important. In many ways, it is because of my grandchildren that I was moved to write this book. I am the last survivor of our group of survivors and I recognize that it is my responsibility to tell what happened. If I do not tell it, who will? If I do not remember it, who will? If the stories of our time in the sewer leave this earth untold it will be easier for future generations to suggest that the Holocaust is a myth, that it never happened.

Thank you as well to my many friends who supported me in this very emotional and difficult task. They, too, helped me to nurture these unhappy memories over the years, by asking me to share them, and recognizing that there were times when I could not.

I also want to acknowledge the caring people at the United States Holocaust Memorial Museum in Washington, D.C., for their deep interest in my family's story of survival, and for taking such extreme good care of my precious green sweater that survived together with me for fourteen months in such horrible conditions. In addition, I am very grateful to the curators at the Imperial War Museum in London for permanently exhibiting my family's story there. Thank you as well to the individuals at the Shoah Foundation, under the leadership of Steven Spielberg, for their tireless efforts in establishing a living, breathing visual and audio library of Holocaust survival stories; I am honored that my family's story is included in this important archive, and that it is being made available for teaching programs around the world.

Lastly, I am especially grateful to Dr. Mordecai Paldiel of the Yad Vashem Museum in Jerusalem, for his essential research, and for his role in sharing my story with future generations.

Who has inflicted this upon us? Who has made us Jews different from all other people? Who has allowed us to suffer so terribly up till now? It is God that has made us as we are, but it will be God, too, who will raise us up again. If we bear all this suffering and if there are still Jews left, when it is over, then Jews, instead of being doomed, will be held up as an example.

—Anne Frank

In the beginning, God created Heaven and Earth. He settled in Heaven and assigned the Earth to the people. And on the Earth, this happened. . . .

—Ignacy Chiger, from the introduction to
his unpublished memoir, *World in Gloom*

The Girl
in the
Green Sweater

Introduction

YES, I REMEMBER

I T IS A FUNNY THING, MEMORY. It is a trick we play on ourselves, to keep connected to who we were, what we thought, how we lived. It is fractured, like a dream that returns in bits and pieces. It is the answer to forgetting.

I remember—the bits and pieces and the entire cloth. My father used to tell me I had a mind like a trap. "Krzysha will know," he would say. "Krzysha remembers." He called me Krzysha. Everyone else called me Krysha, and the difference was everything.

Yes, I remember. If I saw something, heard something, experienced something, I put it away for later, someplace where I could reach for it and call it back to mind. It was all filed away, the stories of my life bundled for safekeeping. Even now, when most of the people I remember are gone, they are here for me like they never left. Like what happened so many years ago happened yesterday instead.

My memories come to me in Polish. I think in Polish, dream in Polish, remember in Polish. Then it passes through Hebrew and somehow comes out in English. I do not know how this works, but this is how it is. Sometimes it has to go through German and Yiddish before I am able to tell it or understand it. All these thoughts. All these moments. All these sights and sounds and smells—tiny, fractured pieces, fighting for my attention, calling me to make sense of the whole. My memories of my family's struggle during the Second World War are the memories of a child, reinforced over a lifetime. They are my memories first, and then on top I have put my father's memory, and my mother's, and even my baby brother's. To these I have added the reflections of others who shared our ordeal, along with the histories I have read. I might have been only a child, but what I saw, what I heard, what I experienced, has been reconsidered many, many times, and it is the accumulation of memories that now survive.

Yes, I remember what it was like to be a small girl in Lvov, a vibrant city of six hundred thousand. People called it "Little Vienna." It was a city of winding cobblestone streets that reached to majestic churches and open courtyards bursting with colorful flowers and lovely fountains. It was mostly Polish, with a great many Jews and Ukrainians as well—one hundred and fifty thousand Jews in all before the war. It was the place of my growing up, a childhood of privilege and hope cut short by ignorance and intolerance. It was where our lives were transformed, first by the Soviet occupation that threatened our freedom and later by the German occupation that threatened our lives. It was where everything went from sweetness and light to desperation and darkness.

I remember our French pinscher, Pushek, his coat the color and feel of soft snow. We called him Pushek because he was soft, like a goose with down feathers. My father brought him home the day my younger brother, Pawel, was born, and he was a special gift. He was with us for two years, all through the Soviet occupation, but when the Germans came we had to give him up. We could not have his barking give us away. My mother brought him to stay with a woman who lived just beyond the city. She did this without telling me, because she knew it would make me cry. It was my first real loss of the war, and of course I cried. Two days later, we heard a scratching on our door. It was Pushek! He came back! All the way from the edge of town, maybe five miles, but that only meant we had to return him to the woman and that I would cry all over again.

I remember our piano, an August Förster, and the German officer who claimed it for himself. His name was Wepke, and he came to our apartment to pick what he wanted from our few remaining nice things. This was how it was, all over Lvov, all over Europe. The fine things of the Jewish people became like a flea market for the German officials, the SS and Gestapo. They picked clean our leavings before we could even leave them behind. This officer Wepke sat down to play our piano, went over the keyboard, rubbed his hands over the fine wood casing, announced that it was one of the finest instruments he had ever seen. I imagine it was. He played beautifully, like a maestro.

I remember hiding in a crawl space beneath our window ledge. Sometimes it was the Germans who came looking for us. Sometimes it was the Ukrainians, who in many ways were worse. My father was handy with tools, and he made us elaborate hiding places, behind false walls, in the backs of closets, where my brother and I would go while my father was at work and my mother was sewing uniforms for the German army at the Janowska labor camp on the hill overlooking town. My father built a false front beneath our window and closed my brother and me inside, sitting on potties for when we had to go. There was no room to move and hardly enough air to breathe. All day long, I worried what would happen if my father did not come home, if he was taken off the streets like so many other Jews. If my mother was shot on the long march down Janowska Road. Who would free us from our special hiding place? Who would even know we were there?

I remember huddling with my family and some men we did not yet know in the basement of one of the ghetto barracks, when a round-faced Polish sewer worker named Leopold Socha agreed to look after us in the underground tunnels and pipes beneath Lvov, to help us find a place to hide, to bring us food and supplies. Poldju, as my father would call him, was a reformed thief and an observant Catholic who believed that in protecting us from the Nazis, he would find redemption. He was kind and generous, with a bright, wide smile that seemed to light our dismal barracks. He saw our salvation as his salvation, but it was also an opportunity.

I remember the simple green sweater my grandmother knitted for me when we still lived in our grand apartment at Kopernika 12. My father's mother. His parents were divorced, his father remarried, but this was my natural grandmother. Always, she liked to knit for me, only I was not always such a good girl. I liked to disturb her knitting. I would take a spool of wool and run with it and hide. Or I would take out the last rows, where she kept her place with the needles. And yet somehow she managed to make me some nice things, despite my mischief. She made nice things for everyone in the family. It gave her great pleasure. This sweater was my favorite. It had a delicate lace neckline. After she was taken in one of the actions, it was even more precious. I wore it constantly. When I put it on, it felt as if I were wearing one of her warm hugs. That I managed to keep the sweater all during the war was just another of the small miracles that found me and my family—and that it stands now on permanent exhibit at the United States Holocaust Memorial Museum in Washington, D.C., is a tribute to the struggles of all Jewish children during the war, as well as to the child I used to be.

I remember the night of the final liquidation, the last action. It was May 30, 1943. Already, more than one hundred thousand of the Jews of Lvov had been transported to concentration camps or killed. I remember the sounds of the commotion and chaos, the shouting and the confusion. I remember the sheer black terror. Around midnight, the Germans started pulling people from their ghetto barracks and herding them onto the trucks that would take them to the Janowska camp or to the Piaski, the sand pits north and west of the city where Jews were lined up and killed. There was our group of a dozen or so, desperate to avoid capture, scrambling to fit through the hole my father and the other men had painstakingly dug. Another few dozen were so desperate to escape, they entered the sewers through manholes on the street. Together, we spilled into the sewer, hoping to find sanctuary among the rats and the filth.

I remember the small, dank cavern where we sat for our first three days underground. It was miserable. There were spiderwebs so thick that they could slow the rats that seemed to occupy this space in droves. Hundreds and hundreds of them. Thousands, probably. We would get used to the rats, and they would get used to us, but we were not so used to one another just yet. The walls were slick with the sludge and dampness of the sewer. Tiny yellow worms covered every surface. The smell was fetid and dank and awful. There was mud and small puddles of wastewater at our feet. The only place to sit was on the wet ground or on two large, misshapen stones.

I remember the dysentery we all suffered those first weeks underground. My brother and I suffered most of all. The constant diarrhea, the nausea, the disorientation. My mother had the idea that if we did our sickness off to the side, we would somehow keep our hiding place more sanitary. It was as though we had to fool ourselves into believing we were still human.

I remember how each day one of the men crawled nearly two kilometers through a maze of small pipes, some only forty centimeters wide, the handle of a kettle clenched between his teeth to collect drinking water from a fountain dripping from the street above. The kettle filled, he would retreat backward, because there was not enough room in the pipe to turn around, and in this way we would each receive three-quarters of a glass of water each day. My parents did not drink their share and gave it to us children instead because we were so sick, but they were sick, too.

I remember, some weeks in, a disagreeable man in our group became so enraged at my brother's crying that he threatened to shoot him. His name was Weiss, and he thought he was in charge. He got it in his head that my brother's crying could be heard on the street above.

I remember the *slosh, slosh, slosh* of Socha's boots as he trudged through the water on his way to our hideaway each morning. The echo of the pipes told us he was coming, along with his coworker Stefek Wroblewski. The sloshing meant we would soon have a piece of bread or some news about the fighting.

I remember the dull cries of the baby born to a young woman

some months into our underground odyssey, a woman whose husband had abandoned her after just a few weeks in the sewer and who kept her pregnancy secret from the others. A woman who had already given her infant daughter to a Ukrainian woman during the early days of the German occupation, hoping this would keep the child safe.

I remember these things and so much more. The fire that almost suffocated us. The flood after the spring thaw that almost drowned us. The times we were nearly discovered. The prisoner who joined our group in the last days of our confinement. There are good memories, too. The satires my father would write for us to perform, to keep our minds from our situation. The joking and the laughter. The unshakable bond that developed among the few of us who made it to our final hideaway, a place my mother called "the Palace" because there was room for me and my brother to stand, room for us to cook, room for us to bathe once each week. There was not a lot of room, of course, but room enough. Most of all, there was the affection we all came to feel for Leopold Socha, who continued to look after us long after our money had run out and we could no longer pay him.

I remember hearing the bombs of the Russian aircraft, when the front reached Lvov and the newspaper accounts we were by now receiving reported a coming end to the fighting. And still we worried that the bombs that would hopefully free us might kill us first instead, trapped as we were in our underground burrow, beneath the very streets that were the target of the bombing. Indeed, those final days were a mix of jubilation and terror, we were all so anxious about what would happen next.

I remember the day of our liberation, when Socha led us to a manhole opening and coaxed us up the iron ladder to a courtyard, where a crowd had gathered to greet us. After so much time underground, without a sliver of daylight, I could hardly see. I was wearing my precious green sweater, which must have looked like a rag. Probably we were all a sight! Our clothes were tattered, our bodies dirty and withered and broken. The day burned orange, like a photographic negative, and it would be a few days more before my eyes could adjust. It was like something out of science fiction.

I remember how we struggled after liberation, as my father looked for work, as we tried to find a home, and to build a life out of no life at all. All this time, we thought that if we simply outlasted the Germans, we would be okay, but it was not so easy. We had nothing. I remember going to school with shoes made from newspaper because we could not afford proper boots. I remember being told by school administrators that it might be better to pretend that I was not Jewish after all. I remember my mother baking latkes for my brother and me to sell on the street after the war, to earn extra money. I remember moving from Lvov to Krakow and eventually to Israel, where it sometimes seemed that every other person on the street had a number burned into his or her skin from some concentration camp or other, where almost every Jew had an unbelievable story of survival to match our own, where almost no one would speak a word of the Holocaust.

Yes, I remember. . . .

One

⤳

KOPERNIKA 12

L ike a princess. That is how I grew up, like a character from a storybook fable. At least, that is how I grew up for a while. I was born on October 28, 1935, at a time when Lvov was one of the most vibrant cities in Poland. It was a magical place, a Renaissance city, only it was not the best place to be a Jew. There were over 600,000 people in Lvov in the middle 1930s, including about 150,000 Jews.

We were Jewish, of course, but we were not terribly religious. We observed the Sabbath. My mother, Paulina Chiger, always lit the candles. We celebrated Passover. But we did not go to temple. On the High Holidays we would go, but the rest of the year we observed at home or not at all. We would light the *Yahrtzeit* candles on the anniversary of a death, but we would not always say the prayers. We were Jewish by tradition more than we were Jewish by faith, yet a strong sense of Jewish identity ran through our household. That came from my mother's side of the family. My father's side did not believe in God. They considered themselves Jewish, so they also had that strong identity, but it was more of a heritage than a religion. They were Socialists and Communists. They were more concerned with social justice. They would not be treated like second-class citizens. In their minds, I think, the thought that all people are created equal was a way to lift the Jews to level ground. You see, even before the war, the Jewish people in Lvov were sometimes made to suffer, usually at the hands of the Ukrainians. People today, they do not talk about this. Or they do not remember. But it was so. My father told me stories about how he used to walk through certain parts of the city and Ukrainian boys would lash at him with razor blades taped to long sticks, tearing at his clothes. He said it was like a game to these boys, taunting and intimidating the Jewish men who crossed their path. This was not the only discrimination my father experienced, yet it is the example that has stayed with me.

I did not know of such things as a small girl. All I knew was that we lived in a grand apartment and that I did not want for anything. I had fine clothes, wonderful toys. My maternal grandmother used to bring me souvenirs from Vienna, where she would go on buying trips for her textile business. She brought me a lovely silk robe, which I remember wearing constantly. I used to jump up and down on my parents' bed, wearing this robe. Jumping with me was my imaginary friend, Melek. This Melek, he was my constant companion. I talked to him. He answered me. Later, when we were in the sewer, he kept me company. I do not know how I came to invent this Melek, how he got his name. It was a nonsense name, Melek. It does not mean anything in Polish. It was just a name. Melek. Together we laughed and laughed, jumping on my parents' bed.

My grandmother also brought me beautiful dolls and a spectacular dollhouse, with a kitchen and furniture. I had the whole set, all the different rooms, all the proper pieces. Today, a dollhouse like that would cost thousands of dollars. It was my most prized possession, and I would lose myself in my imagined world of that dollhouse, inventing fantastic little lives for the people who lived there. The people who lived in my dollhouse were not Jewish or Christian, Polish or Ukrainian, Russian or Hungarian. They were just people, and they were happy with their nice things, their nice furniture, their nice families.

In my imagination, the dollhouse was on a charming street in Lvov, not far from our apartment at Kopernika 12, in the nicest part of the city. This was my reality corresponding to my fantasy. Our building on Kopernika Street is still there, and the street is much the same, but it is darker now, more dreary. It is different from the picture I have carried in my mind for so many years. The colors have all changed. The trees that line the street no longer appear to bloom. Or perhaps they do and I no longer see it. Maybe it is because I cannot look at the city the same way I did when I was a child, when it was filled with fine, happy things. Maybe it is because of everything that happened there, and how violently and suddenly everything was taken from my family, beginning with our apartment. We had four bedrooms, with a nice entry hall, a big dining room, a kitchen, two full bathrooms, and two entrances, one for the labor and one for our family and guests. There were wrought-iron gates opening out onto the street, balconies overlooking the street in front and the courtyard in back, and a vaulted ceiling on top of the interior stairwell, throwing light onto the entryways of each individual apartment.

Absolutely, it was like my special dollhouse, like a fantasy. To me it was like a palace, because I really did feel like a princess. I was an only child for a time, so there was no place else for my parents to lavish their attentions. Everything was made especially for me. I had a nanny, who wore a starched white uniform. We had a housekeeper, who wore a traditional maid's uniform. In our china cabinet, we had a Rosenthal service set for thirty-two, though I do not recall that we ever set our dining room table for thirty-two guests. Still, I believe the contrast of how we lived before the war with how we lived later is important. I do not mean to boast, but to compare. Certainly, we lived well. My mother used to take me for my clothes to a store called Mickey Mouse. It was just the name of the store. It had nothing to do with Walt Disney, but it was a fine clothing store, and I used to stand on a very high stool while a woman pinched here and there and took my measurements to make my clothes.

Like a princess, that is how it was for me. That was my life.

It is hard to imagine what happened to Lvov during the Russian occupation, and how it was torn apart during German rule, but the city I remember was beautiful. There were so many exciting things to do and see, so many wonderful things to eat, so many opportunities all around. It was such a shame to see how it deteriorated, first under the Russians and then under the Germans, because it had been a place of heart and hope and happiness. Even a child could notice the transformation. There was a park down the street from our building, and I used to go there almost every day when the weather was mild. My nanny would walk me there and sit on the bench while I played with my friends. Through the open windows, in summer, you could always hear laughter and singing. We would play in a little courtyard behind our building, until it was time to go inside for supper. In winter, after a fresh snow, the streets were quiet and still and beautiful, like a postcard.

Yes, I had a very good life, only I did not like my nanny very much. This was my one wrinkle. She was very strict. She never laughed. In my family, we were always laughing, always joking, so my time with my dour nanny was very serious. It was not a lot of fun. I remember that she tried to feed me constantly and that I did not want to eat, not with her. I kept the food in my cheeks and spat it out when I thought she was not looking. Perhaps I was just being rebellious, because I never gave my mother any trouble when it came to eating. Or our housekeeper. Her name was Marisha, and she used to say, "Mrs. Chiger, I do not know what it is. With the nanny, she does not want to eat at all. With you, she is finished in five minutes."

My parents owned a textile store called Gold Textiles on Boimow Street, one of the first Jewish streets in Lvov. Most of the merchants on the street were Jewish. There were apartments above the stores, and most of the people who lived there were Jewish, too, but everybody came to our store. Christian, Ukrainian, Russian . . . it did not matter. My parents had good customers from every background. It was a very successful store. My mother worked there full-time, which was unusual back then, but not so unusual for me. It was all I knew, so that was that. My grandmother, my mother's mother, she also worked full-time, so I did not think anything of it. My grandparents also worked as textile merchants, and my parents' store was like an extension of theirs.

A favorite outing with my nanny was to go to my parents' store and wait for my mother to finish her work. Oh, I loved to go to the store, with its wonderful textures and supplies and smells. Such a busy place! There were giant rolls of fabrics, and the people would come and my mother would take down the fabrics and show the customers the designs. She would spread out the material on a big table and run her hands over it, to smooth it down. Her movements were so crisp, so professional. It felt good to be among all those grown-ups, all those nice materials. I was proud of my mother, watching her work in such an important job, moving about in such an important way, helping the people to pick out their materials and to plan their alterations. Everyone was always so excited, coming to my parents' store, because out of that visit would come so many pleasant things like draperies for their home or a new dress for a special occasion. It was a place where people were preparing to be happy.

Some evenings, I would wait for my mother on the steps in front of the store. I can still remember one of my parents' regular customers passing me on her way inside and asking me what color I liked best. She called me by my name, Krysha. This was what everybody called me, except my father, who called me Krzysha. The first was a popular diminutive of my name, Krystyna, an intimacy; the second was especially so. In Polish, you can hear the difference. I answered that I liked yellow, and when she was through with her shopping the customer passed me once again on the steps out in front and handed me a small yellow swatch of material. It was just a little something I could maybe use for my dollhouse, a little something to make me smile.

In the summer, we vacationed in the Polish countryside. This was not so unusual among the Jewish families of Lvov. We rented a house with my aunt and her family. We stayed for two months each summer. My father went back to Lvov during the week, but my mother did not work the entire summer. It was a wonderful retreat. Everywhere you looked, there were yellow sunflowers. Acres and acres of brilliant yellow sunflowers. How I loved those flowers! I spent most of my time running up and down those fields, lost in my own fantasy world. I remember one day, I was asked to do some type of chore around the house, and I did not want to do it. The woman who was renting us the house scolded me and said, "If you do not listen, Baba Yaga will come and get you." Baba Yaga was like a witch, from a popular folk tale. This scared me, but still I did not listen. I neglected my chores and went outside to play. I was afraid, but I was also bold.

My father's name was Ignacy Chiger, and I do not think he enjoyed working at the store. It provided a very good living, and for this he was grateful, but if it had been up to him, he would have done something else. He was a very intelligent man, a very creative thinker. He had a PhD in philosophy and history. He could have been anything, but he attended school at a time when Jews were prohibited from certain occupations. This was the result of a government plan called *numerus clausus*, and it is proof that even before the Second World War, even before the Germans, life was very difficult for Polish Jews. My father would have been a doctor, but he could not study medicine. He could have gone to another country to study, but this was also difficult. It was even difficult for him to finish his studies in philosophy and history. No one would sit next to him in the lecture halls. He might never have gotten his degree were it not for a very good friend, who happened to be Ukrainian and who acted like a kind of bodyguard for my father, protecting him from the young Ukrainian hoodlums who would torment the young Jewish men. Once my father had completed his degree, starting his own business as an outgrowth of my grandparents' business seemed like the best option available to him, and he made a great success of it. The store provided my family with a comfortable living, even if it meant my father could not pursue a life of the mind. He would be a shopkeeper, a merchant, instead of a university professor, instead of a doctor, instead of a well-known writer, and he would continue to read and learn and consider new ideas in his own way. That was just fine with him, because he had a family to support. Nothing was more important.

All was right in our little corner of the world, in our little corner of Poland, until 1939. Early on in 1939, something wonderful happened, but after that something terrible happened, and the two events changed my world completely. The something wonderful was the birth of my baby brother, Pawel. We all called him Pinio. He was born on May 18, 1939. It was a church holiday, and my parents sent me out of the house with our housekeeper, Marisha, as a distraction. My mother was to give birth at home, and they did not want me in the apartment with all the excitement, so Marisha took me to the park and then to the church. She was not Jewish, of course. She wanted to see the service, but I kept tugging at her arm, wanting to go home, knowing on some level that she was keeping me from something. I did not know the first thing about babies and pregnancy, but I knew my parents' moods. I knew there was something they were not telling me. When we finally returned home, my father announced that he had a present for me, and I walked in to see my mother holding Pinio. Here is how he came to us, I thought: my mother placed several cubes of sugar on the carpet by the window, and the stork came and took the sugar and left my brother behind. For years, this was what I believed.

There was another present waiting for me that afternoon— a beautiful French pinscher we called Pushek. The name loses something in the translation, but it had to do with the goose-down feathers that call to mind a fresh snowfall. Our Pushek, he was so little and so white, like a snowball. He joined the two yellow canaries we kept in a cage in our living room to give us a regular menagerie. Now, between the baby and the animals, our apartment was a whirlwind of sounds and activity. So much joyful noise! My father had brought the dog home as a distraction for me, knowing my mother would be busy with the new baby. He did not know if I would be upset about this and thought he would delight me in what ways he could. He need not have bothered, though, because Pinio was delight enough, but now I had my two new playthings to keep me busy.

And then, on the morning of September 1, 1939, there came something terrible. My father took me to the window of our apartment and pointed out the German Messerschmitt planes flying overhead. He said, "Now this is the end." *To jest koniec.* He explained to me what was happening, how the Germans were at war, how they had already attacked the western part of Poland and were now on the outskirts of Lvov.

"My Krzysha," he said with melancholy, "this is the end."

I was confused. Not frightened so much, but confused. I had picked up bits and pieces of my parents' concern about the coming war, through conversations at supper or over the newspaper. I paid attention, because I liked to know what was going on, but of course I was only a child. I was not prepared to hear the bombs. It sounded as though they were being dropped right outside our window, although in truth most of the damage was on the other side of the city. Years later, I read about the famous German-Soviet nonaggression pact, which meant that the planes over the central part of the city were mostly for show, because Russian foreign minister

Vyacheslav Molotov and German foreign minister Joachim von Ribbentrop agreed that the German army would not advance directly into Lvov. Of course, we did not know this just then. All we knew was that we were under attack, so we hurried to the basement of our building, which we used as a bunker to wait out the bombing. I passed the time with the daughter of the concierge, who was about my age. Her name was Danusha, and she had beautiful blond hair. She lived on the first floor of the building, and when the bombing quieted I retreated with her family to their apartment to get something to eat. My mother stayed in the basement with my father and Pawel, while Danusha's mother made me eggs, sunny-side up. I had never eaten eggs prepared in this way, and I liked them very much. To me, at four years old, the discovery of these eggs was as big as the bombing. When I got back to the basement, I told my mother about the eggs, and from that day forward that is how she prepared my eggs, and every time I took a bite I thought back to the German invasion. That is a funny thing about the human brain, the way it can tie two sense memories together, for all time.

The bombing continued for several weeks, but after the first few days we moved to my grandparents' building, because their basement was bigger. I was not used to seeing the streets so empty. There was just my family and probably a few other families, hurrying for safety. I helped to push my brother in his carriage—one of those English prams with the big wheels. My mother carried a few things, and my father carried a few things, and we had placed a few things more inside the carriage with Pawel. After three or four days we were able to return to our Kopernika apartment, and on the way back I could hear my parents wondering how our lives might be different now that we were living under a different regime. I did not know what this meant, a different regime, but it did not sound good. Their worry became mine, even if I did not fully understand it.

Despite all the bombing, we did not see too much destruction on our way to and from my grandparents' apartment building. Most of the damage was in another part of the city, although I suppose it was possible that my mother steered us away from any streets with bombed-out buildings to keep me from being afraid. Such a noise, from all those bombs, for days and days, and I did not see evidence of it anywhere. It is possible that as a child I did not make the connection between the bombs and the devastation, but everything looked as it had always looked. I was only happy that the bombing had finally stopped. I listened to my parents talking and tried to imagine the changes they said were coming, because all around the streets looked much the same.

The quiet lasted only a few days more, because the Germans and the Russians decided to divide Poland. This of course created almost as much tension and confusion as the bombing. Hitler and the Germans were to occupy the west part of Poland, and Stalin and the Russians would occupy the eastern part, which included Lvov. All around, people were talking about which was better, to be under German rule or under Russian rule. Some people said it was better to be ruled by the Germans, because they were cultured, educated, refined. But they were also cruel and ruthless. My father, he was afraid of the Germans. Already, people knew what Hitler was doing to the Jews, and as a result many thousands of Polish Jews escaped to the eastern part of Poland. They could not live under German rule. They did not want to live under Russian rule, either, but they would take their chances. Very quickly, the Jewish population of Lvov grew to over two hundred thousand, because of all the Jewish refugees from western cities like Krakow and Lodz.

Of course, the Russians were not such a good choice, either, as we would come to know. The Communist ideal sounded wonderful in theory, but in practice it could also be cruel and ruthless. And harsh. No, they had not built concentration camps to exterminate the Jews, but they sent a great many people to Siberia, and a great many people died there, too. Jews, Christians . . . it did not matter to them. If you had money, if you owned a business, if you did not work, you were of no use to the Russians. And if you were of no use, they sent you away. That was the Russian way. They confiscated material possessions, moved people from their homes, kept people from pursuing the freedoms they had only recently enjoyed. There was no good choice, the people were saying, and yet among the Jews of Lvov there was the feeling that with the Russians we had been spared an even more terrible fate.

My father considered our situation with a sense of humor, which was how he and my mother tried to approach our ordeal. He called the Russians "our uninvited guests," because they had come to spoil our party. He wrote, "They call themselves our liberators, because they liberate us from everything."

The first change I noticed under the Soviets was that we no longer had a nanny or a housekeeper. We were now part of Communist Russia, and as Communists everyone was treated equally. We were all working class. We would all suffer, and struggle, and starve. These women would no longer work for my family in a subservient role. At first, I thought it meant that these women did not like our family or that they felt they had been mistreated. In any case, it meant that my mother could no longer work, because she now had to stay at home to take care of me and my brother. Actually, this was a welcome change for me. I liked having my mother around all day. She used to tell me stories at the kitchen table. She would make them up as she went along, but by the next day she would forget what she had told the day before. I would say, "What happened to the wolf?" Or, "What happened to the little girl?" I wanted to know what was going on, and she had already forgotten.

The other big change was that I started kindergarten that September, just after the bombing ended, during the transition to Russian rule. The school was two or three blocks from our apartment, and I did not want to go that first day. I cried when we arrived at the school, but my mother convinced me to stay. I held on to her for those first few hours, I could not bear to see her go, but eventually she did go, as did all of the other mothers. I can still picture the classroom, where I had to hang my coat, where the teacher was showing us the toys, the faces of all the other children. The next day it was a little bit easier. We developed a routine. My mother would walk me to school and my father would pick me up in the afternoon, except on one afternoon when my father could not make it, my mother picked me up instead. When my father came home later that evening, he was very upset. He walked in the door and I could see he had been crying. "That's it," he said, handing over the key to the store. "We've lost everything. This is all that is left."

His sense of humor was gone. I looked and looked, but I could not find his smile. My father had known this day would come, but now that it was here he was not prepared for it. On some level, yes; on some other level, no. I listened to him tell my mother what had happened. Some Russian officials had come in and had told him to turn everything over to them. Already, my father had seen other private business owners sent to Siberia, for the crime of being bourgeois, and if he had been thinking clearly, he would have counted himself lucky for merely being sent home. But he was not thinking clearly.

A few days before, the Russians had taken my grandparents' business. They had employed about fifteen people, and what was especially upsetting to my grandparents and to my father was the way these workers responded to the change in ownership. It showed how quickly the people could be brainwashed by the Russians, how Soviet propaganda could poison not only our way of life, but our relationships as well. By coincidence, my father was present when the Russian officials demanded control of my grandparents' business, and my father could not believe how these workers turned on my grandparents. They had all been very well treated, very well paid. They had all been to dinner in my grandparents' home. It was like a family. Yet when the business was taken from my grandparents, the workers seemed happy about it. When the Russian inspectors came in, they told everybody to put their hands up. All of the workers were searched. One of the workers, an educated woman, pointed to my father and said, "Why don't you search him?" For some reason, my father had been overlooked during the first inspection. He was frozen with fear, because he was carrying a gun. For some other reason, the Russian inspectors overlooked the woman's comment and failed to search my father a second time, and it was a lucky thing because if they had found the gun, they could have said my father was a spy and sent him to prison.

I did not know my father carried a gun, but he said he began doing so to protect himself from the Ukrainians. The Ukrainians had a deep-seated hatred for the Jews. The Russians simply hated the upper class. The one was bad enough without the other.

My parents had only a few workers in their store, and none of them turned on my mother or father the way my grandparents' employees turned on them. Almost all of the workers stayed on in my parents' store after it was requisitioned by the government, but my father was forced to look for another job, because in Communist Russia if you do not work, you are a drain on society. He got a job in a bakery that happened to be on the ground floor of our apartment building, which was very helpful when the Russians started to ration our food. There were long lines just to get a loaf of bread or some sugar, and my father used his job so we would not have to wait. Sometimes he would trade an extra loaf of bread for something else we might need. Quite often he would pinch an extra loaf for a friend or family member, as a kindness. Once, there was an extra shipment of sugar and eggs and other foods and supplies, and my father arranged to hide the overage in the apartment of the concierge, Galewski—Danusha's father. Because of this, the two men had something extra to sell or to trade. My father made only about 400 rubles per month at the bakery, which was not enough for us to live on, so he soon took another job. This second job paid about 300 rubles per month. Together, this was almost enough to get by, except we hardly ever saw my father. He was working fourteen hours a day.

In a matter of weeks, the Russians had reorganized all of eastern Poland. In Lvov, all private businesses were nationalized. It was amazing to my father how swiftly the Russian bureaucracy managed to move, how they were able to turn capitalist Poland into Communist Russia in just a few weeks. It was like a trick of black magic. Everything was run by the NKVD—the precursor to the KGB—and the Polish people were terrified of these agents. The Russians, too, lived in fear of the NKVD. They knew everything about us, tracked our coming and going, decided who would stay in the city and who would be sent away. One moment the merchants were running their stores and businesses; the next they were out on the street or in prison. Everybody had to work or risk being sent off to Siberia. You had to wait on long lines and meet with the Russian officials and discuss what kind of work you were qualified to do. My father was always afraid that my mother would be sent away, because she did not work. She had to stay at home to take care of two small children—a logical reason not to work, but the Russians did not always agree with logical reasoning.

As a little girl, however, I did not have any of these worries. Also, I did not mind any of these changes. Most of them I did not even notice. Of course, I did not like the tension in our family, the uncertainty that had crept into our lives, the unhappiness I could sometimes read on my mother's face, but all I really cared about was that I had my mother with me most of the time. I had my imaginary friend, Melek, for company. I had my baby brother and my beautiful French pinscher.

From time to time, when his work schedule allowed, my father would meet me at school and walk me home. Once, he came to pick me up, and I suggested we take a different route back to our apartment. "It will be shorter," I said. My father smiled. He liked that I had figured out a shortcut. He said that this was the problem under Russian rule. Everybody does as they are told. Nobody thinks for themselves. Nobody considers a better way.

Outside of school, I spent most of my time with my mother and brother. My mother would take us on long walks. There was a beautiful park up in the hills just outside of town, and we used to hike there. Wysoki Zamek, this place was called. *High Castle.* From these hills, you could see all the way into town. My aunt would join us, with her children. You would not know we were living in a city in turmoil, on a continent at war, to look at us cousins romping and playing on those hillside trails. I was happy. I ran around with my cousins, smiling and laughing.

It was during the Russian occupation that my mother took me to see my first movie, *Snow White and the Seven Dwarfs.* There was a movie theater not far from our apartment, and it was a special outing, just the two of us. I can still remember looking up at the screen, with all those bright colors, all those cheerful songs, marveling at this new type of storytelling. I had never heard of such a thing as moving pictures, but there it was, and as I watched I never once thought about the tension or uncertainty I could sense at home and all around. For me, from the narrow point of view of a child, this was a happy time.

Sometimes we would go with my mother to visit my father for dinner. We did not see him much, because of the two jobs (sometimes three). He worked in the afternoon and evening at a health club across town. He had always been a strong athlete—he was a volleyball player and a soccer player—and had somehow managed to secure a position at the club. This was considered an important job to the Russians, who placed special emphasis on fitness and physical activity. The health club was a large facility, like a YMCA, with a gymnasium and a swimming pool, although maybe it only appeared so big to me because I was so little. I think I had a chance to go swimming there on just one occasion. It was difficult, with my baby brother, to make the arrangements. Usually, we had only a short visit with my father while he ate a hot meal my mother prepared at home, and then we collected the dirty dishes and walked back to our apartment.

Probably the first I noticed the Russian occupation was when we had to share our apartment. Our landlord had been sent away, but we were allowed to continue living in our grand apartment at Kopernika 12. For some weeks, we stayed on in the apartment with our routines relatively unchanged, except for my father's busy work schedule and reduced income. But then it was announced that the rationing by the Soviets would extend to our living quarters. They set a limit that no individual be entitled to live in a space greater than seven square meters, which meant that our family of four could not exceed twenty-eight square meters. This was now the law, and it meant we could live in only one or two rooms in our big apartment. Rather than wait for the Russians to assign our apartment to a group of strangers, my father reached out through the Jewish community to take in individuals and families in particular need. They would still be strangers to us, but at least we would choose. Soon, we were joined in the apartment by a father and two sons who had escaped to Lvov from Krakow, and by a husband and wife named Bodner. This was a big adjustment. We shared the kitchen, but each family took its own meals. Once in a while, *Bodnerova* would sit with us at the kitchen table over tea and biscuits, and sometimes she baby-sat for me and my brother while my mother went across the street to visit with her sister. Bodnerova would be in her room, but if we called to her, she would come and sit with us until my mother came home.

I had a habit of waking up in the middle of the night. I would call to my mother, and she would come to me and whisper, *"Cicho, cicho, cicho."* Ssshhh, ssshhh, ssshhh. Over and over and over. In Polish and English, it sounded much the same: *'chi-sho, chi-sho, chi-sho.*' Somehow, the sound of her voice, the warmth of her touch, the gentle rhythm of her whisper, made me feel better, and soon I would fall back asleep. One night, I awoke and called out to my mother, but Bodnerova came to my room instead. I was half-asleep. She took me in her arms and whispered, *"Cicho, cicho, cicho."* Over and over and over. Ssshhh, ssshhh, ssshhh. My mother had told her what to do to comfort me, but I recognized this was not my mother's voice and shook myself fully awake. I started to cry. At the same time, I was afraid that if I cried, I would be punished, but then I decided that if my brother also cried, maybe they would forget about my crying. So I stood next to Pawel's crib and cried. Louder and louder, I cried. Finally, Pawel woke up and he started to cry as well.

Poor Bodnerova, she did not know what to do.

It was a big difference to how we lived before the Russians, but not so big after all. When you are little, you can get used to anything, and here I got so quickly used to these other families that it was as though they had always been a part of our household. I got used to all the different foods, and to not having so much money, and to no longer taking summer vacations in the country. I even got used to the language and started to speak a little bit of Russian. Yes, our family business was gone. Yes, there were strangers living in our apartment. Yes, our movements were endlessly tracked by the NKVD. Yes, my parents were in constant fear of being sent away to Siberia. And yet at four and then five years old, my world was little changed. I was no longer a princess, but still I had everything I could possibly want. Not so many fine things as before, but more than enough. I could not be greedy, because in Communist Russia everything was meant to be shared equally. I had my mother, who was with me constantly. I had my father, who smiled with such great pride when I did so little as come up with a shortcut home. He was busy, of course, moving from job to job—for a time, he worked as a medical assistant in a doctor's office!—but he always made time for me. I had my little brother. I had my puppy, and my canaries, and my cousins. I had friends. And so I had my fill.

No, all was not quite right in our little corner of the world, which was now our little corner of Russia, but it was mostly okay. Not like it was, but mostly okay. And yet these things too were about to change—so much now that even a child had to notice.

In June 1941, almost two years after the Germans cut short their approach into Lvov, we heard those Messerschmitt planes flying once again overhead. My parents did not talk about it, but they must have known this would happen. Once again we heard the bombs, and once again we retreated to my grandparents' basement. This time, too, I helped with the pushing of Pawel's stroller, laden with some of our worldly possessions. This time we expected the worst, and on June 29, 1941, when the Wehrmacht marched into the city, my parents were terrified. There was a big panic. The nonaggression pact was no more. The Russians had fled. The Jews were afraid to come out of their apartments. And the Ukrainians were dancing in the streets. This was one of the most disturbing aspects of the German occupation, the collaboration of the Ukrainians. You see, the Germans had promised the Ukrainians a free Ukraine, which was why they were so overjoyed at being liberated from Russian rule. They welcomed the Germans with flowers. The German soldiers paraded through the streets with their motorcycles, with their helmets and their boots and their black leather coats, and the Ukrainian women would walk out among the motorcade and greet the German men with hugs and kisses. We watched from our balcony. My father, he was very upset. Once again, he said, "This is the end for us."

My father did not let us leave the apartment, and he went out only when he had to work or to bring back food or supplies. The Ukrainians were ruling the streets. They were doing the Germans' dirty work even before the Germans could set about it. This was the beginning of the pogroms that took place that summer in Lvov, in which more than six thousand Jews were killed by Ukrainians. There were orchestrated attacks, but there were also small instances and disturbances, not unlike the razor slashing meted out on my father as a young man. A thousand tiny torments, adding up to a riot of violence and torture. Young boys beating on Jewish men with sticks, pulling their beards so hard that they would bleed, following them home and looting their apartments before turning them in to the Germans, terrorizing Jewish women with impunity because they knew their misconduct would be supported by the Germans.

In July 1941, in part to revenge the assassination of former Ukrainian leader Symon Petlyura, the Ukrainians killed more than five thousand Jews. I would later learn about Petlyura in history class. He was a famous Socialist who served as president of Ukraine during the Russian civil war. Under Petlyura, the Ukrainian government perpetrated a series of pogroms that resulted in the killing of as many as one hundred thousand Ukrainian Jews. He allowed the pogroms, it was said, because they demonstrated his people's solidarity. Years later, Petlyura was approached on a Paris street by a Jewish man who shot him three times at close range and cried out with each shot: "This, for the pogroms. This, for the massacres. This, for the victims." My father always believed that the pogroms of 1941 were a kind of payback for that one act of defiance, an endless retribution.

The Ukrainians rounded up the top-ranking Jews in the city—the upper classes, the intelligentsia, the community leaders—and delivered them to the Germans. They worked off target lists of Jews and checked each name off the list as that person was captured. As a small child, from my window, I could see it was terrible. I was not supposed to watch, but I could not look away. With the help of the Ukrainians, I could see, the German soldiers were pulling the Jews out into the street and shooting them on the spot or taking them on the transport to the Piaski, the sand quarry northwest of town where Jews were executed. It was too soon for the establishment of the forced labor camp on Janowska Road, but already large numbers of Jews deemed unfit for work were being sent by transport to the concentration camp at Belzec.

Within just a few weeks, the Germans completely reorganized life in the city. It was ordained that all remaining Jews had to wear a white band with the Star of David on their arms any time they were out on the street. There was a curfew, from six o'clock in the evening until six o'clock in the morning. Separate stores were established where Jews could shop for food and necessities, but only during the hours between two o'clock and four o'clock in the afternoons, at prices determined by the Ukrainians put in charge of the operation.

I do not have any firsthand observations on what life was like in the city in the first days and weeks of German rule, because I did not go outside. I stayed in our apartment on Kopernika Street with my mother and brother, and I could see everything from our big picture window. One night, German soldiers came to search our building. They knocked first on the door of the elderly doctor who occupied the entire first floor. He had a big, beautiful apartment—

ten rooms, the whole length of the building. They took him out into the street. Then they went upstairs and kicked down the door that corresponded to the doctor's downstairs apartment. This was our next-door neighbors' apartment, and the Germans went inside and collected those people as well. But we were spared, because the second floor was divided into two apartments and they searched only the one, thinking the layout was the same as on the first floor.

It was, my father used to say, one of the first of the many small miracles that kept our family alive.

Frequently, the Germans would come to inspect our building, and Galewski, the concierge, would stall them until my father could leave by the back entrance. He was a good man, Danusha's father. He helped us many times. The Gestapo and the SS, they would come for inspection and ask, "Are there any Jews living here?" Galewski would shake his head, *Nein!* Then he would engage the Germans in conversation, knowing my father would have seen them approaching from our upstairs window. Galewski kept them talking, to give my father time to hide or to escape.

Our building was adjacent to another nice building the Germans had commandeered as a kind of headquarters, so many of the highest-ranking German officers regularly walked our street. Many of them eventually came to our apartment, where they took turns picking and choosing among our artwork, our furniture, our silverware. All across the city, the Germans would take what they wanted and leave the rest, setting fire to the buildings after they had looted them. Here, though, we were directly across the street from an old palace that was now occupied by the Luftwaffe. The general of the Luftwaffe had set up housekeeping there, and there were other officers with the idea of turning our building into their living quarters, so they were not about to burn it to the ground.

One by one the officers came to our apartment, and one by one they left with our nice things. It must have been heartbreaking for my parents to see all their worldly possessions being taken from them, but at the same time they were thankful that we were not being taken out into the street along with our things. Soon, all of our furniture was gone, including our piano, a fine August Förster, one of the best pianos ever made. My mother used to play for us, very beautifully, but the piano had been silent since the German occupation. Still, it pained her that this wonderful instrument would be taken from our apartment and that she would never play it again. The piano was claimed by a German officer named Wepke, a man who was acting as the interim governor of Lvov. The only solace was that Wepke seemed to appreciate how fine a piano he was about to receive and that he could also play it beautifully. It was the poetic way to look at the injustice, to see that at least the piano would be enjoyed and put to beautiful use.

I have kept a picture in my mind of my brother and me sitting on the floor of our apartment, our furniture all but gone, the walls checkered with bright squares where our paintings used to hang. In another time, in another place, it would have been a picture of any two children, their household packed for a move out of town. I sat on the floor and watched and listened. I could see the shine of the piano pedals against the polish of the officer's boots. Watching him play, listening to him, you would never think he was capable of cruelty. The splendor that spilled from his fingers! The joy! When he was finished, he stood and complimented my father on the piano. Then he made arrangements for the instrument to be transported to his apartment across the street. Before it was taken away, my father wrapped the piano carefully with a blanket pulled from our linen closet. It pained him to lose the piano, but it pained him more to see it damaged. He stamped it with his name—IGNACY CHIGER—on the small hope that he would someday get it back, after the war. Always, he was thinking ahead to the end of the war. Always, he was hopeful, and so he put his stamp on everything.

Before the piano was taken, another officer came to the apartment and admired it, but my father told him the instrument had already been claimed. My father leapt to his feet with misplaced pride. He said, "I am sorry, sir, but the piano has already been claimed by Officer Wepke." In his voice, I could hear how pleased he was that our fine piano was the focus of so much attention.

The second officer was very angry when he heard this, no doubt because Wepke had him outranked and also because he had gotten to the piano first. Afterward, my father admitted that it had been foolish of him to announce with such pleasure that the piano was not available, because this second officer could have easily shot him right there in our living room. It was just the sort of stupid reprisal he kept hearing about, and he regretted saying anything the moment the words left his lips. Luckily—another miracle!—this second officer did not take his disappointment out on my father, but contented himself with some of the remaining things that had not yet been claimed.

The next day, the piano delivered, Wepke sent an officer back to our apartment with a package for my father. It was our blanket, along with a bottle of wine and a note of thanks for the piano. I was six years old, still a child, and even I could recognize the absurd mix of humanity and inhumanity. It was a curious gesture of civility, we all thought. My father wrote about it after the war, how it was strange to find decent people among such animals. That such a people, with such a high culture, could do such terrible things . . . it was unthinkable.

With our piano now in the possession of such a high-ranking officer, we were left alone for a few weeks. My parents took the opportunity to distribute some of their possessions among their few Polish friends. Silverware, china, jewelry, some furniture . . . whatever the Germans had not claimed for themselves, my parents gave away to non-Jews, with the hope that we might recover the property or that it would at least be enjoyed by someone of our choosing. All along, I had been watching the officers take my toys, and it made me very sad. I wanted to cry, but already I knew not to cry. I did not fight or protest. We gave my dollhouse to my friend Danusha. It made me happy, to see her with my dollhouse. She had always admired it, and I knew we could not take it with us. It was still not clear where we were going, or when, but it seemed a certainty that we would not stay on in this apartment much longer.

One day, while my father was out seeking provisions, another set of officers came by to consider our remaining possessions. My father liked to take pictures. He had a very good German camera, a Leica. The camera was still in our apartment, tucked away in one of my father's bookcases, and one of the officers saw the camera and prepared to take it. Next, he examined some of the beautiful books still on the shelves of our library. My mother noticed him admiring one book in particular, a fine collection of photographs. He turned and asked my mother if he could take it. He did not have to ask, but he asked.

"No," my mother said, "it belongs to my husband. I will have to ask him first."

The officer smiled, a devilish smile. He said, "I can take it without his permission." He said this with some good cheer. Then he paused for a moment, and his smile deepened. "But I will wait for your decision," he said.

When my father returned later that afternoon, my mother told him what had transpired. He was very angry at my mother. He said her head was in the clouds. "He asks," he said of the German officer, "you give it to him." It was a simple equation, as far as my father was concerned, an obvious transaction. He did not like that my mother had put our family at risk.

The next day, the officer returned. He was still in good cheer. "So," he said to my mother, "what have you decided?"

My mother apologized and gave him the book. "It is yours, of course," she said. The officer took it gladly. He was very polite. Then he told my mother that the Luftwaffe was planning to commandeer our apartment the following day. He did not have to give us this information, but he did it as a kindness. He said, "Tomorrow, they will come and you will have to leave. Whatever you still have, you must pack."

There was not much to pack: a single suitcase filled with clothes, some pots and pans. The soldiers and officers had picked our apartment clean. There were no toys left for me to take, no dolls, no special playthings to keep me amused or distracted. Even if there were, I do not think we would have taken the trouble to pack them. My parents did not explain why we were packing or where we were going.

Before we left, my father made an inventory of everything the Germans had taken. He wrote who got what, and where he had stamped his name. He also recorded the names of our Polish friends who had come to collect what was left. And then we prepared to leave. We stood in our kitchen for a moment, before embarking. There was our one suitcase. There was my brother in his stroller. There was a bottle of milk, which Pawel would need for his supper later that night. I pushed the stroller as we left. Always, I liked to push the stroller. It made me feel all grown up. My parents walked a few steps behind. It was the first time I had been outside since the German occupation, and a part of me was glad to be in the sunshine. Around every corner, I imagined Baba Yaga, the witch who haunted the stories I heard as a small child. In my imagination, I was running through the big, open fields of wild sunflowers once more, with my friend Melek at my side. I was afraid, but I was trying not to be afraid.

In museums, you can see photographs of the dispersed Jewish families of Eastern Europe, put out on the streets with all of their worldly possessions. This is the picture we must have made, the four of us, shuffling along Kopernika Street with no clear destination. My father must have known where we were going, but he did not say. We were going, just. And as we walked, Pawel started to cry. I did not like that he was crying. My parents were nervous, because we were out on the street and vulnerable, and their nervousness became my own. I kept whispering to Pawel to be quiet. I was thinking about Baba Yaga, thinking about my dollhouse, thinking about our dog, Pushek, whom we had to give away. It was a lot for a little girl to keep on her mind.

Still, my baby brother kept crying, and so my whispering grew louder. Soon, I was yelling at him to go to sleep. I was so angry. I started shaking his stroller, I was so angry. Finally I said, "Close your eyes forever, already!"

As soon as I said it, I regretted it. I felt so terrible. I was six years old, my brother was two, and I knew this was not something a sister should wish upon her baby brother. Probably, under normal circumstances, this is something a sister might say to her brother all the time and it would be nothing, but these were not normal circumstances. I knew this was not something you say when the Germans and the Ukrainians are taking Jewish children off the streets, when they are liquidating the city. My words hung there in the bright afternoon sunlight, stinging me, making me feel guilty.

Mercifully, my parents did not hear—they were a few steps behind—and I did not tell them. Pawel must have heard, because he immediately stopped crying, or maybe he quieted because of the tone of my voice. He never said anything. He was so young, but he was speaking in full sentences, so he might have said something. But he was quiet. Suddenly, I leaned into his stroller and started kissing him and hugging him. My parents, looking on, must have wondered what had come over me, but I did not say. Already, I had my inside life, the thoughts and dreams and hopes and fears I did not share with anybody.

Two

⤙

THE GIRL IN THE
GREEN SWEATER

My father did not know how miserable the conditions would be for us at Zamarstynowska 34 until we arrived. He had arranged the room through the Judenrat, a Jewish council that operated like a kind of relief organization for the Jewish community. There were Judenrats all across Poland. It was an organization of Jews, for Jews. In one way, it offered relief and support and an important link for Jews anxious to keep connected to one another; in another way, it offered the Germans a kind of bridge between the Nazi government and the ghetto population. The Germans encouraged this arrangement, because they were able to use the Judenrat to communicate with the Jews and to keep us organized, but at the same time it was a useful resource for the Jews as we struggled to survive. My father always said it was a confusing irony, that an organization dedicated to helping an oppressed and persecuted people could at the same time be used to make it easier to oppress and persecute the people it was meant to serve. It was like a helping hand, except that the same hand that lifted you up might also hold you down.

Yet for certain things, like finding an apartment and helping to locate family members and other Jews, the Judenrat was a valuable resource. Someone gave my father the address on Zamarstynowska Street and a man's name: Bahrow. That is all. I do not even know if we ever met this man, Bahrow, but we were meant to ask for him. He would tell us where to go. We walked for a long time, maybe a half hour. I was happy to be outside in the bright sunshine. I had missed the fresh air, but I wanted to know where we were going. It was a long walk for all of us, with all of our things.

There was a bridge that crossed Zamarstynowska Street at the center of town; in a few weeks, the bridge would mark the entrance to the Juden Lager—or Ju-Lag, for "Jewish Camp"—the ghetto area where the Jews who had not been killed or sent to the camps were forced to reside. It would become like a camp itself. Zamarstynowska 34 was located on the near side of the bridge, outside the area that would soon be our ghetto. I looked to the other side of the bridge and wondered what horrors were waiting for us there. I wondered how it could be any different, any worse. Our side of the bridge was bad enough. Even a small child knew to be anxious and afraid.

How we got to Zamarstynowska 34 was another in our long list of small miracles, because it was indeed a small miracle that we found any place at all. Palace, hovel . . . it did not matter. Everyone was desperate for a place to live, so we were lucky to have a roof over our heads. My grandfather had been elected one of the local representatives of the Judenrat, and he knew someone who lived in the building, so he helped my father with the arrangements. We did not know what to expect. What we found was a horrible, dimly lit room, overcrowded with displaced Jewish families. There was one bathroom for maybe twenty people. We were all refugees of one kind or another, thrown from our homes and stripped from our lives.

We were assigned to one room with three or four other families. All these years later, I do not remember the first thing about these families. There must have been some children among them, but I do not recall playing with anyone. There was no real atmosphere for playing. I played with my brother, Pawel. We invented little games we could play in our heads. I told him stories. Always, we were talking, talking, talking. Sometimes we included Melek in our talking. Already I had brought little Pawel into my imagination and introduced him to my friend, and together we were in our own secret world.

We did not take any toys with us when we left our apartment on Kopernika Street. No dolls. Nothing. All I had were the clothes on my back—my cherished green sweater knitted for me by my grandmother—and a change of clothes in the one suitcase we all shared. There was nothing to do but sit and wait for my father to get back. Each day, there was someplace he had to go, to work or to find food. Each day, we waited for him. He was very careful, leaving the apartment. The Ukrainians controlled the streets. He would go through back alleys to get where he was going. Sometimes the Judenrat would arrange a special place where Jews could get food and basic supplies. Word would spread among the Jewish community, and the men would zig and zag through the back streets to avoid capture. Sometimes they did not make it back.

Coming from our grand apartment, where even under the Soviets we were able to meet our essential needs, this was a big
change. At Kopernika 12, our comings and goings were not so
restricted. Our living conditions were not so miserable. The conditions at Zamarstynowska 34 were terrible. Filthy, foul-smelling,
suffocating. There was no furniture, except for maybe a few
mattresses and some chairs. My father was working as a carpenter
and had access to tools and materials, so he built a table, which we
shared with the other families. There was one window, but my
mother would not let me near it. Also, I was not allowed to go outside. This, of course, was not such a big change for me, because I
had not been outside during the German occupation except to
make the long walk to Zamarstynowska Street, but at least at
home I was able to look out the window. Without my window, I
would not know what was going on outside unless news of it was
brought inside, and usually my father would not bring such news
home with him. He and my mother tried to protect us from our dire
circumstances, but I was learning to eavesdrop on their hushed
conversations. Sometimes my parents spoke to each other in Yiddish if they did not want me to understand what they were saying,
but eventually I learned to speak Yiddish. Eventually I heard
everything.

I was very unhappy. We stayed in this room for only about a
week, but that is a long time when you are six years old. My
mother, too, was unhappy. She was used to having her own things,
running her own kitchen, arranging her family's schedule, but
here we could only follow the motions of everyone else. Here we
could eat only when my father was able to bring home some food.
Here we could bathe only when it was our turn, and only with cold
water. And here my mother would have to go back to work. This

was probably the biggest change for me and my brother. We had gotten used to having our mother near, and now she would have to go to work each day like my father, and we would have to wait nervously for her return as well.

We could not stay in Zamarstynowska 34 very long. Soon my father moved us to another apartment. This second apartment was also on Zamarstynowska Street, Zamarstynowska 120, and it was a little bit better. This time, we were on the "ghetto" side of the bridge. We had to cross through a gate to reach the ghetto. At the checkpoint, we had to present papers and say where we were going. Some families were detained if they did not have the proper paperwork or if the German soldiers working the checkpoint decided for some reason they could not pass, but we were lucky. One of the soldiers hit my father on the back with a leather whip, but my father said it was not so bad. He said a lot of people suffered much worse.

Once we crossed into the ghetto, things did not seem any different to me. In fact, this next apartment turned out to be bigger, less crowded. The man who rented us our new room was also a carpenter. Perhaps this was how my father came to know him. He had a woodworking shop in the basement. I can still smell the fresh wood shavings. The smell filled the whole building, and it made me feel clean, brand new, like a fresh start. Even today, when I smell fresh wood shavings, I am taken back to that woodworking shop in the ghetto. It is a happy sense memory, even though it was not a happy time.

We stayed at Zamarstynowska 120 from February 1942 until August 1942. The conditions there were a little bit better than at Zamarstynowska 34. At first we lived with my aunt and two cousins, all in one room, until one day my uncle came and took his wife and children to Warsaw. I liked this second apartment on Za-marstynowska Street because there was a courtyard in the back of our building, and my mother would sometimes let me go outside to play. This was a great treat. There were fresh mushrooms grow-ing just beyond our courtyard, in a field behind our building. I had never seen fresh mushrooms. At first, I thought they were big white stones. I had to ask my grandmother about the stones when she came to visit, and she explained that they were mushrooms and that we could eat them. This was so surprising to me. We collected some of the mushrooms and brought them home to eat. I could not believe it, eating those big white stones. They had no taste, but I convinced myself they were delicious.

I had begun to pay a lot of attention to food. Before the Soviet occupation of 1939, I did not care about food. As I have written, sometimes I would not even eat, just to torment my poor nanny. But now food was scarce and precious, so of course I ate. I did not like being hungry, which was why my discovery of the mushrooms was so special and why I remember it. I also remember how I used to peel potatoes for my mother, to prepare for our dinner. I used a knife, because we did not have a potato peeler, and my father taught me how to shave the skin so slight, so thin, so I did not waste a bit of potato. In the beginning, I would peel and my father would watch, until he thought I had mastered it and could be trusted with the task. I peeled those potatoes so carefully, it was almost as if I were whittling. I did not waste a bit. It was a habit I could not break, even long after the war, when potatoes were once again plen-tiful. To this day, someone seeing me in the kitchen peeling pota-toes will wonder how I learned to do such a thin, fine job of it.

Now that I was allowed outside to play, I could see the reality of our situation up close and firsthand. One afternoon, through an opening in the fence behind our building, I saw a group of Ukrainian teenagers beating up an elderly Jewish man. They were hitting him with sticks. The man was not resisting. He was screaming in pain, calling for help, begging for the teenagers to stop. After a while, the Ukrainians grew tired of the beating and walked away, but the man continued to moan. I ran upstairs to tell my mother what I had seen. I thought maybe she could help this poor man. I did not know how to help him myself. My mother, what could she say? What could she do? She was very upset about it, but at the same time she told me not to pay attention to such things, to mind my own business, because getting involved in something like this could only lead to trouble. This was not the kind of person my mother was, not the kind of person she wanted me to be, but this was how the war had changed us, how the Germans had changed us. The Ukrainians, too. If we tried to help this man, the Ukrainian boys might take offense and start beating us with their sticks.

We did not have running water at Zamarstynowska 120. For bathing, yes; for drinking, no. We had to go outside to a pump, and I would sometimes go with my grandmother. This was our special time together. My grandmother would carry the bucket when it was empty, and I would carry it back when it was full. I liked that I was big enough to help in this way, and on this one day, returning to our apartment with a full bucket of water, I noticed two young Ukrainian women approaching us on the street. They did not look as though they meant us any harm, but they were Ukrainians. In my head, I decided to blame the women for the way those Ukrainian boys beat up on the old Jewish man in the courtyard. It had just rained, so there were puddles in the street. I stopped by one of the biggest puddles and waited for the two women to approach. Then, just as they came close, I jumped in the puddle and splashed them with water.

My grandmother, she was furious with me. And the Ukrainian women, they shook their fists and chased after me. They shouted, "You Jewish bastard!" They did not catch me, though—I was very fast—and they did not chase after my grandmother. Perhaps they did not know we were together. I felt so good, splashing them like that, so powerful. It was nothing, just a little bit of water, a little bit of mischief, but it made me feel that I was not so helpless after all. Of course, I got in a lot of trouble when we got back to our apartment, but I did not mind. It made me feel we could stand up to the Ukrainians, to the Germans, to whatever might happen next.

It was good to be a fast runner, especially during one of the actions, when the Germans would come in force and sweep the streets of Jews. At all other times, it was unsafe to move about the city without proper papers, but at these times it did not matter even if you had proper papers. During an action, the Germans would mobilize their entire police force: soldiers, Gestapo, SS. They would go into the apartments where the Ukrainians had told them the Jews were living and drag us out into the street. Sometimes they would throw grenades into buildings if they suspected there were Jews hiding inside. They would capture the Jews and load them onto lorries for transport to the Janowska labor camp, on the hill overlooking town, or to the Belzec extermination camp. Sometimes they would just shoot the Jews right there in the street or take a large group to the Piaski sand pits and shoot them there. It was a concentrated effort, to kill or capture as many Jews as possible, in as short a time as possible, to tighten the grip of terror over the Jews who managed to survive. Follow-

ing each action, the surviving Jews were made to move deeper
into the ghetto. It was like a funnel. They pushed all the Jews into
smaller spaces, until finally there was no place left for us to go.

I can still recall the very first action. At least, it was the first action I remember. We were still living at Zamarstynowska 120, and
my mother was home with us at the time. We heard noise on the
street outside our window. We heard the footsteps of the Germans
bounding up our stairs. We heard them banging on the doors of the
apartments below. We heard the cries of the other families as they
were pulled from their apartments. My brother and me, we hugged
my mother close. She tried to comfort us. She kept saying, "Don't
be afraid, don't be afraid." But, of course, we were afraid.

And then she did the strangest thing. She started pinching our
cheeks. Over and over, she pinched our cheeks. We complained
because the pinching started to hurt, but still she kept pinching.
She said, *"Cicho, cicho, cicho,"* to keep us calm, to let us know everything was going to be all right. Ssshhh, ssshhh, ssshhh. And
still she kept pinching. She explained to us quickly, quietly, that
she wanted our cheeks to look healthy, she wanted us to look well
fed and well dressed and well mannered. She made sure there was
a nice picture of me and Pawel displayed on the table by the apartment door. And all the time she was pinching, pinching, pinching.

Finally, some Germans came into the apartment. They did not
knock. They just burst through the door. The man who appeared
to be in charge looked around. He did not look like a terrible person. He did not seem much more than a boy. He studied me and my
brother. He could see we looked clean and healthy. Our cheeks
were so red, from all the pinching! We were wearing nice clean
shirts. On top of my shirt, I had my special green sweater. We

stood perfectly silent and still, not because we were so well mannered, but because we were too scared to say anything or to move.

The German, he looked us up and down. Then he noticed the
picture by the front door and he compared our faces with the faces
in the picture. Then he said to my mother, "Doctor?" They were
Wehrmacht, these soldiers—not Gestapo, not SS, just regular German army. Always, they were a little bit easier to talk to, a little bit
more human. This was what my parents always said.

My mother shook her head.

"Professor?" the German asked.

Again, she shook her head. *"Nein,"* she said. *"En airbrecht."*
No, I am just a worker.

Once again, the soldier studied us. *"Das en dein kinder?"* he
asked. These are your children?

My mother nodded proudly.

He looked at us once more. For the longest time, he looked at
us. Then he said, *"Bleiben sie."* You can stay.

This is how we survived our first action, by another small miracle, by pinching.

The next day, another German soldier came. My mother went
at us again with her pinching, and again we were allowed to stay.
Where she learned this trick, I never knew. Later that second day,
a Ukrainian soldier came through the door, and he ordered us to
leave with him. This time my mother's pinching was not so effective. The soldier told my mother that one of our neighbors had
reported that there were Jews living in this apartment, and this
was why he came. My mother tried to talk to him, but he would
not listen, and as they talked my father returned home. It was a
lucky coincidence. Right away, my father began to bargain with
the Ukrainian. The Ukrainian decreed that my father could stay

with us children but my mother would have to leave with him since she did not have the proper paperwork. My father asked the soldier to name a price. The Ukrainian asked for 500 zlotys—about $100—which my father happily paid, and we were free for another day.

During the next action I remember, I was with my cousin Inka, who was two years older than me. We were living together at Zamarstynowksa 120 at the time. We had learned to be extremely careful when we were outside playing. Normally, we did not go outside, but in this one courtyard it was felt we would be protected. Still, we were constantly looking, left and right, up and down, fearful of the Germans, fearful of the Ukrainians, constantly listening. Action or no action, it was much the same. Every day, they were killing Jews, taking Jews, punishing Jews. But when it was a big effort, they gave it a name. They called it an action. In the meantime, they did it anyway.

We were like animals, attuned to our environment. Any sudden movement, any unexpected noise, and we would run. And that is just what happened. Suddenly, I heard some German voices, and I looked up and could see some German soldiers. I could hear noise and activity as the people spilled out onto the streets. I told Inka to run, and she did, only I ran a little bit faster. I managed to duck into an alley to hide, but Inka was not so lucky. One of the soldiers caught her and took her away.

I ran upstairs to tell my mother what happened, and we were so upset. Everyone was upset. It was the way of the ghetto, we were all learning. One moment you were with someone and everything was fine, and the next moment that someone was gone and everything was no longer fine, and underneath our sadness was a kind of knowing that something like this was going to happen.

After Inka was taken, I thought I would never see her again, but later that day I saw her. I heard some commotion in the street and I looked out our window. There, on the lorry, pressed together with dozens of other Jews, I could see Inka. She was with my grandmother—my father's mother, the one who knitted me my cherished sweater. I did not know until just then that the Germans had caught my grandmother in the same action.

At some point, my grandmother looked back toward our window. Probably she knew I would be looking. She knew I would be frightened for them. I do not know that she saw me, but she imagined I was there, so she waved. Just a little twist of her wrist, just for me, just in case I was looking. Probably she did not think any of the soldiers guarding the lorry would notice, but one of them did. Probably he did not like that this woman was waving to someone. That she was smiling. That she was being brave. So he hit her. With the butt of his rifle, he hit my grandmother, and Inka reached to comfort her, and that was the last time I saw either one of them.

After that, I did not go outside.

Already, I was learning that there was no room in our lives for tears. Later, when we were hiding in the sewer, so close to the street where children were playing, I could not cry because my tears would give us away, but here, watching my cousin and grandmother being taken to their certain deaths, I was all through with tears. My parents were trying to be so brave, so strong. They were so focused on keeping the four of us alive that to mourn too deeply for those we were losing might take away from that focus. They did not have to speak these things to me. We were all sad, to think what had happened to Inka and my grandmother, what might be happening still, but there was only so much time for sadness, so we put it out of our minds. Not because we did not love them or cherish their memories. Not because of any kind of disrespect or detachment. No, it was because there was no longer any room for crying. Also, you could not openly demonstrate your sadness. Not in the ghetto, not any longer. Why? Because all around everyone else was experiencing their own sadness. We were all watching our friends and our family members being taken to slaughter. At any other time, we would have been collapsed in grief, but at this time we could only hope that we would not be next.

My mother was not in control of her emotions. She had a small breakdown after the first actions, after losing her mother-in-law and her niece. (Her sister-in-law, Inka's mother, was also killed in this same action, we later learned.) She was normally a very strong person, but this was too much. She stopped going to work, for a time, and stayed in hiding. My father did not even tell me and my brother she was hiding. He was afraid that if the Gestapo came to search our apartment, we might accidentally give her away. She was hiding in the sofa bed. My father folded her up inside and covered the opening with a blanket. Every morning, I thought my mother had gone to work for her regular shift, but she moved instead to this sofa bed. All day long, I thought I was at home alone with my brother. I became suspicious only when I heard my father talking to an empty room. He was standing in the doorway, talking, talking, talking, and no one was there.

I said to my father, "Who are you talking to?"

He said, "No one, Krzysha. I am just trying to gather my thoughts."

Later, I could hear him still talking. It was almost comical. This time he was asking the room for advice: what to do about the children, what to prepare for dinner, what clothes to put out for us. This sounded so strange to me, to hear my father talking about such details to an empty room, until finally I heard my mother's voice in answer. It was coming from the sofa bed, and she was telling him what there was to eat.

This went on for a few days, until my father could convince my mother that this latest action was over and that she would be safe, but even I could see my mother was changed by what was happening. She became very superstitious. One day, Pawel announced that in his dreams he saw the Germans coming back to our apartment, and so she retreated once again to our sofa bed. Sure enough, another German soldier came to our apartment the very next day—and once again, we were spared.

Little Pawel's premonitions came into play another time as well. Like a lot of Jewish women in the ghetto, my mother had begun carrying vials of cyanide, which she meant for us to swallow in the event we were captured. This was to be our last resort. The Germans would not take us alive, she vowed. She carried three vials: one for herself, one for me, one for Pawel. Presumably, my father carried his own. My mother had taken to carrying these vials pressed beneath her watchband on her wrist, and one of them happened to break one evening as she was preparing something for Pawel to eat. My mother did not know at first that the vial had broken, but somehow Pawel knew not to eat. How he made this connection, I will never know. My mother tried to force him to take a bite of whatever it was she had made, but he would not open his mouth. Over and over, she tried to force him, but he would not eat. He started to cry. Usually, he was very good, and he seldom cried, but here he was, crying. We could not understand it.

Of course, I did not know anything about these vials of cyanide, and Pawel, he was too young to understand, yet on some level he must have known something. Finally, my mother noticed the vial had broken and that the cyanide had surely spilled into Pawel's food. She raced over to him and covered him with hugs and kisses, and from that moment on she believed he might be a kind of prophet. He was only three years old, yet he dreamed the Germans were coming back, and he knew not to take a bite of the poisoned food. For the rest of the war, my mother would ask him, "Pawelek, the Germans are coming?"

I do not really believe my brother was psychic, but we were all changed by these first few actions. We were all broken, bent, beaten—so much so that my mother was willing to believe my little brother could see into the future. In this way, you could see how we were being psychologically defeated by the Germans. My father always talked about this. First, he would say, our freedoms were taken from us by the Russians. We were separated from our lives and fed all of the Communist propaganda and made to feel we were no longer human. Everything went from a straight line to a crooked path, and nothing was as we had known it to be. Next, after the Russians, the Germans continued with our dehumanization. We were reduced by what we were being made to endure. We were made smaller. Because we could no longer feel for the loss of our loved ones. Because the liquidation of our Jewish population was all but inevitable. Because we began to believe it was our fate and we were helpless against it.

I did not need to be an adult to recognize the feelings underneath this type of thinking. I could see that I had been changed by what was going on. I could see that where I would have once cried for my grandmother, I could now only shudder and wince and take a deep breath and move on. And for this, I blamed the Germans. I blamed them for making my mother weak and afraid, even if it had been for only a few days. I blamed them for taking my grandmother and my aunt and my cousin—and, soon, for everyone else they would take from my family. Most important, I blamed them for taking away my tears.

This was unforgivable.

Our comings and goings were soon manipulated by a terrible man named Joseph Grzymek, the SS Obersturmführer assigned to the Lvov ghetto. Whether we would live or die was determined by this man, who was known as an expert liquidator. This was his specialty. Years later, it was revealed that Grzymek was not only SS, he was a high-ranking Nazi official, who was eventually tried for war crimes. At the time, we knew only that he had been sent to organize the ghettos and to choreograph the killing and incarceration of the entire Jewish population in that city, and when word came that he was being sent to the Ju-Lag, the Jewish people of Lvov were panicked.

Grzymek's arrival coincided with the closing of the ghetto. There was a fence surrounding the ghetto, with a gate by the bridge that crossed Zamarstynowska Street. Until August 1942, the gate was more of a checkpoint than a barricade; you could come and go with the proper papers, as we had done when we crossed the bridge to move into the apartment at Zamarstynowska 120. The ghetto was a marked-off area, but it was not yet a closed-off area. However, following the so-called August action of 1942, the "open" part of the city was liquidated and the remaining Jews were fenced inside the Ju-Lag. Once again, this was part of the Germans' strategy, to confine us into smaller areas, to make it easier for them to control us, to torture us, to eliminate us. We were the "leftover Jews," my father used to say, restricted now to a

small area of just a few streets behind four-meter fences. Guards
were posted along the fence with shotguns every few meters. If
you had to work outside the ghetto, you were permitted to leave as
long as you marched in line with the other workers. Always, you
had to be counted.

My mother, who worked the day shift for Schwartz Co.,
the manufacturer of German army uniforms at the Janowska
camp, was given a big "R" to wear on her clothing. The "R" stood
for *Ruestung*—German for daytime. Workers on the night shift
wore the letter "W," for *Wernacht*—German for nighttime. Sometimes they used the letters to divide the Jews. Sometimes there
would be an action, and only the workers with the letter "R"
would be taken. Sometimes they were looking only for the workers with the letter "W." Somehow, I think my father had two letters. He was assigned one, and he forged the other. Each day, he
wore whichever letter he thought would do him the most good.

He was good with forgeries, my father. He once forged a document called a Meldecarta, which was a difficult document to obtain. You needed to produce the document and have it stamped at
certain checkpoints or risk being sent to one of the camps or killed.
My father received one of these documents for himself by legitimate means, but he wanted my mother to have one as well, and I
remember one night in our apartment he sat huddled with some
other men, falsifying another set. They used the thin membrane
from an egg to transfer the ink and make a copy to another set of
papers, to transfer the legitimate Meldecarta of someone who had
already been killed by the Germans into my mother's name. I do
not know where he learned this technique or how exactly he managed it. Years later, I watched the movie *The Great Escape*, and
there was a scene where the British prisoners made a forgery using

a similar method, and I thought about my father and these men in our apartment.

The August action was particularly devastating. It lasted for ten days, from August 12, 1942, until August 22. The Germans liquidated over forty thousand Jews during this time, including most of my father's family and most of my mother's family. Add to that the tens of thousands who were killed or captured in previous actions and the incidental killings between actions. The Jewish population of Lvov was decimated, and so particularly was our family. After this August action, we had only one another. My father's father managed to survive, and my stepgrandmother, and so did my uncle Kuba, who had been married to my father's sister Ceska, Inka's mother. Also, my mother's father was still alive at this point. But everyone else—aunts, uncles, cousins—was gone. My father wrote after the war that in all of Lvov only three Jewish families had survived intact. Only three! Ours would be one of them. But this was only nuclear families.

My father woke up early on the morning the August action began, and he noticed how unusually quiet everything was. The streets were empty. He was curious and wanted to see what was going on, so he went outside and moved carefully among the buildings until he reached the hospital on Zamarstynowska Street. There he saw that all of the Jewish patients had been emptied out onto the street. There were lorries stationed out front, and the patients were being loaded onto the open carts like cattle. Some could not even walk. My father described this for us when he returned. He told us that the German soldiers were standing to the side with guns, ready to shoot any of the patients who complained or tried to escape. The patients were then taken to the Piaski sand pits and emptied onto the ground, where they were promptly shot by German soldiers.

On August 22, the last night of the action, we were visited by my father's uncle. He had been living just outside the city, but he had come to see who in his family had survived. Like my father, he was very careful moving about the streets. He moved only at night. My parents were asleep when he arrived. I woke when I heard their voices. I remember that my mother made tea for my father's uncle and that he sat with my parents at our table, talking. He said to my father that everyone else in their family had been killed or captured. My father was very saddened by this, but he knew as much. He could see the desolation and the killing outside our window. Then my father's uncle told my parents about some money and valuables he had saved. He told my father where it was hidden and drew him a map. He said that since no one else in the family had survived, he wanted my father to know where these things were located in case anything should happen to him.

After he left our apartment, my father heard a gunshot. He looked outside into the night and saw his uncle's body lying in the street. It is possible his uncle was the very last victim of the August action and that his very last act was to pass on his valuables to my father.

We were right to be afraid of this man Grzymek. The August action was only one indication of his capacity for cruelty, of his madness. He was also a very thorough commandant, very fastidious, and this became apparent when life was supposedly "normal" and there was only the killing in the meantime, between the actions. To Grzymek, order was everything. He placed signs throughout the ghetto declaring, "Order must rule!" *Ordung muss sein!* Also, he was very sadistic. He was famous for giving his prisoners impossible tasks and then killing them when they were unable to meet those impossible tasks. If a man could carry only one hundred pounds, Grzymek would command him to carry three hundred pounds. This was Grzymek's method. This was his idea of order.

There is an expression in Polish to describe someone who has come up from nothing: *Z chlopa pan.* From the peasant to the king. It is said with disdain, and it is meant to deride a pretender to power, someone who was not born into authority or who does not deserve it or who has not acquired it by noble means. This was my father's opinion of Grzymek, a man of modest intelligence, from modest beginnings, who demanded that he be treated with respect and dignity. On their own, the people did not shower him with praise. On their own, his subordinates did not bow to him. Yet when he arrived in Lvov, he ordered a procession in his honor. He ordered all the people to assemble in the main square, in two neat rows, one on either side of the street.

I did not go to this procession. Like most of the Jewish children who had survived to this point, I no longer went outside, but I could see some of the activity from my window. I peeked from behind the curtains. I could see the shiny black leather of Grzymek's boots and his jacket. I could hear him barking his commands. He rode through town in a stately carriage pulled by two beautiful black horses. It was a big show of power. He looked like the Roman emperor Nero, my father said, riding through the square. He drove his own carriage. In one hand, he held the reins; in the other, a Russian machine gun known as a *pepesza.* Every now and then, just to show that he could, Grzymek shot and killed one of the Jews in the two neat rows, and when he did the people stood straight in horror, afraid to move.

Finally, Grzymek pulled in the reins and the horses came to a stop. He stepped down from the carriage and began to inspect his two neat rows of Jewish prisoners, for we were all now prisoners of the Ju-Lag. What was once merely one of the poorer neighbor-hoods of Lvov was now like a concentration camp, suitable only for the warehousing of the city's Jewish population. Grzymek would not step too close to any of the Jews, because he was afraid of the lice. He said, "Stand back, so your lice will not jump onto me." *Darnit euch die laeuse nicth enfrienen.* This was in part a show of disrespect to the Jewish people, a way to denigrate us as filthy human beings, but it was also rooted in an unfortunate truth. The living conditions in the Ju-Lag were horrible, the inevitable result of so many people living in such unhealthy, unsanitary conditions. And so yes, many of the Jews struggled with lice. We were living in filth, and Grzymek did not like that we were living in filth, and when he was through with his inspection he waved his hand and ordered everyone to clean the streets.

In time, we would learn that Grzymek was also famous for his obsession with cleanliness. It was like a phobia. Everything had to be perfect, and if it was not, he would shoot whoever was respon-sible. Always, he would ride up and down the streets in an open car or an open carriage. Always, he would stand, waving, holding his Russian rifle, ready to shoot at anyone or anything for any rea-son. If he saw a dirty shop window, he would stop his car and ap-proach the window and break it with the butt of his rifle. If he saw a cigarette butt in the street, he would shoot the man or woman or child standing closest to it. Very quickly, the Jewish people of Lvov came to look on this man not with the respect he seemed desperately to crave, but with fear. And it was a fear born of crazi-ness. He was worse than a murderer, Grzymek; he was a madman. You never knew what he would do. He would shoot you for no reason or look away for no reason. Even children, he would shoot. Oh, he hated Jewish women and Jewish children, especially *dirty*

Jewish children. My father used to say that Joseph Grzymek would prefer a dead baby to a dirty baby. This was our conquering ruler.

During this first inspection, when Grzymek was paraded down the street in his horse-drawn carriage, my father made a regrettable mistake. He made himself known to this maniac. There were tens of thousands of "leftover Jews" when Grzymek came to Lvov, and it would have been nothing for my father to pass anonymously among them, but that was not to be. When Grzymek gave the order for everyone to clean the streets, my father stepped from his place in line and asked to be put to more productive use. He introduced himself to Grzymek and told him he was a skilled carpenter. This was true. He also told him he worked with a group of skilled carpenters throughout the ghetto. This was also true. Then my father suggested that perhaps the Obersturmführer might assign him and his fellow craftsmen a task more meaningful than simply sweeping the streets. Grzymek would not be spoken to in such a disrespectful manner by a filthy Jew, so he reached for the leather whip he kept on his belt and lashed my father across the face with it a few times. My father was cut in several places, and his left eye started to bleed. From that moment on, my father could not see properly with his left eye. Then Grzymek handed my father a shovel and a mop and told him to get to work. This my father did, in terrible pain, his face covered with blood, until Grzymek continued with his procession and my father could sneak into an alley and seek help for his wounds. He found a friend of his, a locksmith, who took my father to his wife, who cleaned my father's cuts for him.

Certainly, my mother could have attended to my father's wounds, but she was working. By the time of the August action, she was working at the Janowska labor camp, making uniforms for the German army. Schwartz Co. was probably the largest employer of Jews at that time; their factory never shut down. My mother had to work or risk being shot, which meant she had to leave me in charge of my brother, Pawel. For the first time since the Soviets commandeered my parents' business, my mother would not be at our side. She worked now in twelve-hour shifts. Some days she would leave the apartment at five o'clock in the morning and return at seven o'clock in the evening. Twelve hours for working and one hour each way for marching. Other days she would work at night, on the reverse schedule. I liked it when she worked at night, because in the day she would be home. When she was working in the day, we were alone, because my father was also working. When she was working at night, I tried to keep very quiet during the day so she could sleep. I looked after my brother. I remember feeling so relaxed, so good that my mother was home. It made me strong. But it did not matter how quiet we children were, my mother could not sleep during the day, and she saw what happened at the Janowska camp to workers who fell asleep on the assembly line. She was afraid this would happen to her.

Such a long shift, twelve hours a day, seven days a week. And for what? Two bowls of soup. That is all. Two bowls of soup and the privilege to continue living and working under such oppressive conditions. If she did not work, she would be killed. You worked to demonstrate your usefulness, not to earn money. And so my mother accepted her soup as payment and worked without complaint. She would have to march several miles to work, back and forth along the Janowska Road, and she used to tell us the long march was the most difficult part of her day. Walking in rows, flanked by Germans with rifles. If someone fell out of line, they would be hit or shot. If someone was tired and could not keep up, they would be hit or shot.

One evening, my mother came home covered in mud. She was crying. I reached for a wet cloth and helped to clean her up. I said, "Mama, what happened? Who did this to you?" She answered only that it was some bad people. Always, she tried to protect me from the truth, but I learned later there was a group of Ukrainian children making mud balls and throwing them at the Jews. This was a game to these children! And my poor mother was made to suffer this torment without stepping out of line.

"Dirty Jew!" they shouted. "Dirty Jew! Good for you!"

One by one, step by step, she was hit by wet clumps of mud. The mud was hard and filled with small rocks and other debris, and it must have stung terribly when it hit her, but more than the pain there was the anguish of the moment, the humiliation. Of course, my mother was not alone in this indignity; the other Jewish workers in the line were also under attack. But my heart ached only for her. More than once this happened. It made me very angry. My father, too. But what could he do about it? Shake his fists and shout? What could any of us do about it but continue on?

I have always told people that fourteen months in the sewers of Lvov was not so bad compared with hiding aboveground with my brother during the days both my parents went to work. Next to this, the sewer was nothing, and yet the people look at me as if I am fooling with them. But this was so. Underground, at least, I was with my parents. Underground, at least, we had one another. I did not care so much how we suffered as long as we were together. Aboveground, alone in the apartment, I had only my brother. We were children. It was frightening and bewildering, never knowing if my parents would return. I was like a parent and a sister to my baby brother, but this was too big a job for such a small girl. In this way, I had my childhood taken from me. The Germans, they did not take me, but they took a part of me. This part.

All the time, we discussed with my parents what to do when we were alone. What to do if I heard the Germans coming. What to do if there was an action. What to do if my father did not come home. What to do if my mother did not return. What to do—God forbid!—if both my parents were taken. My parents had us very well trained, because all around us other parents and children were being taken out into the street. All around us, families were being separated. So every night my mother would lay out a set of clothes for me and a set of clothes for Pawel. If we heard anything during the night, we were to jump into our clothes and run. Or hide. My mother would help Pawel to get ready, and my father would help me. That was the plan. At the end of each day, I would slip out of my cherished green sweater and lay it out at the foot of my bed or on the floor at the foot of my mattress, the arms opened wide and waiting for me to slip them back around me. Sometimes we did not even bother to take off our clothes. We slept fully dressed, ready to flee. Always we slept with one eye open, one ear listening.

After we left Zamarstynowska 120, we moved frequently. Sometimes we moved because my father arranged for a better, safer place or a place where we knew somebody. Sometimes we moved because the Germans had taken our building and we had no choice. Each day, when my parents were out, Pawel and I would sit quietly and wait for them to get back. For me and my brother, this was terrible—to be left alone, for so many hours, when all around us people were being pulled from their apartments and out onto the streets. Pawel may have been too young to dread those long hours the way I dreaded them, but I was anxious enough for both of us.

In one of the apartments we moved to after Zamarstynowska 120, my father built for us a special hiding place beneath our window ledge. It was good for us that he was handy with tools, that he had access to materials, and that the Germans would not question him if they caught him with his supplies because he carried the proper papers and wore the correct letter. The special hiding place was like a small compartment directly beneath our window ledge. It looked only like an extension of the ledge itself, and my father fashioned a false wall extending beneath the ledge, which he painted over so you could not see a difference against the rest of the wall. Behind the false wall, he removed a layer or two of bricks, to give us more room. He had to finish the wall from the outside, sometimes with nails to keep the opening closed, sometimes with a fresh coat of paint, so we could not escape unless my father came home to free us.

The people in the ghetto came to know my father as handy and capable of building good hiding places, and soon they called on him to make such places for them in their apartments. This he always did. But it was in our apartment that he worked hardest and longest. It was for us that he saved his best work: little closets inside our closets, false walls in the back of our wardrobe. You would have had to be a detective to discover some of his hiding places. In the bathroom of one apartment, he built a special hiding place for all our important papers and some jewelry. Probably the papers and the jewelry are still there, because I do not think my father ever went back to claim them, and certainly no one could have found them. The space he built for us beneath the window ledge was very ingenious, very clever. There was hardly enough room for my brother and me. You would have never imagined that you could fit two small children in such a space. We sat close, face-to-face, as if we were still babies in my mother's belly. My father placed two potties in the space for us to sit on, in case we had to go to the bathroom during the day. If there was talk of an action, or if there had not been an action for some weeks and my parents were growing worried that it would soon be time for another, we would climb inside this space before my father left for work in the morning. Then he would close up the wall behind us and move a big heavy table in front of the window, for camouflage.

I do not remember if my father built any airholes into this false wall so that Pawel and I could breathe inside, but I believe now that he must have. Always, he thought of everything. But if there were any airholes, they were concealed even from us, because it was pitch-black inside our tiny space. My brother and I could not see each other. We could only hear each other breathing. This was comforting at first, but as the hours passed it became also terrifying. To hear only your breathing, only your brother's breathing, louder and louder, all day long, with time moving so slowly that it might have stopped. The noise was so loud, I could not hear the prayers inside my own head. Even my imaginary friend, Melek, was silent underneath such a noise.

For me, these long, endless days in our hiding places were the worst part of the war. Absolutely, this was worse than losing our apartment at Kopernika 12. Worse than losing all of our fine, nice things. Worse than the beatings we sometimes suffered or that we were made to watch. Worse than the fourteen months underground in the stink and waste of the sewer that was still to come.

And it was not just one time. Many times we were made to crawl inside a hiding place and wait for my parents to return. In one apartment, my father made our hiding space in the kitchen. In another, the bathroom. And always, we were so scared! Our tears would run without noise, we were so afraid to make a sound. We could hear the footsteps of the Gestapo as they made their inspections. This happened frequently. We were not allowed to lock our apartment doors. Anyone could come in, at any time. There was a characteristic sound to the footsteps of the Gestapo, with their heavy boots. There was no mistaking it. In and out they would come. Gestapo, SS, Wehrmacht . . . they all took their turns.

My brother, he was also scared and crying silent tears. I held his hand and whispered to him that everything was going to be okay. He was so good, so brave. I tried to be good and brave like Pawel, but there was no one to hold my hand. There was no one to tell me that everything was going to be okay. All I could think was what would happen if my father was taken from the streets before he could make it home. What it would be like to be left inside this small space.

Sometimes, when there was no talk of any action, we would not have to hide. My parents would just leave us in the apartment. We were not to go outside, of course, and I was to stay away from the window, to make sure no one could see me from the street below. I learned to tell which noises were to worry about and which noises were okay. If I heard a suspicious noise, we were to hide. I used to stuff poor Pawel into our one brown suitcase. This was not a strategy I discussed with my parents beforehand, but a course of action I came upon myself. One day I heard the Gestapo marching up our street and into our building. I saw the suitcase underneath the bed. I thought this would be a good place to hide my little brother.

He was barely able to fit, but if he curled up in a tight little ball, I could close the lid. He did this without complaining. Then I slid the suitcase underneath the bed—it was so heavy!—and stepped into the closet behind one of my mother's robes, careful that you could not see my feet sticking out on the bottom. In the closet, holding my breath because I was afraid the sound of my exhaling would alert the Gestapo, I counted out the seconds before Pawel would suffocate. Usually, I would wait for a full minute or more after the disappearing sound of the Germans' characteristic foot-steps, before escaping from my closet and rescuing Pawel.

For months and months, this was how things were—and I prayed constantly for a time when my family could be together, all the time together, without my brother and me being left on our own. It would not happen the way I prayed it would happen, but it happened just the same.

Three

HERE THE GROUND IS SUFFERING

W ith each action, the ghetto became smaller, our situation more precarious. There was no end to our suffering. We went from a city of 150,000 Jews, to a city of 200,000 after the Germans and the Soviets divided Poland in 1939, to a city that now could count us in the tens of thousands. Our numbers were dwindling—and so was our resolve.

Here is just one example of how we were weakened. When we were still living at Zamarstynowska 120, the Ukrainian militia discovered a cache of fur coats in the attic of our building during a routine inspection. The coats did not belong to us, and they did not appear to belong to any of the other families currently occupying the building, but somehow my father was considered responsible. The soldiers determined that we had to pay a fine of 7,000 zlotys—about $1,400 at the time—as punishment for having these coats. If we did not pay, they said, they would take my father. Of course, we could not allow this to happen. My parents had money, my grandfather on my father's side had money, but this was a lot to pay for the crime of living beneath an attic full of someone else's fur coats. But we paid the fine. After all, this was what our money was for, to buy us our continued freedom. It did not matter that the Ukrainians kept the coats and probably sold them on the black market. It did not matter that the punishment did not fit the crime, because in fact there was no crime.

Here is another example: on Yom Kippur, the holiest day on the Jewish calendar, the ghetto commander, Grzymek, issued a special work order requiring all Jews to once again clean the ghetto. He ordered the men to their knees, to scrub the cobblestone streets, to pass the day that should have been spent in meaningful prayer in meaningless toil. Naturally, they knew it was an insult to require Jews to work on Yom Kippur. The work itself was an insult, so they added insult on top of insult and hoped to weaken us in this way as well.

In one important way, Grzymek and his cohorts nearly did succeed in breaking my family. Like all Jewish parents in Eastern Europe, my parents worried how to keep their children safe. It was a constant concern. My parents knew that many other Jewish families had placed their children with non-Jewish families and hoped in this way that their children could survive the war undetected. Some of these arrangements were permanent and some were meant to be temporary, with the children to be returned to their true families as soon as circumstances allowed. These were the so-called hidden children of the Holocaust, and they were great in number. Usually, there was some payment involved, some money that passed from the Jewish family to the non-Jewish family to be used for the child's safekeeping. Sometimes there was an additional payment or exchange of property, to compensate the adopting family for the risk they were assuming in taking in a Jewish child. Many Aryan families were put to death for harboring a Jewish child; many more were sent to prison just for suspicions of the same; more still lived in fear of being found out. Some of these situations were successful, and some ended in the discovery by the Germans of the deception. Very often, the children were so young that they did not remember their biological parents and grew up without ever knowing the circumstances of their adoption; many did not even know they were Jewish.

Some months into the German occupation, my parents looked into making just such an arrangement for me. I did not know about it at first. They began making discreet inquiries until finally they located a woman who was willing to discuss the matter. The woman they found wanted only me, not Pawel. It was difficult to find a family willing to take in a boy, because of course all Jewish males were circumcised and therefore easy to identify as Jews. But with girls it was not so easy to tell, Jewish or not Jewish. This was why so many of the surviving "hidden children" were girls.

This arrangement was probably a long time in planning. It is surprising to me now that I did not know about it beforehand or read it on my mother's face. Usually, I could hear my parents talking at night. We were living in only one room, and there was no space for secrets. However it happened, they found time to make the arrangements, and one afternoon a young schoolteacher came to our room to meet me. She had brown eyes and brown hair. She was a very nice woman, but I could not understand why she wanted to meet me. We did not have visitors very often.

My mother explained that this teacher wanted to take me. "She will be like a mother to you," she said. "You will go with her."

I understood immediately what they were doing, and I told my mother I would not go with this woman. It was difficult for me to be so strong in my argument because I was only seven years old, but I was firm. I said, "I will not go."

My mother said, "You have to go. There is no other way."

I said, "I am not going. Whatever will happen to you will happen to me. I do not want to live if it means I will not be with you."

I did not feel as though my parents were trying to get rid of me. I understood they were trying only to save me. But still I would not go. I would not be saved. I would not be removed from my family. Thankfully, mercifully, my parents listened to my appeal. They did not want to live without me, either, apparently. Looking back, I find it unbelievable that two such caring, thinking, desperate adults would listen to the pleas of a child on a matter such as this, but that is just what happened. They listened. They accepted that what might be an agreeable solution for other families was disagreeable to ours, and after a few minutes the nice young teacher left. I remember she had a warm smile.

It was an impossible puzzle: how to save at least one child, even if it meant breaking up a family, how to do your best when all around there was the worst. I did not understand this then, but I understand it now. It was a difficult time, with no sure or easy path for Jewish families. Each day, there was a new dilemma, another puzzle. I am still haunted, for example, about the circumstances of one particular day. It was early in 1943, during an action that was focused on the children. I was seven and a half. My brother was not yet four. We were living in the barracks in the heart of the Ju-Lag. All over the ghetto, the Germans were going from apartment to apartment, taking only the children. I imagine that for the Germans this served the double purpose of eliminating a large segment of the Jewish population and at the same weakening the will of the surviving adults.

During this action, my father hid us in the basement, where he had made one of his double walls. Our barracks was a large brick building with a large cellar, and he had fashioned this hiding place in such a way that the basement room where he put it up simply looked smaller than it actually was. You could never tell this hiding place was there, behind the false far wall of the room, if you were not looking for it. The cellar in this barracks building was where people took their things to be repaired, where the men would meet to discuss the situation with the Germans. My mother was working at the Janowska camp when we climbed into this hiding place. There was a small entrance. We had to crawl to enter it, but once we were inside we could stand up straight. There was no light, and we held each other's hands, for comfort. We were pressed in like sardines, and on the other side my father concealed the opening and closed us in. He put up some tape and some wood and painted over it so no one could tell that anything had been touched.

My father was nearly finished when my mother completed her long march home from the Janowska camp. All the way home, she said, she worried about me and Pawel. She knew the Germans were taking the ghetto's children and that we were in danger. She went first to our apartment, and of course she panicked when she discovered we were not there. "My children!" she cried. "Where are my children?!"

One of the women we were sharing the apartment with told her my father had taken us downstairs, and my mother rushed to the basement to make sure we were okay. She was overjoyed when she found us alive and well. Frightened, of course, but alive and well, and she joined us in our hiding place, so my father closed her inside as well. She would not leave us alone at a time such as this. Our fate would be her fate as well.

Again, I did not know this at the time, but there were those three vials of cyanide pressed into my mother's hand. All the time, she held these vials, thinking that if we were captured, there would be time to place the poison under our tongues and put a quick end to our suffering. Thank God it never came to that.

Some hours later, we could hear the Germans searching our building. It was just one German, as it turned out, but from our hiding place it sounded like an army. We could hear him thundering through the building with his heavy boots and his thick, gruff voice as he talked to himself. He was in the basement for the longest time, and we could hear all of this moving about. We stood very still. We did not make a sound. My brother was still very young, but my father had been hiding us for so long by this point, so many different times, in so many different places, that Pawel was good at keeping still and quiet. I held his hand tight, and he was quiet.

Finally, the German lifted his voice, as in discovery. "Wet wall!" he said. "Wet wall!" *Nass Wand! Nass Wand!*

The German soldier had been tipped off by another Jew in our building that we were in hiding and on inspection recognized that the false wall my father had built was a slightly different color from that of the other walls and wet to the touch because the paint had yet to dry, so he took a hammer to the spot and started to bang. I cannot be sure it was a hammer, but there was a lot of banging and commotion on the other side of the wall, and inside

our tiny hiding space we were terrified. Pawel at last started to cry.
I think I might have screamed. My mother did not move to hush
us, because we had been discovered.

When the German broke through the wall, he seemed more
puzzled than angry. He was surprised at the good job my father had
done in hiding us, almost pleasantly so, and he stood back from the
wall as if to admire my father's handiwork. The German soldier
would not have recognized it were it not for the wet paint, and for a
moment I thought he might congratulate us for fooling him in just
this way. My mother spoke German, and she understood that the
soldier was marveling at my father's ingenuity. But then he pulled
us out and started beating us with a leather crop. He hit me, over
and over. My brother, too. We both cried, I think. He hit my
mother. She did not cry, and I was proud of her for not crying.

And then, shortly after the beatings began, as if by some great
coincidence, my father came home. Probably somebody had gone
to tell him what was happening. He saw right away what was going on. He said, "This is my family. Please. Let them go."

He started to beg. It was not like my father to beg, but he would
do anything for his family.

The German, he was curious. About the wall, about the begging. He said, "Why did you hide them?"

My father said, "I hid them to save them. From the action. You
are taking all the children." Then he dropped to his knees and
begged again for our release.

The German became so frustrated with my father's begging
that he took the butt of his rifle and bashed him on the head with it.
The German, he was just a boy. He hit us like he was supposed to,
like he was following his orders, but it was not like he meant it. It
hurt, but my father said later it could have hurt a lot worse.

It was my mother who came to our rescue. She had a small handbag with her, and it was filled with food. Sardines, ironically, and some bread and biscuits. She did not know how long we would be shut inside our hiding place, so she had come prepared. She too must have sensed that this young man was uncertain of his role. She handed the bag to the German soldier. "Here," she said. "Take this." Then she handed him the gold watch from her wrist.

The German studied the watch as if it were a prize, and after a moment or two he said, "I will give you a choice. One watch, one child."

My poor mother, how could she choose? She was horrified. This was the difficult choice she could not be expected to make, the difficult choice she nearly made with the teacher who came for me, the difficult choice Jewish mothers were undoubtedly making all over Poland. She said, "These are both my children. I cannot take one and leave the other to die."

My father, too, was outraged at the suggestion. He could not choose between his children. He held out a photograph of me and my brother and shouted, "You see, they are both my children! You cannot make me decide!"

My father was bloodied from the blow to his head, but he kept begging for mercy, for our release. He believed that he could get what he wanted by the strength of respectful argument, by reason. He urged the German soldier to take him and to leave his wife and children behind. This was a choice my father could make, a choice he could die behind.

The young soldier seemed to consider this option, and then he quickly rejected it. He waved his hand in a dismissive way and said, "Stay!" *Bleiben sie!*

And so we were given a reprieve. My mother was so overjoyed

by this sudden show of kindness on the part of the German that she invited him upstairs to our apartment for something to eat. I did not understand this at the time, but I know now that she wanted to repay his kindness. She also wanted him to stay for protection. She could see that he was human after all. Also, she knew that if he left, there would be others coming to look for us. She knew that as long as the young German soldier stayed with us in the apartment, we would be safe.

Our apartment was on the first floor, directly above the basement, so we went upstairs. My mother was so happy that this latest threat had passed, almost giddy. She asked the German what he wanted to eat, and he answered that he wanted eggs with onions. *Ein mit ʒwiebel.* Even today, whenever I catch the smell of scrambled eggs and onions, I think back to that tense night in our kitchen, in that overcrowded apartment. I remember the German soldier who swung at us with his leather crop, who told my mother to choose between my life and Pawel's, and the way my mother and father managed to turn him from our enemy to our protector, to find the kindness beneath the cruelty.

My mother went to the kitchen and scrambled some eggs with onions for the soldier, and of course we all followed. She made him a heaping plate—six eggs, as I recall—and we settled in to watch him eat. As he ate, we could look through our kitchen window to the courtyard below and see that it was full of people. Jews, mostly, and they were frantic and frightened. All of our friends and neighbors had been emptied from their homes and onto the streets, where they were lined up in the gutter and waiting to be herded onto the transport. Some of them had already been shot, but most were just waiting or looking hysterically for their loved ones. Up and down the street, I could not see any children. They had already been taken away. All that was left were their grieving parents and grandparents, who were themselves about to be taken away.

Somehow, my mother managed to spot her cousin in the crowd, from the safety of our kitchen window. She pulled from her belongings another fancy watch and handed it to the German. She said, "Now *I* will give *you* a choice. One watch, one member of my family." Her German was perfect, so she was able to plead a convincing case. She pointed to her cousin and said, "That woman out there, that's my cousin. Go and bring her back to us. Please."

The German, with his full belly and another fine watch for his trouble, went downstairs and called the name of my mother's cousin, but she was too afraid to respond. She thought the man was just singling her out and that to follow him would be to go to her death. She did not know he was trying to save her. She did not know that her cousin, my mother, had sent him. She did not know that all she had to do was stand in answer and she would be led to safety. And so she sat with all the others and refused to acknowledge the soldier when he called her by name.

We looked on from the window, unable to help her, unable to signal that it was okay for her to go with this man, that it had been prearranged, and after a while the German simply gave up and left her in the crowd. And of course the Germans did come and take her away, and we never saw her again after that. But our German soldier came back to our apartment. He stayed with us a while longer, protecting us, sharing our food, talking to my father about how he had built this or that hiding place.

Soon after the transport was gone, a few thousand of our friends and neighbors dead or on their way, we heard some muffled crying from the kitchen window. Always, after an action, there would be a time when those who had been in hiding would get the courage to go outside and see what the Germans had done. And now, after our ghetto had been cleansed of virtually all children, I could hear these particularly sorrowful noises through the walls of the apartment and up on the roof. I looked outside, and everyone seemed stunned, ashen. It was, I realize now, the face of grief. And along with that face came something else. When I stepped away from the window, I heard a loud thud. It sounded like a sack of potatoes hitting the pavement below. Then I heard another loud thud, another sack of potatoes. I raced back to the window to see what might make such a noise, but my mother stopped me. She did not want me to look. She did not want me to see the grieving mothers, their children now taken from them, jumping to their own deaths from the roof of our building.

Our German soldier stayed with us until early that evening, when the other Germans left and the action subsided. For a few days or weeks, it was calm. For a few days or weeks, we felt secure. But then, every few weeks it was something else.

Somehow, my father's actions during Joseph Grzymek's grand procession had placed him on the mind of the SS Obersturmführer. Since then, they had many encounters, with the ghetto commander trying to get the better of my father and my father trying warily to outsmart his adversary. It was unusual for a German of such authority to pay attention to a Jew of such little consequence, but in my father's mind they became like rivals. Back and forth they went, as in a chess match. Grzymek had the advantage, of course, because he stood with the strength of the German army, the Gestapo, the SS.

Certainly, my father would not openly cross Grzymek. He knew what would happen. He had seen it with his own eyes. Once, my father recalled, a group of Jews was made to stand in a row. They were given some mops, some brooms, some shovels, and told to clean the streets. After some time, the SS man in charge told the workers to put down their tools. He told them that they were being taken to the Piaski. Of course, the Jews knew what this meant. They knew they were being taken there to be killed. One of them, a doctor, stepped to the front of the line and screamed, "You cowards! You are afraid of our mops and shovels! You are only strong in front of people who are unarmed!" Then he spat in the face of a high-ranking German officer, and when he did this the SS took out their revolvers and shot him. The rest, they corralled onto a transport and killed in the Piaski.

Another time, a group of Jews killed an SS man in the ghetto. This happened every now and then, a small uprising among a group of Jews who had been pushed to their limit, and when it happened this time, Grzymek decreed that fifteen hundred Jews would be taken as retribution. Fifteen hundred Jews for one German. This was the price of this one small uprising.

With my father and Grzymek, it was a more subtle conflict. Grzymek would deliver a difficult assignment for my father, and always my father would manage to complete it. Always there was something, and all of these somethings nearly came to a terrible end when Grzymek was preparing new living quarters for himself. He had placed my father in charge of some aspect of the renovation. My father had an impossible deadline to meet, and as it happened he did manage to complete the work in the time allowed. However, the paint on the interior staircase railing was still wet when Grzymek made his inspection. This, to Grzymek, was a punishable offense, so he decided that my father deserved to be hanged.

Every day, there was a lineup in the ghetto's main square, and Grzymek would make his pronouncements while the Jews stood in line. On the day of this "failed" inspection, Grzymek pulled my father from his place in line and told him he would be hanged. There was another worker assisting my father on this job, and this man was told the same. Their families, Grzymek said, would be sent to prison. My father knew Grzymek was crazy and that to say anything would be to make the situation worse. He had seen the way he could put down any Jew who made his life difficult. Even so, my father feared for his family, so when he was not being observed, my father passed a note to a friend asking him to tell my mother that she should take me and my brother and flee. This we did. We had been in our first-floor apartment and ran to a third-floor apartment in our building, where a kind tailor with a sewing machine helped us to hide.

My father and his coworker were taken to a corner of the square where the Germans had erected a gallows. Soon, Grzymek arrived and the ceremony began. Always, with this man, there was a ceremony. My father told us later that he was numb to what was happening. It was like a dream. He was told to empty his pockets, remove his belt, remove his clothes. He stood naked on the platform as they placed a noose on his neck. The other man was also made to strip and to receive the hangman's noose.

It was Pawel who noticed the commotion from our neighbor's upstairs window. He looked outside and said to my mother, "Look, Mama, they are going to hang someone." He did not recognize that this was my father.

My mother came to the window, and she knew right away this

was my father. I looked, too. We were on the third floor, and this was happening directly below our window. I recognized my father immediately. I wanted to scream, but I knew I could not.

My mother did not want us to watch. She said, "Don't look, don't look, don't look." She said this over and over, as if she were in a trance.

But, of course, I watched. Pawel was in my mother's arms, and she held his face to her chest in such a way that he could not see out the window. I looked over to her and saw that she was watching, too. She did not want to watch, but she could not look away.

My father wrote later that he was resigned to his fate, that it was as if he were inside his own bad dream. He stood and waited for the hanging to proceed, and then, inexplicably, Grzymek gave a dismissive wave of his hand and said, "Ah, you can stay alive." As if it were no longer worth the trouble to proceed with the hanging. He offered no explanation, and my father did not want to wait around for him to change his mind.

My father was stunned. Happily so, but stunned. The other man was also waved free, and he too did not know what to make of it. My father turned and bowed to Grzymek, as if he were thanking him for his freedom, and then he turned and began to step down from the gallows. As he did so, a German voice called him back: *"Halt!"*

My father thought, What could this be? Was this Grzymek playing with him again? Another round of cat-and-mouse? A cruel back-and-forth? *You will be hanged, you are free, you will be hanged, you are free.* This was Grzymek's nature, my father realized. This was just like him, to set him free and then hold him back. For amusement. But it turned out Grzymek merely wanted my father to take his things. His clothes, his belt, his shoes, his watch. Grzymek said, *"Hole dir deine sachen, wirst doch nicth so mit dem macketen schwanz herumlaufen.*" Take your things because you cannot leave with your naked penis.

My father had been walking away without any of his clothes, completely naked. He was so swallowed up by the moment that he had not realized, so he hurriedly collected his clothes, stepped into his pants, and walked quickly from the scene.

I remember hugging and laughing and crying with my mother and brother as we watched this. Hugging and laughing and crying, all at once. It was so unexpected, to look out the window to see my father about to be hanged, to see him suddenly set free, to see him scurrying away from the gallows without his clothes. There was nothing to do but hug one another and laugh and push away our tears. We had all been so scared, so terrorized, and we were now so weakened by our fear and overcome with relief that we could not help but find this picture a little bit funny, this picture of my father standing naked before the ghetto commander.

My father did not come home right away. He did not know we were in the tailor's apartment. Also, he did not want Grzymek's men to follow him, so he hid for a time in another building, and sure enough Grzymek sent the Gestapo to look for him. When they found my father, they brought him back to Grzymek. Once again, my father thought the game was continuing.

"Where were you?" Grzymek said. "I was looking for you."

"I was hiding," my father said.

"You are a coward," Grzymek said. "You are the biggest coward I ever met."

My father thought, I am the coward? In Grzymek's apartment, he has twenty-four-hour guards. He hides behind his guns and tanks and grenades. And I am the coward? He did not say anything, my father, but this was what he thought.

This would not be the last time the two would meet. Sometimes they would meet by chance, and sometimes Grzymek sent for my father. For whatever reason, Grzymek appeared fascinated with my father. Maybe he liked that he kept turning up, like a bad penny. Maybe he saw in my father the face of humanity. Certainly, the ghetto commander's inhumanity toward the Jewish people of Lvov was in full evidence, yet he had spared my father from hanging, and he would spare him several times more.

Once, Grzymek tried to ask my father about his background, as if to gain understanding. He said, "Who is your father?"

My father lied and said his father was an Austrian doctor. This seemed to impress the ghetto commander. He said, "Ah, so you have German genes! This explains it!"

Next he asked about my father's mother. Again, my father lied. He said his mother was a Russian princess. He was toying with Grzymek, manipulating him.

"Where were you born?" Grzymek asked.

"Turkey," my father said. It was like a friendly interrogation, and my father wanted to give Grzymek something with one hand and take it away with the other. This was how he explained it. He would let Grzymek think my father was of German descent and then infuriate him with the part about Russia and Turkey. He was a very proud man, my father. His back was not always bent. He would not be humiliated by this madman, yet to engage in a battle of wits with a witless German official was very dangerous; but my father believed Grzymek would not lash out at him if he remained intrigued. Also, my father knew that Grzymek needed him. Why? My father had developed a reputation as one of the finest carpenters in Lvov, and there was much work to be done.

Somehow, for some reason, Grzymek let my father go once

again, but he was determined to kill him with his own hands. This was what he said to his soldiers, my father learned later. Indeed, after the final liquidation, Grzymek was seen on Zamarstynowska Street searching frantically for my father. "Where is Ignacy Chiger?" he shouted. With everything else that was going on, he was going crazy that he could not find my father. There were not many survivors of this final liquidation, but one man who survived told my father about it after the war. He said Grzymek seemed obsessed.

The two would meet one final time, in 1949. Grzymek was on trial for war crimes at a court in Warsaw, and my father went to testify against him. Of course, my father was not the only person to testify, and I do not even think his testimony was central to the case, but he was looking forward to it because now Grzymek could not hide behind his bodyguards and his guns and his uniform. Now they would be equal. All during his trial, Grzymek denied everything. He did not admit to the actions, to the establishment of the Ju-Lag. He did not even admit to being in Lvov during the liquidation. And then he saw my father and his expression turned. It was, my father said, the strangest thing. The judge asked him if he recognized my father. Grzymek said he did not, but his expression gave him away. Eventually, his interrogator pulled the truth from Grzymek's lying lips. The questioning came back to the subject of my father, who was still in the courtroom. This time Grzymek said, "I know him well. Chiger. He was the main contractor in the Ju-Lag. He built all the bunkers. He checked all the canals. He was an artist."

Then Grzymek told the whole courtroom that he knew my father would survive. Among all the Jews, he knew, Ignacy Chiger was the one who would survive.

In the end, Grzymek was sentenced to death, and I could not say which my father seemed to relish more—that the SS Oberstürmführer finally received the punishment he deserved or that he at last acknowledged my father in this admiring way.

One of the last places we lived before being sent to the Ju-Lag barracks was in a small house at Kresova 56, with my grandparents on my father's side. We lived in the kitchen. There was a large credenza and a big old oven. The floor was made of raw wooden planks. I remember the planks because I spent so much time on my hands and knees scrubbing that floor for my mother. We were living in desperate circumstances, and sleeping on the floor, and still my mother wanted to keep a clean house.

My grandfather came home one evening and told my father we had to run. Something had happened, and the Germans were looking for his entire family. He said, "Tomorrow, they are coming for us."

My father, he did not want to run. He did not want to take his wife and children deeper into the ghetto. My grandfather Jacob, he was insistent. He said to my father, "You have to save your family." This was always the most important thing to my father, to protect his family. If he had been on his own, he might have fled Lvov some months earlier or entered the resistance movement. He might have joined one of the uprisings. It was not his character to quietly accept such cruelty and hopelessness. But he had his wife and children to think about.

Finally, my father relented and my parents packed our few things. My grandparents would leave in the morning, but we would leave in the middle of the night, because my father thought it would be safer for us to move about under darkness.

My grandfather lay down next to me while my parents were making ready to leave. He said, "Sing to me, Krysha. Sing me our lullaby." Always, I would sing him a lullaby before I went to bed:

Za gorami. (Behind the mountains.)
Za lasami. (Behind the forest.)
Tancowala dziewczyneczka z ulanami. (A girl is dancing with the soldiers.)

Always, I would sing and he would give me a kiss. It was our special routine. So I sang him our lullaby, and he kissed me and hugged me, and then we stood in the doorway and said our good-byes.

My grandfather had a fine gold pocket watch. He wanted my father to take it, but my father refused. My grandfather was insistent. He said there would come a time when we would need it to buy our way out of trouble, so my father took it. My grandfather's second wife—my *step*grandmother, a sweet, kindly woman whom I also loved—gave my mother a bottle of milk to carry for my brother, and then we went out onto the street. All of this happened in the doorway at Kresowa 56, before we disappeared into the night.

It was the last time I ever saw my grandparents.

Later, as we walked to some new place, my mother tripped and dropped the bottle of milk. It shattered on the cobblestone street. My father yelled at her. It was one of the only times I can remember him yelling at my mother. Probably his yelling had to do with something other than the milk. I was only seven, but I realized this.

My father doubled back the next morning to see which direction my grandparents were headed, hoping maybe to reconnect with them later, and he watched as a German soldier shot his father. There was nothing my father could do but watch. He did not see what happened to my grandfather's wife, but he expected the worst. He said it made his stomach turn to watch them shoot my grandfather, but this was what it meant to be Jewish in the Lvov ghetto in the early part of 1943.

Here is a curious memory. In our last proper apartment before we moved at last to the barracks of the Ju-Lag, my parents participated in a séance with a noted Jewish spiritualist. My parents did not believe in such things, but a group of people had gathered to listen to this man, and so my parents listened. The man's name was Dr. Walker, and he said he could predict the future of everyone who participated. He could tell who would survive the liquidation of the ghetto and who would not. He made a demonstration. There were about twelve people sitting around the kitchen table. Everybody was holding hands. At some point, the table began to knock. I do not know if it was the table itself that was knocking or if Dr. Walker was making the noise. The people all seemed to be hypnotized. Dr. Walker asked, "Who will stay alive?" Then he went around the table and the knocking stopped only when he reached my parents. He said this meant that they would be the only two who would survive. This was an ominous prediction to make among such a group, but Dr. Walker seemed to be somewhat hypnotized himself.

During the séance, an SS man appeared. Someone had left the door open and he stepped inside to see what was going on. He could see right away it was a séance. Everyone was startled by the noise of his arrival and awoke from their trance. They were scared that they

would be shot, because of course it was against regulations to engage in any kind of spiritual activity, but the SS officer sat down at
the table and said, "Continue." He was intrigued. Very often, this
was our experience with the Germans in authority. In a group, they
were brutal and heartless. Alone, they could be curious and feeling
and human.

Next, Dr. Walker moved to a part of the séance where the spirit
was spelling out certain words, like you sometimes see with a Ouija
board, only it was not a Ouija board. It started to spell out the letters "H" and "I." My mother told me later that everyone thought it
was going to spell out Hitler's name, but instead came the letters
"H-I-L-F-D-E-N-J-U-D-E-N." *Hilf den Juden*. Help the Jews.

The SS man appeared startled. He stood and left. The others
watched him go and considered the strangeness of the moment. To
be huddled in a séance with an SS man, in the middle of the ghetto,
in the middle of such terror and turmoil. Sure enough, the others
at that table would be killed. Dr. Walker himself was killed during
the very next action. And, just as Dr. Walker's table had predicted,
only my parents would survive.

For a few weeks more, my mother continued to work. Always, it
was very difficult for her to leave us each day because Pawel
would cry. He did not cry when she was gone, when we had to
hide, but he cried when she had to leave. The separation was
painful. He did not want her to go, and all day long he would wait
for her to return. Together, we would worry we might never see
her again. We would run to my mother at the end of her long day,
and we would hug her close and fill her with questions. We were
hungry for information about what was going on in the city, on

the other side of the ghetto fence. What the other people were doing. What the other children were doing. We were trapped inside, so long inside that any piece of news was welcome.

The Janowska camp was still being operated as a labor camp, but it was also a death camp. At its busiest, the Schwartz Co. plant employed over four thousand workers, and there were other manufacturers based at the camp as well. If you were young and strong and healthy, you were sent to Janowska and put to work. If you could not work, you would be shot. There was nothing in between. Sometimes the Germans would take you to the Piaski sand pits for the shooting, but sometimes they would just shoot you right there in the Janowska camp. It was not a place built for the execution of Jews, but it became a convenient place for it. Of course, the camp was not just for the Jewish people of Lvov, but for those from all over Poland, all over Europe. Over time, the Germans would kill over two hundred thousand Jews at the Janowska camp, although this number probably included the Jews who were shot at the Piaski nearby. The sad irony was that my mother went to work at the camp every day, sewing uniforms for the men who were out to kill us all.

Today, if you go to the Janowska camp, you will see a sign at the entrance. In English it reads, "Passerby, stop! Bow your head! There is a spot of the former Janowska concentration camp in front of you! Here the ground is suffering! Here the Nazis tormented, taunted, executed innocent people and sent them to the gas chambers. Let the innocently undone victims be remembered forever! Eternal damnation on the executors!" I think it is a moving inscription to commemorate the lives lost in this place. I read this and I get goose bumps, because this was where my mother worked each day, where so many members of my family were taken, where surely the earth must have absorbed so many tears, so much anguish.

It was around January 1943 that my father first started to think about where he would take his family when we were pushed at last from the ghetto. Already, he was running out of hiding places. For a time he considered fleeing. He had an Aryan friend named Michat Kollerny. They had played together on the national volleyball team before the war, and he had brought my father some false documents with our pictures on them that we could have used to negotiate our escape. There were four complete sets of papers, one for each of us, but my father determined it was too dangerous. He was too well-known because of his flirtation with Grzymek, so we abandoned this plan. We kept the papers, but my father was afraid to use them, except as a last resort.

Another plan was to build a bunker beneath the ghetto commander's quarters. My father thought this was an ingenious strategy—to hide beneath the very nose of the man who had vowed to kill him with his own hands. My father believed Grzymek would never search for him below street level, so he dug a tunnel from an unoccupied house across the street from the German command center. For several weeks, he prepared a bunker for us, while he was doing legitimate work on a greenhouse for one of Grzymek's men. The bunker was just beyond the ghetto fence, and each day my father would do his work on the greenhouse and then some extra work on our bunker. This went on for several weeks. He completed the tunnel. He put in supplies: an electric light, two beds, food, some pots for cooking. All by himself, he did this. It was, he thought, a good place to wait out the war with his family. Dangerous, but probably not any more dangerous than what we were facing aboveground. All that remained was to wait for the day when we would have no choice but to descend to this bunker and continue our lives there.

We were confined now to the barracks in the deepest part of the ghetto. The living conditions were miserable. The people were miserable. One night my father was doing some repair work in the basement of one of the barracks and noticed that it would be possible to enter the city's sewer system from this place. It would take some digging and some calculations to determine the precise spot for the digging, but it would certainly be possible. Later that same week, when he was hiding once again from Grzymek, my father escaped through a manhole into the sewer. He wanted to see what it was like beneath the city streets. The bunker he had built for us was really only an extension of a basement. It was not so deep underground that it could not be discovered. Perhaps it was not such an effective plan to hide us there after all. But the sewer! There were miles and miles of pipes and tunnels and good hiding places. They would not be pleasant hiding places, of course, but they would be safe. Certainly, my father thought, no one would look for us in the sewer, just as no one came looking for him when he escaped through the manhole. He found his way below by calculating the location of the streets above, and in this way he was able to resurface through another manhole in a different part of the ghetto without being detected.

This notion, that the sewer might offer us sanctuary, was a revelation for my father. He remembered when he was a small boy, when the Peltew River was open, before it was covered with stones by Italian POWs after the First World War. The Peltew was the main waste waterway for the city sewer. Back then there must have been a terrible smell by the river, which was probably why city officials were forced to cover it. My father watched the workers dig the first canals and set the stones for the retaining walls. He knew where the river ran in relation to the streets that had since been built above. It was not so long ago that the river was covered. It was not hard to reimagine.

At around this same time, my father met a man named Jacob Berestycki. The two men had good friends in common. They were told they could trust each other, and so they got to talking. Berestycki knew my father as someone who was very good at building hiding places. He wanted to talk to my father about building some kind of bunker beneath the city where together they could hide from the Germans. He was not thinking about the sewer necessarily, just some space below the street level. Someplace like the bunker my father had recently completed and stored with supplies. My father wanted to talk to Berestycki about this idea he had of using the sewer for sanctuary. Berestycki mentioned that he knew someone in one of the other barracks who was pursuing a similar plan. This was how it started: a group of Jewish men, reaching for some last, desperate measure, looking for someplace to go to escape the Germans.

Berestycki introduced my father to a man named Weiss. I remember going to meet this man with the rest of my family. I remember I did not like him. To be fair, Weiss did not expect my father to show up with his wife and children. He was expecting a secret meeting to discuss a delicate matter with a man he did not know. Still, I did not like this Weiss. He had some other friends with him, and I did not like them, either. They were all so sour, so miserable. We met in the basement of Weiss's barracks, and my father huddled with the men in one corner while my mother sat with me and Pawel in another. The men talked for a long time.

Weiss did most of the talking. He was like the spokesperson for his group. He had most of the ideas, but really it was just one idea: to descend into the sewer and follow the river to the outskirts of the city. My father did not think it was a good strategy to try to escape to the countryside with a wife and two small children. If he had been by himself, possibly he could have taken his chances. With his family to think about, however, it was better to find a place where we could hide for an extended period. His plan was to build a kind of bunker for us in the sewer where we could wait out the war, but he thought it might be profitable to continue his association with Weiss and these other men. He thought they could help one another.

Together, the men recognized that it would be possible to descend into the sewer undetected from this barracks basement. Weiss had heard of my father's facility with tools and carpentry and thought he would make a good addition to his group. Berestycki said he could be trusted. And so a partnership was formed. Weiss claimed to have a lot of money. The other men in his acquaintance also claimed to have a lot of money. My father, too, had money. Where he kept his money, I never knew, because at this point he had only the clothes on his back and perhaps another change of clothes. Probably he built good hiding places for his money and valuables the same way he built good hiding places for his children. Always, the Jewish people of Lvov were sewing money and jewelry into their clothes, so probably this was what he did. Wherever his money was, there was always enough to pay our way out of trouble, always another fine watch to replace the ones we had to trade for our freedom.

Very quickly, the men determined a good entry point into the sewer and began digging a tunnel through the basement floor of

Weiss's barracks. They took turns with the digging, using spoons, shovels, picks . . . whatever they could find. The floor was made of cement that had been laid directly upon the soil. The cement was cracked and broken in many places before the men even started to dig, so they targeted an area where the floor was already compromised, to make the digging easier.

With this new plan, my father abandoned the bunker he had made beneath the ghetto command. This would be better, he said. This would be our best chance.

My father built a false wall surrounding the area where he and the other men were digging, so that upon casual inspection it would appear that the basement was slightly smaller than in fact it was. The false wall concealed an interior room of about one meter wide and two or three meters long, and it was in this room that they did their digging. They dug very quietly, usually at night. Sometimes my mother would take me and Pawel and we would stay with my father while he dug. We did not like to be separated, but there was not so much room behind the false wall for all of us and the other men. There was not enough air to breathe. The men worked by candlelight, and the flame swallowed up oxygen, so it was difficult to get a full breath. Difficult, but not as difficult as being separated. During the day, the men would cover up their work with a carpet, a table, and some stools. Then they would go off to whatever jobs they were assigned in the Ju-Lag camp. During the day while the men were at work, we would sometimes use the concealed space to hide, if there was an action or some other uncertainty that required it.

We were not living in the same barracks as Weiss, but we spent a good deal of our time in that basement. I do not think Weiss and the other men appreciated having my mother, Pawel, and me around. It was such a small space, and everyone was nervous about being discovered. They must have worried that we might scream or cry and give us all away. My father was not worried about this. He knew we would be good, and he knew we wanted to be near. But the other men did not know us or how well we had been trained. They looked at us and assumed we were like other children, when in truth we were like animals. We knew only how to survive.

It took about eight days to dig all the way through the cement floor to an opening into the sewer. I remember it as taking much longer—weeks and weeks and weeks—but in his journal my father noted that it took only eight days. Eight very long days, from a child's perspective. Usually, my mother and father would work their regular shifts during the day, and at night we would meet in Weiss's cellar. Usually, we children would sit nearby with my mother and Weiss's elderly mother while the men did their digging. Most nights we fell asleep in the cellar, huddled in my mother's arms. Here again, the intrusion of children into this dangerous scene was not especially welcome by the others in our group, but my father did not give them any choice. He would keep his family near, he said, or he would lend his tools and his ingenuity to some other escape plan. He did not tell the others about the bunker he had already prepared, but he kept it in the back of his mind, as an option, in the event this uneasy alliance came apart.

Finally, the opening to the sewer was finished. It was small, about seventy centimeters in diameter, barely enough room for an adult to slip through, but it would have to be big enough. When the opening was ready, a group of the men decided to go through it, to make a kind of trial run. My father was among this group, along with Weiss and Berestycki. It is possible that they were joined in this by my uncle Kuba, my father's brother-in-law, whose wife and daughter had been taken in the action with my grandmother some months earlier, but I cannot be certain. Also, my mother's father, Joseph Gold, was still alive and living in another barracks, and he was included in our plans as well, although I do not remember my grandfather participating in the digging.

The group descended into the sewer with a lantern and some tools. There was a ledge above the Peltew, and the men walked along it for several hundred meters. The ledge was too narrow for regular walking; the men had to move with their backs against the stone wall, shuffling their feet from side to side.

My father reported that it was very dark and very noisy. The rushing water of the Peltew was like a thousand waterfalls. The men walked for several minutes, not knowing what to expect, not knowing what they were looking for. What most impressed them, my father said, was the absolute blackness. When the lantern was out, they could not see one another even though they were standing close together. They could not imagine how it would be possible to survive in such darkness for an extended period of time, but this was the last option available to them, they all felt.

The following day, my father and the others made another descent into the sewer, this time to look for a place that might provide adequate shelter. This time, as they stood sideways on the ledge above the Peltew, they saw another lantern swinging in the distance. This was terrible! The men thought they had been seen and would soon be captured. It never occurred to them that the lantern might have belonged to another group of Jews also seeking refuge. They thought it was the Gestapo. There was no place to run. They could only turn off their lantern and hope that whoever it was holding the other lantern had not seen them and would turn

back before they reached them. They could not turn back themselves, because without a light to guide them they would surely
fall into the rushing wastewaters of the Peltew below. So they
stood still and silent, the sound of their breathing swallowed by
the sound of the rushing water.

Finally, the lantern illuminated the faces of my father and his
companions. In the light, my father could make out the features of
the round-faced man who held the lantern. It did not appear to be
the face of a fellow Jew. This face was so round, so ruddy, it was
almost cherubic. The man who wore it did not seem to mean them
any harm. He seemed more curious than intimidating, my father
said. Behind this man, my father could make out the features of
another man, his face in shadow. And behind him stood a third
man.

"What are you doing here?" the first man said. He was dressed
like a sewer worker, with tall rubber boots and a cloth cap on his
head. His tone was pleasant.

"I am looking for a place to hide my family," my father said.

"Here?" the first man said, incredulous. "In the sewer?"

"It is the only place left," my father said.

The first man considered this for a moment, and then he whispered to the men who stood behind him, who were dressed in the
same manner. From their whispers, my father could hear that they
were discussing whether or not to turn them in to the Gestapo.
This seemed to be the preferred action of the two men in the background, but the first man who held the lantern seemed to have a
different notion.

After a short while, the first man spoke: "So it is not just the
group of you, then?"

My father shook his head. "I have a wife and two small children," he said.

The man with the lantern seemed to consider this. "Take me to them," he said.

It is interesting to me now, in the retelling, that my father did most of the talking, because up until this moment Weiss had presented himself as the leader of the effort. It was Weiss's initiative, Weiss's basement, Weiss's operation. He was always the big talker. But in the sewer Weiss was mostly silent, leaving my father to make this all-important first connection to the man who would ultimately become our savior.

My father and the other men retreated along the ledge above the Peltew the same way they had come in, their backs to the wall, their feet moving side to side. The three other men followed. They stopped when they arrived at the tunnel to the basement floor. The man with the lantern looked up at the opening. "Look at this," he said, marveling at the group's handiwork. "Look at what you have done." He was silent for a while, and then he said, "Maybe we can help you. For a price, maybe we can help you."

This was a welcome thing for my father and the other men to hear, because they did not know if these men were SS, or Gestapo, or Wehrmacht. They did not know if they had been captured and the three men were merely looking for accomplices before shooting them on the spot, or if these three men had no more official business in the sewer than they had themselves. It was a very tentative few moments, my father recalled.

The man gave his name as Leopold Socha. He was a sewer worker, he said. He introduced his partners, Stefek Wroblewski and Jerzy Kowalow. Kowalow was the foreman of their group, and he was said to be more familiar with the pipes and tunnels and crawl spaces of the sewer than any man in Lvov. Under the right terms, they would consider helping my father and his family, but first there would be much to discuss.

And then Leopold Socha fit himself through the narrow, spooned-out opening to the basement floor of the barracks above. The sight of his cloth cap peeking through the hole in the basement floor fairly startled my mother, who was expecting my father or one of the other two men. She was sitting and waiting for their return from their underground exploration, my mother having ssshhhed us to sleep some hours earlier. The last thing she expected was to see the cloth cap of a complete stranger. And then, beneath the cap, the stranger himself! My mother pulled us close. Her sudden movement awakened me, but I knew to keep quiet. I was on one side and Pawel was on the other. My mother did not know what to expect. Probably she was terrified. And as for me, probably I was more excited than scared. I took one look at this man's face and his warm, beautiful eyes, and I could not be afraid of him. I wondered, Who could this be?

Socha noticed my mother and smiled. He later said that it was at that moment that he decided to help us. The sight of my mother holding us close, like a hen and her two chicks. *Kania z piskletami.* This became his name for us. And this began a dangerous relationship that would not only save our lives, but also, Leopold Socha hoped, save his soul as well.

Four

⤝

ESCAPE

On May 30, 1943, SS Obersturmführer Joseph Grzymek staged his final ceremony. He organized a concert in an old gymnasium and ordered all surviving Jews of the Ju-Lag camp to attend.

It was another absurdity, forcing this group of oppressed, frightened, grieving, tortured, doomed people into a gymnasium for a party. And yet, my father related, there stood Grzymek by an old gramophone the Germans had carted into the hall, his face beaming, his manner drunk from power and happiness. Everything about the ghetto commander's appearance was an indication of his self-importance: the leather of his boots had been polished to a sinister shine; his uniform was crisp and perfectly appointed; his hair had been groomed into place. He was in his element, my father said. One of Grzymek's subordinates played popular Polish records of the 1930s as the ghetto commander encouraged his prisoners to dance. Whether they did so under fear of punishment or simply by coaxing was not clear, but—surprisingly, tellingly— quite a few of them did indeed dance, maybe under the confused thinking that there was something to celebrate or that by dancing, they would somehow win Grzymek's favor. Or maybe they danced just to dance.

My father could not understand why Grzymek staged this concert, what he was thinking. Perhaps it was a strategy to lull the Jews into a kind of complacency, like a decoy for what would happen next. Perhaps even in 1943 the pacifying power of music was known to the Nazis. Perhaps Grzymek truly meant it as a kindness, to make a gift of music and dancing to his condemned Jewish prisoners. Perhaps it was a final opportunity for Grzymek's inferiors to witness the superiority of the ghetto commander. Who can say? He was a twisted madman, so it is difficult to judge his motive here.

Of course, Pawel and I did not go to this concert. It was not a place for children. Also, the ghetto had already been liquidated of all children, so to make an appearance would have meant certain death. My mother did not go. She stayed in the barracks with us, fretting over what the music might mean. My father went to the gymnasium for a short time to make an appearance, before disappearing to the basement of Weiss's barracks to continue with his digging. He had learned since his unfortunate introduction to Grzymek to call as little attention to himself as possible and to move furtively about the ghetto. But at the same time, my father had to assume the Germans were taking note of the Jews in attendance and that to not attend the concert at all would have been more than just an insult; it would have been reckless. He certainly did not want the Germans to come looking for him.

The ghetto was otherwise still. It was a warm spring night. We could hear the sounds of the records through the thin wooden walls of our barracks apartment and through our one window. My father could hear the music from his tiny, suffocating basement work space. I recognized the polka "Roll Out the Barrel." Such a bouncy, playful tune that on this night sounded so chilling. It has been almost sixty-five years, and each time I hear that song I am taken back to this strange gymnasium concert. Once again, the power of sense memory is in full evidence; I close my eyes and picture that terrible man Grzymek, smiling insincerely, clapping his hands, trying to show the people a false good time, just as my father described him.

Even a child knows when a happy sound is laced with sadness. I knew that this concert could only mean that the Germans were once again going to do bad things to the Jews. To us. All along, my parents had done an admirable job protecting us children from what was happening. They wanted us to hold on to our childhoods as long as possible, to not be afraid. I figured out what was going on only in pieces. But here was something beyond my understanding. Here was bouncy, joyous, celebratory music, set against our hopelessness and despair. It made no sense, this concert, this evil, twisted ghetto commander ordering the people to dance and celebrate, and yet it could only mean that something bad was about to happen. This I knew.

We did not talk about it in our small barracks room. My mother tried to put us to sleep early that night, probably because she had some of these same dark thoughts, and I remember fighting sleep as the spooky sounds of these joyful polkas spilled into our room. In fact, I could not fall asleep right away. Of course, there was no bed-room. There was no bed. There was no mattress, even. I remember sitting on the floor with my mother, my brother sleeping in the crook of her one arm and me lying in the crook of the other, trying to get comfortable. All the time now, I slept with one eye open, but on this night the other eye would not close, either.

Prior to this night, my father had enjoyed several visits with Leopold Socha, the Polish sewer worker who would be our great benefactor and guardian angel. He had come up four or five times from the sewer to our tiny hiding place in Weiss's basement by prearrangement to meet with my father and the other men to de-velop the details of their plan. Sometimes he came by himself, and at other times he was accompanied by Stefek Wroblewski. My fa-ther and Weiss and probably Berestycki were always there to meet them. There were others, but I did not know these men yet. Al-ways, Socha would ask for my mother and us children, the hen and her two chicks. This was how he began each meeting, and my father said this greatly annoyed Weiss. He did not like how it moved the emphasis away from his group and seemed to inflate my father's role.

Socha did most of the talking during these meetings. The men were afraid that if they asked too many questions, Socha might realize some new difficulty and decide to abandon the plan, but I did not get the sense that Socha would ever abandon us. From the very beginning, I could see this was not his nature. Yes, I was only a child, but I was a good judge of character, and I liked Socha's character, so much so that I came to look forward to his visits. Pawel, too. Socha used to take Pawel into his lap and play with him while the men spoke. He had a daughter of his own, he told us. Stefcia. She was about two years older than me. He liked children, he said. He had a quiet, gentle demeanor. He used to bring us a special piece of bread or something else to eat, some treat we could not get in the ghetto. He knew how much this meant to us. The other men could not understand how this man they were counting on to save us could spend so much time on foolishness such as playing with my father's two small children. My mother and father liked that Socha showed us this kindness. It meant he could be trusted and that he saw us as human beings instead of as a group of desperate Jews willing to give him some money for protection.

I liked that Socha took Pawel on his lap. I liked that he gave us attention. I liked his bright smile. He had such beautiful white teeth, and when he smiled it filled the barracks basement as if with sunshine. He was always saying to me and my brother, "It will be okay, little ones. It will be okay." It was such a great comfort, hearing this, because he said it in such a way that I could not help but believe it.

How it would be okay, the men could not yet say for certain. Even Socha could not say for certain. The only certainty was that my father was pleased to have a course of action. It was a good and necessary thing, he said, to be taking control of our own destinies instead of having our destinies controlled by the Germans. One of the first issues the men were made to consider was payment for Socha's protection. The three sewer workers were asking for 500 zlotys per day, about $100. It would have been a small fortune in any city in Eastern Europe in the early 1940s, but it was especially so in the Ju-Lag of Lvov in 1943. No Jews had any money anymore. No Jews had a paying job. All we had was what we had managed to save and secret away.

On the one hand, yes, 500 zlotys per day was a lot of money, but the zloty had been so devalued during the war that it was difficult to gauge its worth. This daily amount was four or five times the weekly wage of the average Polish laborer, yet there was very little you could buy with it in and around Lvov. What good is money when it does not circulate among the people? Many of the goods and services in the ghetto were bartered, and many more were exchanged on the black market. The Jews, of course, could not buy anything, but even if you were Polish, it was difficult. Still, there was always the chance it would be worth something again after the war, and for this daily amount the sewer workers were promising to find us a safe place to hide, to bring us food and other necessary supplies on a regular basis, and to protect our hideaway from being discovered by the authorities in whatever ways they could. There were no guarantees, but under the agreement they would make every effort to protect us, until such time that our protection was impossible. They would use the money to pay for our food and supplies and divide what was left among the three of them—and even with these deductions and the devaluation of the zloty, there figured to be a rich windfall.

Weiss and the others wanted to negotiate with Socha on the price, but my father had already agreed to it. His consorts told my father he was crazy, to place such trust in the hands of a stranger. What if Socha took the money and turned them in to the Germans? What if he took the money and abandoned them to the rats and the filth and the rushing waters of the sewer? My father responded that they had no choice but to trust this man and his colleagues. Anyway, there was nothing else he could do with his money other than to use it for his family's protection, until it ran out. There were no other options: soon the Ju-Lag would be no more, soon even the Janowska camp would be liquidated of all Jews. And so it was settled. My father would pay half of the quoted amount; the other men would all contribute to the remaining total. The women and children would not be counted. They would pay Socha and his colleagues for as long as they could, never thinking that they would count their confinement for any longer than a few weeks.

This decision by my father to accept Socha's terms caused significant tension among the group. In the beginning, it was Weiss who was in charge—it was his plan, his basement, his initiative—and yet when the three men were first discovered by the sewer workers on their exploration of the sewer, it was my father who did the talking. This was a reflection of their personalities: my father was gregarious and personable; Weiss was gruff and miserable. Still, Weiss considered himself the leader of this loose operation, and most of the other men looked to him in this role as well. In addition to the men I have named, there were others, probably half a dozen or so, and these men too looked to Weiss. For my father, a simple carpenter who had come late to their discussions, who had the temerity to bring his wife and two small children into their midst, to agree to such a steep price on his own authority was a cause for concern. Yes, it was true that my father had agreed to carry half the burden, but this was a small point. My father had not accepted these terms to challenge Weiss's power, and yet that was how it must have been perceived, because it shifted the power among the group. My father had his own ideas about how to protect his family, and he would not bend to the majority if he felt that to do so would jeopardize his family—a family that now seemed to occupy a special place in the affections of Leopold Socha. Also, my father must have known how much money he had, how much jewelry, how much silver, and he must have calculated that if he alone could afford half of Socha's fee, he did not need to consult with the others on price.

On these visits to Weiss's basement barracks, Socha developed a kind of friendship with my father and a fondness for my family. This closeness also contributed to the tension in our group, as more and more it seemed to the others that Socha was working for my father and not for them. My father started calling Socha "Pol-dju," a familiar variation of Socha's first name, Leopold. They talked about the war. They talked about what was at stake for Socha and his colleagues, what they were risking by protecting us. They talked about what might happen to us if we were ever discovered in our underground hideaway. Also, they talked about Socha's family and his background, and these things together helped to convince my father that Socha was a good man.

While it was true that my father, Weiss, Berestycki, and the others had nothing to lose by placing their fates in the hands of these three Polish sewer workers, the sewer workers themselves were risking everything by their association with us. Even before we descended into the sewer, the fact that they were meeting with us in our basement barracks and discussing our safekeeping was enough to get them hanged—along with their wives and children.

Socha's colleague Jerzy Kowalow located a safe place for us to hide, and Socha arrived in Weiss's barracks basement one evening to give my father and the other men the location. He drew a map and told them how to get there. He also told them where he and Stefek Wroblewski would leave supplies for them in one of the underground passageways—some planks of wood, some cleaning materials, and other items the men would need to prepare the hiding place for our arrival. We would need boots, the sewer workers said, because where they were going they would have to slog through several feet of water and mud. Immediately, my father went with Weiss, Berestycki, my uncle Kuba, and another man who had joined our party named Mundek Margulies to begin preparing the hiding space. Margulies was a barber by profession. He was short and scheming and adventurous. Everyone called him Korsarz, because he looked so much like a pirate. (*Korsarz* was the Polish word for "Corsica," which was the term used for pirate.)

The men went two and three at a time, every evening after work, making ready. I do not think my mother's father, Joseph Gold, took part in these preparations, but it was understood that my grandfather would escape with us into the sewer when it came time. This was where the men spent their time when they were not working for the Germans. Mostly they were moving the dirt and debris from the hiding place discovered by Kowalow, trying to make it habitable. There was so much silt and mud and cobwebs that it took a lot of effort, yet no matter how much they worked, there was no disguising this place for anything other than what it was—a small, disgusting chamber in the depths of the city's sewer system.

On these trips to prepare our hiding place, Weiss would once again claim a kind of control. He told the men what to do, where to clean, how to organize. It was, he wanted everyone to think, his operation. It was his hiding place, open only by his invitation. Most of the other men involved in this effort were friends of his, of one kind or another. And yet whenever Socha was present, the authority would shift to my father. When Socha was elsewhere, Weiss felt he was in charge.

On one occasion, a group of the men crept into the sewer for a cleaning expedition when they once again saw the light from a lantern approaching from behind. Once again, they thought they had been discovered. They heard a voice command them to stop, in German. But the men did not stop; they ran. They shuffled along the edge of the Peltew, one hand pressing the wet stone wall behind them for balance. Just then, they saw another light in the distance, this time in front. They thought, We are caught! Trapped! The men did not know what to do. There was no place to turn. In front of them was the light from one lantern, behind them the light from another; to one side was the stone retaining wall of the sewer, to the other the killing white waters of the river.

My father told me later that his instinct was to continue forward, but really it was instinct and logic both. One thing was certain, he said: the voice from behind was German. One thing was uncertain: the light up ahead could have been held by friendly hands or unfriendly hands. It was a mathematical decision, reached on an impulse but at the same time by the process of elimination: their only chance was to press ahead, and as it turned out, the lamp ahead was in the hands of Socha and Wroblewski. What a piece of good fortune—another of our many small miracles!

There had been a big commotion on the streets of the ghetto following another small uprising. The Germans had discovered the body of an SS man hanging from one of the manhole openings. A group of Jews had banded together and attacked this German, who had apparently been alone at the time and was therefore vulnerable. The SS were searching the sewers trying to find the culprits. Socha and Wroblewski had gone down into the sewer to warn my father and the other men, who they knew would be preparing their underground hideaway.

The sewer workers quickly explained to the group what was happening and pushed my father and the other men into an opening just off the main canal. It was fortuitous that there was such an opening nearby and that it would lead them back to the basement opening they had prepared. Already, the men had made so many descents into the sewer that they were beginning to know their way through some of the canals and tunnels. Berestycki was able to lead the group back to the tunnel they had dug through Weiss's basement floor, where they sat and waited for word from Socha. At the same time, Socha managed to conceal the passageway the men had used to escape the canal, so the approaching Germans would not notice it in the near darkness. He and Wroblewski waited for them to approach, as if to receive instructions. They pretended to be in cooperation with the Germans and the other sewer workers conducting the search and allowed themselves to be led in some other direction to find the men thought to be responsible for the hanging. The Germans asked about the other group of men that now seemed to have disappeared from the canal, and Socha answered that it was another team of sewer workers off in search of their culprit. All of this my father learned the next day, when Socha returned to Weiss's barracks basement for their next consultation.

Socha told of the fear he and Wroblewski felt at the charade they created, because of course if the Germans had ever suspected they were not telling the truth, they could be blamed for the hanging of the SS man. This was the first time that Socha and his colleagues were made to realize how dangerous it was to associate with us. They knew it on one level, philosophically, but here it was presented in real terms. Kowalow and Wroblewski would actually press Socha into giving up the scheme of protecting us after this incident, but Socha would not consider it. He told the others that he would continue without them if he had to and that they would miss out on their share of the money. Apparently, this was enough to convince them to stay on. The danger was too real for any of them to ignore, but at the same time the money was too rich for them to turn away.

Meanwhile, my father and the other men continued with their preparations. They worked their various shifts for the Germans during the day and then retreated to Weiss's basement and to the chamber below at night. I do not know when they found time to sleep—probably they did so in shifts or not at all. Back and forth like this was how it went, leading up to the night of May 30, 1943. My father did not know when our party would at last have to disappear into the sewer, but he was determined that we would be ready. On this, the men could all agree, and our sewer chamber was as ready as it would ever be. There is only so much you can clean a sewer! The area had been swept. The men had stored their provisions—pots, pans, some canned goods—and they had prepared a small sitting area, using the left-behind planks of wood.

Of course, my father did not share any of these details with his seven-year-old daughter. I did not know that he was planning for us to hide in the sewer. I did not know fully where he went each night with the other men. I could guess that he was preparing some sort of hiding place, probably like the hiding places he had been preparing for me and my brother for the past year and more, but the sewer was never discussed in my hearing. Also, I understood that these other men were involved in some sort of larger plan and that Socha and his colleagues would also be participating, but that was all I knew, so it was a great surprise to me when I was awakened by the tumult of the final liquidation. Such chaos! There were people running everywhere. There was noise all around. There was such a terror that I started to cry. It was not like me to cry, but still I cried. This night was different. This night was the worst.

I was already dressed. I was wearing a simple white blouse and a dark skirt, with my beloved green sweater to keep me warm. Already, the sweater reminded me of my grandmother and what we

1939—This is one of my favorite photographs of my father, Ignacy Chiger.

1939—My mother, Pepa Chiger, standing on the balcony of our Kopernika apartment with my maternal grandparents, Shlomo and Hana Gold. The picture has special meaning to me because my mother was pregnant with my brother Pawel at the time.

1939—My grandfather, Jakob
Chiger, with my baby brother Pawel.

1939—My cousin, Inka Leinwand,
Kuba's daughter. I saw her captured
by the Nazis from the window of our
ghetto apartment in 1942. She was
killed soon after in the Brzezinka
concentration camp.

1943—My uncle, Kuba
Leinwand, who drowned in the
sewer in 1944.

 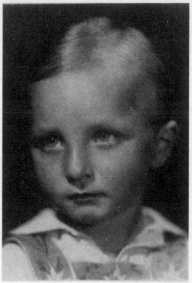

1943—This is a picture of me taken in the Lvov ghetto, not long before the final liquidation. When I think of myself and my time in the sewer, this is how I look in my mind's eye.

1943—My brother Pawel, also taken in the ghetto. This is how I remember him during our time in the sewer. Look how sweet, how innocent he appears.

(Undated)—Another cherished photo of my father. Notice the worn and tattered condition of the picture. This is because my parents kept it among their things while we were in the sewer.

1945—Leopold Socha with Mundek Margulies, taken in Katowice, Poland.

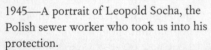

1945—A portrait of Leopold Socha, the Polish sewer worker who took us into his protection.

1945—A dinner celebration with Leopold Socha seated next to Klara Margulies. In Socha's arms is Henry Margulies, son of Klara and Mundek. Standing behind Socha is his daughter Stefcia, next to Halina Wind. The woman seated to Klara's right is unknown to me.

1947—Our family portrait, taken in Krakow, where we lived for a time after the war.

1991—Klara and Mundek Margulies, with an unnamed friend, standing in the same courtyard where we first saw daylight after fourteen months in the sewer. The manhole at Klara's feet is the same manhole we crawled through almost fifty years earlier.

1997—With my own family, standing in front of a photo of me on display in the Cannon Rotunda in Washington, DC. That's my husband Marian on the far left, next to my son Roger. I am standing next to my son Doron.

2000—Me, with Henry Margulies and Henry Berestycki, at the Imperial War Museum in London, in front of a display commemorating my time in the sewer together with Socha, my family and their parents.

2006—Me and my husband Marian standing alongside the green sweater that has come to symbolize my family's ordeal, and the suffering of Jewish children during the Holocaust, at the United States Holocaust Memorial Museum in Washington, DC, where it is on permanent display.

2006—Here I am standing in front of the Statue of Neptune on a return trip to Lvov. The fountain was one of our main sources of fresh water during our time in the sewer.

ПЕРЕХОЖИЙ, ЗУПИНИСЬ!
СХИЛИ ГОЛОВУ!

Перед тобою місце колишнього
Янівського табору смерті!
Тут стогне земля!
Тут мордували та знущались,
тут розстрілювали
та відправляли до газових камер.

ВІЧНА ПАМ'ЯТЬ НЕВИННО ЗАГУБЛЕНИМ!

ВІЧНЕ ПРОКЛЯТТЯ КАТАМ!

Встановлено 19 листопада 2003 року
Міжнародним центром „Голокост" ім. доктора А. Шварца
до 60-ї річниці ліквідації Янівського концтабору.

PASSER-BY, STOP!
BOW YOUR HEAD!

There is a spot of the former Janovska
concentration camp in front of you!
Here the ground is syffering!
Here the Nazis tormented,
taunted executed innocent people
and sent them to the gas chamblers.

LET THE INNOCENTLY UNDONE VICTIMS
BE REMEMBERED FOREVER!
ETERNAL DAMNATION ON THE EXECUTERS

Established by the International Holocaust Centre named after Dr. Alexander Schwarz
on November 19, 2003 to the 60-th anniversary of the liquidation
of Janovska concentration camp.

2006—A photo of the sign outside the Janowska camp memorial on the outskirts of Lvov. After so many years, the sentiment is still so moving to me.

2006—A recent photo of our apartment building at Kopernika 12, where I was born.

had lost. There was nothing really to prepare, nothing to pack. My parents simply awakened me from my fitful sleep and told me to follow them. I remember insisting to my mother that I wanted to wear my white-and-blue sandals. I thought they were so pretty. She wanted me to wear my heavy boots. "The place we are going, you cannot wear sandals," she said. I asked her where we were going, but she could not answer. What could she have said? In the end, though, she let me wear my sandals. What did it really matter?

I took my father's hand, and he led me toward the small basement hiding space where the tunnel had been dug. I said, "Where are we going?"

He said only, "Don't worry, Krzysha. It will be okay." He was comforting me, soothing me, telling me only as much as I needed to hear, each step along the way. In his voice I could hear the same reassuring tone we had grown accustomed to hearing from our new friend Socha, and I believed it, that we would be okay. I was scared, a little, and crying, a little, but at the same time I trusted my father and Socha to take care of us.

I will never forget the panic I felt that night when we finally descended into the sewer. It was a panic shared among the surviving Jews who must have known this was their final hour. *Our* final hour. Throughout the ghetto, there was a pandemonium of the kind I have never experienced since. People running for their lives, screaming for their loved ones, fleeing in terror. It was something no child should have to experience, this measure of alarm, and the most unsettling piece was that we had all known something like this was coming. It was in the air and all around. And yet when the moment was upon us, it was as if it had come from nowhere.

We were prepared and unprepared both, and while we were in its middle there seemed no end to it.

In the quiet just after the absurd concert in the gymnasium, the Ju-Lag had been quickly surrounded by SS, Gestapo, and Ukrainian militia. Perhaps the music had had the desired effect, because many of the Jews in the ghetto were caught off guard. SS Obersturmführer Grzymek had ordered heavy trucks to be driven into the camp, to transport the people who were to be rounded up for execution. We had seen these trucks before, but never so many, all at once. The noise of the trucks outside the thin wooden walls of our barracks was sickening, not only because of the noise itself, but because of what the noise represented. The previous actions had all been terrible, but this final action was terrible and more. There were not so many Jews left in Lvov to begin with, and here the Germans were out with a show of force that seemed to have us substantially outnumbered. There were more of them than there were of us, it seemed, and they also had guns and grenades and leather crops and other weapons to use against us. It was an excessive display, a brutality on top of a brutality. Everyone was running, pushing, crying. It is a wonder that my parents were able to hold on to us children, let alone keep us safe and whole.

I still had no precise idea where we were going. I held my father's hand as he led me to the small basement alcove where he had done his digging, and then I watched as he began to slither into the small hole he and the other men had dug into the floor. Someone held a lantern to light our tiny space, but there was barely enough light for me to recognize all the people. I could see my uncle Kuba. I could see my grandfather, my *dziadziu*. I could see Berestycki. I could see Korsarz, the Pirate. Weiss and his fellows, I could not make out in the commotion. Already, I had decided that I did not like these men. The others who had come and gone from Weiss's basement to discuss these secret plans, I could not say for certain which of these people I saw on this night. My goodness, there were so many people. More than I had ever seen in this particular barracks. Some I had never seen before. There was Weiss's wife and mother and daughter. Apparently, he meant to escape with his entire family. And there were others who were drawn to the sewer as a means of escape. They had thought of this on their own, without any help from my father's organized group, without any digging or preparations or protection from Leopold Socha and his sewer worker colleagues. For us, it was a calculated plan; for the others, it was a last resort, a shared desperate measure.

I was confused for a moment when my father disappeared through the hole in the basement floor, into a shaft about seven meters in length, and down to the floor of the sewer. I could not see him in the darkness below, so I called out to him. He called back to me. His voice sounded so near, near enough to touch, but I could not see him. He was urging me to follow him, but I could not. I was frozen with fear. I was with my mother and brother. Korsarz was trying to gently push me through the hole to the chamber below, but I was pushing right back, maybe not so gently. He was encouraging more than pushing, but I was resisting with all of my strength. I did not want to go. I did not like that I could not see what was at the bottom of the shaft. I did not like all the noise and confusion. I did not like being pressed together with so many people. My father was trying to be encouraging, trying to ease my concern, but there were so many people yelling at me in the basement, telling me I was taking too long, that I was holding up the line, that all I could do was stand there.

I was not the only one unwilling to go into the sewer. Weiss's wife and daughter also would not go. They realized where they were going and what misery awaited them there and refused to descend through the hole the men had dug. Weiss went anyway, leaving behind his wife and daughter. This was something my father could never understand; it would color his thinking about Weiss for the rest of their time together, that he would abandon his family in such a circumstance.

Meanwhile, Korsarz kept up with his pushing, a little less gently with each moment that passed. My mother was trying to be patient, but she quickly ran out of patience. It could not have been easy for any of them, this escape, and I was certainly not making it any easier, until finally I dropped to the cement floor and dangled my legs through the hole. I was only seven years old and fairly slight of build, and I could see that it would not be easy even for me to fit my way through the small, jagged opening.

I went first, followed by my brother and then my mother. My father reached up to grab my legs, and I made a small leap into his arms. Then he set me down on the muddy ground at my feet and turned to grab little Pawel. Someone held a small lantern, but still I could not see very well. I held fast to my father's coat as he reached to collect my brother and then my mother. I did not want to lose him—it would have been too easy to be separated in all the excitement. I was crying, screaming. Pawel was crying, screaming. If I listened carefully, I could make out the cries of other children. This surprised me. I had thought Pawel and I were the only children left in the ghetto, because it had been so long since I had seen another child, but these voices were unmistakable to me. I heard them crying, screaming, and wondered where they had been hiding.

Probably this happened in just seconds, this climbing through our basement floor to the sewer below, but it was an agonizing few moments. There was my hesitancy, and the refusal of Weiss's wife and daughter, and then everything happened quickly. The people kept coming through the small opening into the sewer, but also they kept coming through other manhole openings on the street. They did not care about disappearing undetected through some secret shaft. All they wanted was to disappear, and they were quickly spilling into the pipes and tunnels of the sewer, like rushing water. The Germans knew that people would seek asylum in the sewers, so they ordered the Ukrainian militia to throw grenades through the manhole openings. Up and down the streets of the ghetto, the Ukrainians were prying open the manholes and dropping grenades into the sewer below, setting off a series of explosions that surely left dozens of Jews dead.

The noise of the explosions. The darkness. The scary noise of the rushing water. The terrified screams of so many desperate people confined into such a desperately small space. The echo. It was beyond imagining. And just then, at seven years old, clutching tightly to my father's coat, I could not comprehend it. What would make such a noise? I wondered. What was happening?

Somehow, through the darkness, my father managed to move along the ledge of the main canal, which was directly alongside the opening he had dug through Weiss's basement. This was even more terrifying because of the enormous sounds of the rushing Peltew. It was like Niagara Falls, the way the noise bounced from the pipes and reverberated in the echo. A horrifying clamor! Oh, I was so scared! It could have been anything, this noise: a hundred rushing trains, a thousand waterfalls, a squadron of German fighter planes . . . My father had been along this main canal several times already, so he knew what we would find, what we would hear, but he did not tell me or my brother what to expect.

I remember the hard edges of the stone wall along the ledge above the Peltew. The ledge was narrow and slippery, and I pressed as close to that wall as I could. At one point, my uncle Kuba lost his footing and fell into the water. My father lunged to save him, and when he did he lost the small knapsack he was carrying with some of our possessions. Probably this was the knapsack with my boots, because I did not see my boots after this and I was left only with my sandals. My father did manage to rescue Kuba, however, so it was a good trade. We counted ourselves lucky yet again, because all around us people were slipping and falling into the water and they were not being rescued. The currents were swallowing them up.

My father walked in front of me, holding my hand. My mother was behind me, holding my brother's hand. I kept asking, "Where are we going? How much longer?"

My father kept answering, "A little bit longer, Krzysha. A little bit longer."

At one point, I was moving so slowly that my father lifted me up and put me on his shoulders, which must have been very difficult for him to do as he shuffled side to side above the river. I do not know how long we walked in this way. Maybe for ten or fifteen minutes, but it seemed like hours. Finally, we came to a bridge, which led to the other side of the river, where my father and the other men had prepared our special hiding place. Unfortunately, there were so many people in the sewer that we could not safely cross the bridge to our own haven. It was at this point that we lost contact with my grandfather. My mother, she was so upset when she realized *Dziadziu* was no longer with us, but probably she thought we had just been momentarily separated and he would meet up with us later.

There was such a surge of people, such a rush of activity and tumult. My father must have considered our circumstance and recognized that if we headed for our underground hideaway, we would have been followed by a mob of desperate people. We would have all been trampled! Or we would make such a noise that our voices and clambering would be heard on the street above. Either way we would have been doomed, so we kept walking. Probably my father was thinking we could double back once the surge of people had dispersed deeper into the sewer. Still the people kept screaming and crying, and still we kept walking, right past the hiding place my father and the others had worked so diligently to prepare.

My father had not expected such a crowd. He realized later that so many people in the Ju-Lag had known his reputation for building shelters and hiding places that they were sticking to him and his family in the sewer. Probably they were thinking, Wherever Ignacy Chiger is going, that is where I am going.

We stopped at another bridge that led to another network of tunnels and pipes. It was not so much a bridge as a few loose planks spread across an open span. Once again, I froze briefly. There was nothing to hold on to, no railings or stone wall for support, and the planks seemed so unsteady that I worried they might snap. They had been left behind by some sewer workers and had been crossed countless times by men who undoubtedly weighed four times as much as me, but I did not trust those planks. It was only a few meters across, but I could not get myself to cross until finally my father took my hand and began to pull me along. He did not wait for me to gather my resolve, as before. There was no time for resolve.

Somehow we managed to separate from the rest of the people.

My father turned us one way while the others continued on, and in this way we came upon another small chamber, along with Jacob Berestycki and Uncle Kuba. There was about a foot of raw sewage at our feet. It was the worst place imaginable. The smell! The spiderwebs! You could not move an inch without getting caught in a giant web. Also, it was terribly cold. It was spring already, but in this part of the sewer it was like winter. My mother could not understand what my father meant for us to do in such a place. To sit? To wait? For what? And she was so upset about losing my grandfather. She knew he would never find us in this secret place. She was very nervous, very unhappy. For a moment, it was like the small breakdowns she used to have when we were living at Zamarstynowska 120. Soon, she would develop the strength and will that would help us survive our underground ordeal, but for these first few moments she was very tense, very worried.

During the weeks of preparation, my father had most likely told my mother that the men were cleaning a bunker where we could hide for an extended period. She understood that the bunker was to be in the sewer, but she did not fully make the connection to what this might mean. Or maybe she did and was persuaded that this was the last sanctuary available to us. In any case, the prepared bunker would have been a four-star hotel compared with this small, dreadful place. It would have been swept clean, at least. It would have been somewhat habitable. There would have been something to eat, someplace to sit and rest, some heavy blankets to keep us warm. My father and the other men were counting us lucky for stumbling upon this terrible place, for separating ourselves from the pack of people, but my mother was afraid to move or sit down or stay in this place any longer than absolutely necessary. Pawel and I, we did not complain like my mother, but we did

not like it, either. Everywhere you looked, there were rats under-
foot. Hundreds of them. Thousands, maybe. And worms—a thick,
slimy layer of worms, worms of all sizes, covering the walls, the
rocks, the mud. Too many worms to count. It was worse than our
worst nightmare, and we were inside of it.

We were in this place only a few short moments when we heard
a cry that seemed to be coming from the main canal. Kuba and
Berestycki went immediately to investigate. We did not want to
give up our privacy and once again be tossed about with the rest of
the crowd, but the men could not let this scream go unchecked. It
was different from the other cries. It was the cry of someone in
pain. After they left, it was very quiet in our small chamber. The
four of us—me, my brother, my mother, and my father—were
afraid to move. We did not want to touch anything. There was no
place to sit. There was nothing to say. And so we stood, still and
quiet. It felt to me as though the worms were crawling up my leg. I
looked down and tried to shake them off, but they were not there.
They were all around, but they were not crawling up my legs.

We stood like this for several moments, until another cry shook
us from our thoughts. This time, it sounded like my uncle Kuba,
screaming for help. At first, my parents did not seem to hear. Or
maybe they did not recognize the voice as Kuba's. So I told them,
"It is Kuba. Don't you hear? It's Kuba."

My father ran for the main canal, but first he gave my mother
instructions to stay in this terrible place with the children. She was
not happy about it, none of us were happy about it, but there was
no place else to go. Also, to leave would mean to risk separating
from my father, and she had already become separated from her
own father. My father would come back to this place to find us.

Next, my father retreated to the ledge along the Peltew, and there he saw Kuba, flailing about in the rushing water. My uncle had managed to grab a small promontory reaching out from the wall toward the river and had kept himself from being swept downstream. As before, he had slipped and fallen, only this time my father had not been right there to rescue him. Berestycki was off someplace else, the two men must have gotten separated, which left only my father to save his brother-in-law. He did this by following Kuba's cries until he reached him, then pulling the belt from his pants and tossing one end into the water, so Kuba was able to grab it and my father could pull him to safety. It was a dramatic rescue, to hear them tell it afterward. Kuba was so heavy, my father said, and the current so great, it was like pulling a fallen tree limb from the banks of a river.

Unfortunately, this piece of good fortune came with some bad luck beneath it, because my father and Kuba somehow lost their bearings and could not find their way directly back to our disgusting chamber. It was easy enough to follow the river, upstream or downstream, but the pipes and chambers and other small openings that fed into the main canal were sometimes difficult to locate in the near darkness. We waited and waited for them to return, but they never came. My mother could not wait so long in that disgusting place. She could not understand what was taking my father so long. She did not say anything to me and Pawel, but she started to think he and Kuba had drowned. The uncertainty, the conditions . . . it was just awful! I did not know to think that something bad might have happened to my father, and I did not mind the conditions so much because I was with my mother. It was horrible, but I did not mind. After all those hours, day after day, hiding in those confined spaces my father had built for me and my brother, never knowing if or when my parents would return, this filthy rat hole was like nothing, because my mother was with us. And I was conditioned by this point to expect my father to return. Always, whenever he left, to go to work or to run an errand of some kind, he would come back to us before long. It was the way of our family, the way of our circumstance. But my mother could not stay there. It was unbearable. She said, "Whatever will happen, will happen." She said that even if the Gestapo found us, it would be better than staying in such a hellish place. She must have known this meant we might not find my father in the maze of tunnels and pipes and chambers, but she did not speak of this. Anyway, it did not matter. She could not stay there.

And so we left. We had a small light my father had left behind, and my mother used this to help us return to the main canal, to the slippery ledge above the Peltew, and we continued in the direction we had been going, the river to our right now that we had crossed that first bridge. We did not walk side by side, as before. We moved instead like a tight sandwich, my brother pressed close to the wall, my mother squeezed into the middle, and me on the border of the ledge. It was difficult footing. My mother held my hand tightly, and it was a good thing too because I kept slipping. Every few steps, I lost my footing and fell knee-deep into the Peltew before my mother could snap me back up to the ledge like a rag doll.

It was so dark. We had the light, but we could not easily use it. My mother did not have enough hands to hold the light and at the same time hold me and my brother. She would not trust the light to me or Pawel; we might drop it into the river or onto the stone ledge. So we fumbled our way through the darkness. I was scared, but not so terribly scared. I did not mind dipping into the water because I knew my mother would snap me right back up. She was strong, and I was little. It might have been a game, had it not been so dark and dirty and dangerous. We walked and walked along the river, not really knowing where we were going, just going.

It is interesting to me now that I did not once ask for my father as we were going against his instructions. I was old enough to realize that by leaving this terrible place, we might never reconnect with him, but I did not say anything and did not question my mother. I was also happy to leave this disgusting, filthy place, so I did not think too much about my father just then.

We walked along the main canal for several minutes. I kept slipping into the water and my mother kept pulling me back to the narrow ledge. Finally, we saw another lantern ahead, and now suddenly I thought of my father. I screamed, "Daddy, Daddy!"

And that is who it was. My father wrote later that my mother was so desperate, so crazy, when she reached him that it was a long while before he was able to calm her. She had not shown her panic to Pawel and me, but she was hysterical with concern over my father. She did not think we would ever see him again, and once we were reunited she nearly broke down. Probably she was overwhelmed with grief and concern for her own father at the same time she was overjoyed at finding her husband. This lasted only a few minutes, and then she was back to herself, but in those few minutes her desperate, crazy happiness at finding my father became mine. Pawel's, too. We could not believe our good fortune at being by his side once again, even though we had moved from that terrible place where he had left us without really knowing where we were or how we might reconnect. It was certainly an odd, unsettling sequence of events, with the momentarily joyful outcome that we were reunited once more.

Berestycki, meanwhile, had located Socha and the other members of our group, and Socha had asked him to retrace his steps and hopefully find our family, so Berestycki doubled back along the main canal and managed to intercept us during our joyful reunion. He reported on Socha's whereabouts. He told my father and Kuba that all along the Peltew there were people falling to their deaths. Already, we had seen some of this for ourselves, but not to the extent Berestycki was telling us. So many people! So many tragedies! From the different manholes on the street, people were spilling into the sewer, dozens and dozens of people, and in the panic and disorder most of them were drowning. It was a tragic irony, the men agreed, that so many people should descend into the sewers to escape certain death only to find certain death in the currents of the river.

Socha was with Weiss and the others, Berestycki said. They were with quite a lot of people, including many women and possibly even some children. These other people from outside our group did not know what to do with themselves. They did not have a plan. Weiss and the others had not made it to the special hiding place they had worked so hard to prepare. Everyone had been swept up by the noise and confusion and pushed along in the surge of people. When Socha arrived among this group, they descended upon him like famished prisoners seeking a small piece of bread. What they were hungry for, Berestycki said, was a small piece of hope, and this was what Socha represented. He stood before them as their salvation, and they quickly surrounded him, begging for him to save them from this dreadful situation. At this, Socha stated very clearly that he would offer what help he could, but only for Ignacy Chiger and his family, the hen and her two chicks. *Kania z pisklet-ami*. The others, he would continue to help as well, but our family was his priority, he said. He would help the others because by doing so, he would also help our family, because he knew we would need several sets of hands to help us survive our underground ordeal.

My mother asked Berestycki if he had seen her father in the forward group, but he could not be certain. Probably he knew my grandfather was not among Weiss's party, but he did not want to be the one to tell her.

I listened in, but I could not be scared. I was too happy to learn that our beloved Socha was looking for us here in the sewer, because I knew that under his care we would be okay. This was what he had told me during all those visits to Weiss's barracks basement, and I fairly flew to the area where Socha and the others were wait-ing. Of course, it was another long walk along the difficult, narrow ledge and through a small pipe, but I did not notice the time or the difficulty. When we finally arrived, Socha was standing with the others, and when he saw us his face bloomed with light.

Socha was happy to see us, but I could see on his face that he was also frustrated and worried. He did not know what to do with such a large group of people. There were over seventy of us now, in the side canal where he had gathered the group. He was also angry at Weiss. He was a smart man, Socha, and he suspected that Weiss was somehow profiting from his association with the sewer workers. There were so many people gathered around Weiss, ad-dressing him in familiar, entitled terms, that Socha began to think Weiss had collected money from these people and in exchange had offered Socha's protection. Probably Weiss did not think Socha was so smart and was trying to put one over on him. These people were not complete strangers, as Weiss would have Socha believe; a great many were likely friends and associates to whom Weiss had promised some measure of safekeeping. Socha was never able to confirm this, but this was what he suspected, and my father would come to share his suspicion.

My mother's eyes searched frantically among this group for her father. She called his name. She asked people in the crowd if anyone had seen him, but many of these people were also looking for friends and family and could not be troubled. She was caught in the space between hoping for the best for herself and her own little family and believing the worst about her father.

Whether or not Weiss took money from these others, their presence was a big problem. To look after so many Jews in the sewer was a big undertaking, and a big risk. Socha did not think it was a good idea for us to remain with such a large group, that it would put our family at risk. Also, it would put him and his colleagues in jeopardy. It was too dangerous, this many people, too difficult. Socha did not like that he had been put in this situation, to have to determine the fates of all these strangers. Plus, there were children among this group, and Socha did not wish to turn his back on a child. He and his colleagues had not agreed to these terms. He would not play God for these people, he said, because even God would not undertake a doomed enterprise.

Socha took my father aside and told him he would have to think about what he would do next. He would have to consult with Kowalow to determine a new strategy, whether to find a new place to hide this big crowd of people, whether to find a new place to hide only the original group, whether to abandon the plan altogether.

After a few moments, Socha and Wroblewski left, promising to return when they could do so safely. The strangers among our group were very angry at this, and they began yelling and screaming once more at Weiss and his fellows, but there was nothing Weiss could do and no place for any of us to go. Seventy people in such a small place was quite a lot of people, and we could not move about so easily. We were huddled in a small tunnel. My father recognized the location. He determined that we were beneath the corner of Cebulna and Boznicza streets, where during the day there was a farmer's market in the square. At least, before the war there had been such a market, where the local women sold fresh bread and produce. I remembered going to this market when I was a small girl, the smell of the wonderful Kulikowski bread, the bustle of activity. I could not understand how this terrible place where we were standing could be directly beneath the place of such warm, wonderful smells. I closed my eyes and tried to imagine it. My father whispered to me that it would soon be morning, and I realized I had not thought about what was happening outside for the longest time. It could have been daylight. It could have been darkness. It made no difference to us.

Another sense memory: the smell of the Kulikowski bread has stayed with me. I remembered it as a small child, trapped in the sewer, and I remember it still. When I finally came to the United States, to New York City, I was tired of the processed white bread that was sold in most stores. It was the 1970s, and all there was in American supermarkets was Wonder Bread. But then, as we were driving one afternoon on Broadway, around 80th Street, those same wonderful smells came to me through the open windows of our car. Immediately, I shouted out, "Kulikowski bread! Kulikowski bread!" I was so excited. I got out of the car and followed my nose across the street to the bakery section of Zabar's, surrounded by all these fresh breads that smelled fantastically like the fresh breads they used to sell at the market

above our first underground hiding place. I had never heard of
Zabar's, but this is how I discovered it, by what I remembered.

There were not so many dry places to sit in this small tunnel
where Socha had left us. Most of the people were standing. My
mother found a stone to sit on and made a place for us on her lap.
She held us close and tried to rock us to sleep, but of course I could
not sleep. Pawel slept for a while, but I held tight to my mother and
ached for her as she wept silent tears for my grandfather, for all of
us. My father stood huddled with some of the men, discussing a
strategy. Everyone was speaking in a whisper, careful to keep our
voices from being heard. When people yelled, it was also in a kind
of whisper, and I remember thinking it was somewhat funny, that
people were angry enough to raise their voices but not so angry
that they would lift the volume as well.

After a while, it became difficult to breathe. Some people had
brought candles, and the candles kept going out because there was
not enough oxygen to feed the flames. Once we realized what was
happening, we used the candles sparingly. A few people carried
flashlights, but these stopped working before long. We spent most
of the time in darkness. There was nothing much to see, anyway.
In each sliver of light I could see hundreds of rats scurrying about.
It was better, I thought, not to see at all.

At the time, I thought this tunnel was a big open space, but it
was only about three or four meters wide, maybe six or seven meters long. This explained why the candles kept going out—we
were pressed together close, breathing one another's air. We were
sitting up against the legs of the other people. From my perspective near the ground, I could see the legs of another few children.
Already, I had heard their voices, but now, in the flickering candlelight, I could see them, and I tried to remember the last time I

had seen another child. I wanted to call out to these children, but I could not. I did not know how to raise my voice and still keep to a whisper. I could only keep still and quiet in this horrible place. Everyone was so quiet, so nervous. We were careful not to make any unnecessary noise, wondering what was happening above us on the street. In the quiet, I imagine all these strangers were wondering about their families. For us, this was not a worry, because the rest of our family had been taken. There were only the four of us and Uncle Kuba.

I thought of my imaginary friend, Melek. I would not speak openly to him in this place, inside such a commotion, but I talked to him silently, in my thoughts. I was glad to have him near. I said, "Well, what do you think?"

He answered, "It is not so bad, Krysha."

This was Melek, trying to lift my spirits. This was me, trying to convince myself that everything was going to be okay.

Outside, it was the end of the Ju-Lag. We learned the details later, but on this first night we knew it in our hearts. We were 150,000 Jews before the war, and after this final liquidation we would number only 5,000 at the Janowska camp. My father received a report that piles of corpses were being thrown into Grzymek's waiting trucks, which were then driven to checkpoints outside the city before returning empty to receive more bodies. The action continued for three days, and at the end of these three days the ghetto was reduced to ashes. What they could not shoot or capture, the Germans burned to the ground.

During the next few days, Socha and Wroblewski managed to bring us some bread. Each day there was a big round loaf that Weiss and the others would pull into many small pieces. There were only a few loaves for so many people, and this further enraged the men who seemed to have made a separate arrangement with Weiss. Socha stayed only long enough to deliver the bread and to discuss a few things quietly with Weiss, Berestycki, my father, and a few of the others. He also brought some carbide for the carbide lamps he left behind. I remember that there was a lot of tension and misery among our group. Some of this tension was because of our miserable conditions and general discomfort, and some was over the arrangements our group had made with Socha and his colleagues. There was no drinking water, no room for everyone to sit at the same time. I remember that when people had to go to the bathroom, they did so in the corner, pretending at privacy, as if this made a difference. My father tried to keep his sense of humor, even about this. He said we were sitting in sewage, so what did it matter if we did our business off to the side? He said this to my mother, only she did not think it was funny.

On the third or fourth day, Socha returned and announced that he could not continue with such a large group. My father guessed in his journal that this happened on June 4 or June 5. The group did not at first understand what Socha meant by this. There was a good deal of anxious murmuring and uncertainty as Socha explained that it was too difficult to gather sufficient food and other supplies for so many people and that to keep us safe and relatively comfortable (and quiet!) was also impossible. It placed him and his colleagues in danger, and it placed the entire group in danger as well. It would be better to save only a small group, he said, as originally planned, and he told us he would select only a few of us to follow him deeper into the sewer. My parents were not so worried about this because they knew we would be among those to be saved, but the others were alarmed. The men begged Socha to continue with his protection. The women threw themselves at his feet. The children began to cry. It was a wretched scene. My mother pressed me and my brother into her coat so we would not have to look and covered our ears so we would not have to listen.

Somehow, Socha separated a group of twenty-one from this large mass of people. How he arrived at this number, we never knew. How he made his selections, we also never knew. Among this group were Pawel and me, my mother and father, Uncle Kuba, Weiss and his mother, Berestycki, Korsarz, two disagreeable brothers named Chaskiel and Itzek Orenbach, another disagreeable fellow named Shmiel Weinberg and his wife, Genia, and another nine individuals. Weinberg and the two Orenbachs were part of Weiss's crowd, and Socha was persuaded that our group would be better able to continue with his payments if they were included among us.

The other fifty or so, they begged and begged to go with us. One man, a well-known jeweler before the Soviet occupation, approached Korsarz and offered to give him a bundle of diamonds if he would put in a good word for him with Socha. Korsarz could keep the diamonds himself or share them with the sewer workers, the man said. There was pushing and shoving and excitement, and in the confusion the man with the diamonds somehow stumbled and the handkerchief containing all his diamonds fell into the water. This was the measure of everyone's desperation. All the jewels in the world could not have changed Socha's predicament, which was now our predicament as well.

Our smaller group was haunted by the pleas for mercy offered by the larger group we were leaving behind. We would hear their remonstrations in our dreams. We worried over their fates, but at the same time we knew they would not fare well. Even to a child, this was clear. It is amazing to me now that none of these people followed our group as we moved deeper into the sewer. They argued Socha's decision, but they did not go against it.

Some weeks later, after our group had been settled for some time in a nearby chamber, Korsarz would return to this place and discover the bodies of many of these people. Some of them had drowned. Some of them had apparently gone off on their own in search of sanctuary. Some swallowed the cyanide poison that most Jews had taken to carrying, their bodies now eaten away by rats. Korsarz was very upset when he came back to our group after his discovery. He told my father what he had seen, and he was very upset, too. But they did not talk about it after that, because of all the difficulties we would face during our underground odyssey, leaving behind these other desperate people, these families, these children, was probably the most difficult.

After separating from the large group, we walked along the Peltew for another stretch, until Socha led us into another side tunnel. This tunnel was so narrow and the bottom was curved in such a way that there was not enough room for us to walk with our two feet together, so we moved heel to toe, heel to toe. One foot in front of the other. Pawel and I could walk normally, but the feet of the adults were too big to fit comfortably. Also, there was waste-water at the bottom of this pipe, in some spots reaching almost to the hips of the grown-ups. For me and Pawel, it was almost above our chest. The water level made our forward movement very slow, very difficult, and it only got worse. There were so many of us in the narrow opening—twenty-three counting Socha and Wroblewski—and we displaced so much water as we moved through the pipe that the level reached higher and higher as we filled the space. Before long, my father had to carry me, and my mother had to carry Pawel, to keep our heads above water.

From this pipe we moved into an even smaller pipe, this one maybe seventy centimeters in diameter. It was the first time we had to crawl through the wastewater that accumulated on the bottom of these pipes, and we tried not to think about it. Socha and Wroblewski were crawling, too—Socha in front and Wroblewski in the middle of our long, snaking line. Each held a carbide lamp to light our way. Finally, we reached a hatch in the roof of our pipe, and Socha stopped to pry it open. Through it, there was an iron ladder built into the stone wall, and we climbed up this ladder to another narrow pipe and continued crawling. Socha climbed the ladder first and helped us from above. Wroblewski crawled past the hatch and waited for the rest of our group to pass through it before bringing up the rear. No one spoke as we moved. No one complained. It was very tight inside the pipe, very close, and there was not a lot of room to wiggle through, even for me and Pawel. But somehow everyone managed.

At one point, one of the carbide lamps caught our movement in such a way that it put a picture in my father's mind of a group of trapeze artists at the circus, climbing a thin ladder to reach the high wire. It takes a certain personality, I realize, to compare what we were doing with the actions of circus performers, but my father was always considering our circumstances in the most positive way. To me, we were not like circus performers. To me, we were like animals. Wherever our sewer workers told us to go, we went. Whenever they told us to sit, we sat. Whatever they gave us to eat, we ate. Whatever we had to crawl through, we crawled through. Even old Mrs. Weiss, the oldest of our group, was on her knees and elbows, crawling through mud and sewage, and no one complained. No one talked. We just did as we were told and hoped for the best.

Five

~*

OUR LADY OF THE SNOW

I must pause here and share what I know about Leopold Socha's background, because it is useful to understand what motivated this man to help us the way he did.

He had not lived such a happy or noble life, our Socha, before meeting my family. He had been in and out of prison. As a child, he got into all kinds of trouble. He was orphaned at a young age. He was a ruffian. School was not important to him. It is a heartbreaking thing, to know someone and to come to love and admire that person and then to discover that he had such a difficult childhood. That is how it was with Socha. He ran with a group of young men who did not respect other people. He was never violent, but he was disrespectful. Certainly, he did not respect other people's property; he became a petty thief. His concept of right and wrong seemed to have more to do with what he could get away with, whether or not he would be caught. He was good at stealing, but not so good that he could avoid the police. By the time he had reached his middle twenties, he had served three separate three-year terms for robbery—once for a bank job that had captivated all of Lvov for its brazenness and careful planning, and once more for a petty break-in at an antiques store.

The bank job was well-known in Lvov. Socha entered the bank through the basement, approaching by the sewer where he would later work and where we would seek our sanctuary. It was quite a clever plot, the authorities said, and after Socha made away with the cash, he stowed it in one of the pipes leading away from the Peltew River. My father remembered reading about it in the newspaper. Indeed, Socha might have gotten away with the heist if he had not been so reckless with his spending and with his tongue, and the lesson he learned was to choose his words and his audience very carefully. His great worry, during the long months he was protecting us, was that one of his colleagues would have too much to drink and boast about the Jews they were hiding in the sewer. Already, he had learned this lesson, and he knew that to violate it here would mean certain death.

The antiques store robbery was a great coincidence. It was the sort of break-in Socha and his hooligan colleagues performed regularly, only here he happened to target an antiques store owned and operated by my mother's uncle. We discovered this association some months after our first meeting. Socha took some silverware, some jewelry. My mother remembered this incident, and now she was sitting across from the man who had perpetrated it. Of course, it no longer mattered about the silverware and the jewelry, but it was a strange point of connection just the same.

Somehow, Socha met and married a good woman named Wanda. She convinced him to turn his life around. He took a government job as a sewer inspector. He did not consider the irony: the very sewer where he had staged his greatest robbery, where he had stowed his loot and plotted his escape, would now deliver him a second chance. Since adolescence, most of Leopold Socha's life had been spent behind bars of one kind or another. Now that he was married, soon with a young daughter, he was looking to change. He was still a young man when he started meeting with us in Weiss's basement. He had just rediscovered his Catholic roots. With his wife he attended church regularly, something he had not done since he was a child. He prayed. He came to believe deeply that by redeeming himself in his present life, by living in a good, purposeful manner, he might absolve himself of past sins.

This was his character when he met my father and the other men on their exploration into the sewer. He had not counted many Jewish people among his friends prior to this meeting, but he did not like how the Germans were treating them. He did not understand it. At the same time, he liked that these Jews were refusing to accept such treatment. He liked their willingness to fight. He wanted to help them because they reminded him of how he used to be when he was up against authority and because he had learned in church that by helping others, you can help yourself.

There was also the money. After all, it was Leopold Socha who put the price on his kindness. It was Socha who came up with the figure of 500 zlotys per day. It was a lot of money, to be sure, but he had to use some of it to purchase bread and our other essential supplies and to divide what was left between Wroblewski and Kowalow; so the money alone could not account for his generosity. Some months into our confinement, when our money would finally run out, it would be Socha who would convince his colleagues to continue with their protection. It might have started as an opportunity, but in the end it would become a lifeline. He would come to consider it his life's work, helping us to hide in the sewer, protecting us from the Germans, returning us to the rest of our lives just as he hoped to return himself to the life he had nearly squandered as a young man.

It must have been difficult for the adults in our group to remain hopeful, considering our dreadful position. For me and Pawel it was not so difficult because we were in the dark. This is an appropriate phrase, because for most of the time we sat quietly in the dark and also because we did not know what was going on. My mother was still distraught over what might have happened to her father. My father, he was distracted by the change to our plan. He had not been preparing to spend so much time in such a small, disgusting space, with such a group of terrible people. He may have been thinking that we would have been better off in the original bunker he had prepared by himself beneath the ghetto command.

Of course, I did not like our present situation, but I was also hopeful. It is a child's nature, I believe, to think positively, to be encouraged toward a happy outcome, and even after everything my family had endured, I was still in this one respect a child. I did not have it in me to think we were doomed. Do not misunderstand: I did not like it very much, sitting there in the sewer, but I did not mind it so terribly much, either. Not at first. A little bit later, I would mind. A little bit later, I would become sullen and noncommunicative; that is how much I would long to breathe fresh air, to play with other children, to return to a normal life. My nature would change. As I remember it, this change to my outlook happened some months after we went into the sewer. As my father remembered it, though, this change happened straight away. Either way, it happened. I went from a happy, good-natured little girl to a hardened, desperate creature; my time underground would go from a necessary adventure to a hardship. But in those first days and weeks, all I cared about was that I was with my parents, that my family was together.

I did not know most of the other people in our group just yet. I had not even seen their faces in the darkness, but I would begin to know some of them by their voices and by the unreasonable demands they would make on Socha and Wroblewski. For the first time, listening to the disquiet of our new companions, I realized how difficult it was for them to sit quietly and uncertainly in the darkness. For me, it was not so difficult. After all that time in hiding, I did not think it was so bad. My parents were near, and this was enough for me. I was not yet conditioned to think in worst-case scenarios, so I trusted my parents to see me and Pawel safely through. There was nothing else to consider.

Our dark, dismal quarters were only a little bit better than the elliptical tunnel where we had been staying those first few days. The mood of our group, however, was little improved. This second place was more like a room than a tunnel. We were not pressed so tightly together. It was also wet, fetid, and cold, but there were places to sit. There were stones here and there, and this was where we sat—me on my father's lap, Pawel on my mother's. I cannot imagine that it was comfortable for my parents, sitting on those stones hour after hour, but it was better than standing, better than squatting among the rats in the film of dirty water at the curved bottom of the pipe in our first hideaway.

The rats were one of our biggest problems in the beginning. We would eventually get used to them, but during these first few days we were still somewhat frightened and disgusted by them, so my father and some of the other men positioned themselves over our group with sticks, and they were constantly swatting at the swarm of rats at our feet. The men worked in shifts, so that there was almost always someone assigned to chase the rats, but of course this was a futile exercise. The rats were everywhere! The swatting would cause them to scatter, but then they would return. The effect was like a crash of waves against the shore; the water would go out and then it would come back in again. Eventually we realized that we could no more chase the rats from this chamber than they could chase us, and my father took the philosophical position that we would have to adjust to each other.

This new chamber was located beneath a church called Maria Sniezna. Maria, Our Lady of the Snow. I remember thinking this was a good omen, to hide beneath a church. We were Jews, of course, but it made me feel protected. As though God were watching over us. Our God, their God . . . it did not matter. My mother would come to regard Leopold Socha as our guardian angel, and already he was watching over us in the shadow of the Maria Sniezna church, helping us to stay alive. My father remembered that on June 10, 1943, just a few days into our stay in this new place, the churchgoers above celebrated the feast of Corpus Christi. He remembered that from our underground bunker we could hear the sounds of the procession, the ceremony, the voices of the children singing. In his journal he noted that I was saddened by the apparent contrast between our lives underground and the lives overhead. I must have expressed to my father that I wanted to be outside, gathering flowers and playing with the other children.

My father knew precisely where we were in relation to the streets aboveground. He knew this church and the surrounding square. Underground, he was not always so sure how to get from place to place, but he was proud of how well he knew the streets and buildings of Lvov. He took such enormous pleasure in this. I was proud of my father, too. He was also our guardian angel. And he knew so much! About so many things! My father could tell you when this church was built, when that road was expanded, when this part of the sewer was finally covered. Whatever you wanted to know about the city, he would tell you. He would come to know the underground pipes and tunnels as well as he knew the streets and alleyways of Lvov, but in the beginning Socha had to draw him a map.

The chamber beneath the church was about ten meters by twelve meters. At the bottom of the far wall, there was an opening to the pipe that was our only safe exit. On the other end of the chamber, above our heads, a manhole led directly to the street. There was an iron ladder bolted to the wall, reaching to the manhole cover, and we sometimes used this ladder to hang our few things, to dry our clothing if it was wet, to keep any extra food from the reach of the rats on the floor below. We were so close to the church and its surrounding square that we could hear the people talking on the street above our heads. We had to remind ourselves to keep very quiet in this underground space, because of course if we could hear the sounds from above, then we could be heard from below. I could hear the children playing. Always, they were playing. This was how we could tell day from night. If we could hear the children playing, it meant the sun was shining.

I did not like this place. I did not mind it, but I did not like it, either. What was there to like? It was dark, and foul-smelling, and wretchedly cold. It was uncomfortable sitting so long on those round stones, and of course there was not enough ceiling height for the adults to stand straight. They had to walk stooped over. Pawel and I could stand and walk about, but the adults were too tall. Even Jacob Berestycki, whom I now noticed had an unfortunate hunchback, could not manage to reach his full height.

The pipe leading into our hideaway had a radius of only forty centimeters, yet my father and the other men had to crawl through it each day in order to retrieve drinking water for our group. It was an arduous task. It seems almost impossible to me now that this was what the men had to do in order to supply our group with drinking water, but this was how it was. Socha estimated that it was about two kilometers to the dripping fountain that was the source of our freshwater, a long way to go when you are crawling, holding a teakettle in your teeth by its handle, in a pipe so narrow that there is hardly room to move. At the other end, after the men reached the fountain, they would have to retreat backward, because there was not enough room in those forty-centimeter pipes to turn around. In the seventy-centimeter pipes you could turn around, but not in the smaller ones. The men would go two and sometimes three at a time to fetch the water, and the round-trip would take nearly two hours—a long way to go for such a little bit of water. Sometimes it was such a tight squeeze, my father would come back with his arms all scratched and bloodied from the hard, sharp edges of the pipe and the bolts that jutted into the passageway. His clothes would be torn.

From time to time, a group of men would make other excursions in search of material and supplies. They did not yet know their way underground so well and could only retrace their steps, so several of these excursions were return trips to our basement barracks, to the opening they had dug in the cement floor several weeks earlier. There they would find discarded household items like pots and pans, and these articles were as precious to us as jewels. Whatever we needed, we could usually find there, until one of our group became careless. He was spotted one afternoon through the barracks window, rummaging through our left-behind things, by a Gestapo officer. Immediately, the German gave chase, but the men were able to retreat safely to the sewer. The next time they returned, however, they found the basement opening had been covered with boards.

Socha and Wroblewski also used this forty-centimeter pipe, which opened into our one small room. It was the only underground passageway that led to where we were sitting, so there was no other option. My father and the other men were not yet used to moving about in such a tight, narrow space, but Socha and Wroblewski were used to it. This was how they moved about in their underground world, how they got from place to place. Every day, they would bring a little bit of food for our group. Usually, it was just a loaf or two of bread, although my father wrote in his journal that they also brought sausages. I do not remember the sausages, but that might be because I soon became very, very sick and was not interested in eating. I developed a violent case of diarrhea and dysentery that lasted for weeks and weeks, beginning almost as soon as we made camp beneath the church. Pawel, too. In fact, everyone became sick in the beginning, in our small chamber beneath Maria Sniezna, but no one was as sick as Pawel and me. This was when my parents began giving their daily ration of freshwater to me and my brother. They collected their share—three-quarters of a glass—but they would not take a drop; they saved it for me and Pawel and in this way probably kept us alive. My father wrote later that he was so sick himself, and so thirsty, that he sometimes drank the sewer water to quench his thirst, thinking it could not make him any sicker than he already was. Probably this was not such a good idea, but he did it anyway. He did not think it was possible to become sick on top of sick. No one could determine if we were sick from the germs in the freshwater, from the food, or from the bacteria in the air, but it was a debilitating, exhausting sickness. Disgusting, too, although I cannot say that our diarrhea and nausea contributed in any meaningful way to the waste that was already all around.

For many years, I remembered that Pawel was sickest of all during these first days and weeks and that my parents were frantic with worry about his health, but when as an adult I finally read my father's manuscript, I realized I was the sick one. I was so disoriented, so dehydrated, that I placed the worst of my sickness on my little brother. Already, I had spent most of the previous four years taking care of little Pawelek, protecting him, collecting his hurts, that to carry the full force of our sickness must have seemed to me my due.

In addition to food, Socha and Wroblewski would bring us supplies—carbide, for the lamps they had given us to use; tools and materials, so that the men might improve our living conditions; medicine, if one of our group was sick. One day Socha brought a curative for Pawel, who was suffering from some angina and strep throat. This was my mother's diagnosis, and she wanted him to have some medication. Socha and my father, however, were worried that if Socha went too many times to the pharmacy, it might alert the authorities, and we could not afford to arouse suspicion or have Socha followed. He actually went to the pharmacy, but then he turned around and left without trying to purchase anything because he was so worried, and the next day he came back to our chamber and asked my mother if there was something else he could bring for my brother. She suggested a home remedy known as a gogel mogel, which was popular among Jewish families across Eastern Europe. The precise recipe changed from family to family, from region to region, but my mother made it with eggs and sugar. The mixture was said to be very good for the throat. She mentioned this to Socha, who promised to return the next day with the ingredients.

A few hours later, however, we heard a clamoring in the pipe that opened into our chamber. Someone was coming! My father stood by the opening with a stick, thinking this might be an intruder, and then through the opening we saw Socha. This was such a surprise! He had not wanted to wait a whole day to deliver the remedy for Pawel, so he had gathered the ingredients and crawled once again through the forty-centimeter pipe for the second time that day. He had crawled with four eggs tucked carefully inside a handkerchief, which he had knotted on the sides and carried in his teeth, like a St. Bernard. Can you imagine? Crawling through several kilometers of pipes, carrying such a delicate thing as four eggs with his mouth, to make certain they would not break. This was why my mother thought of Socha as our guardian angel—and soon enough the rest of us would think of him in this way as well.

Socha and Wroblewski were extremely careful about their daily trips to our hideaway. They came to us each time from a different street entrance, and we could hear them sloshing through the mud and water for a full half hour before they actually arrived. Such a noise they made, clambering through that pipe! Always, their colleague Kowalow was stationed as a lookout on the streets above. The sewer workers had a ready alibi in case they were discovered. They were always dressed in waterproof overalls and rubber hip boots, carrying appropriate tools and lanterns, so if they were ever questioned, they could convincingly maintain that they were on legitimate sewer business. And, indeed, they often were, because there was usually some proper assignment for them to carry out as well. It was the contents of their satchels that worried them—how to explain the food and other supplies—so they determined that if they were ever confronted, they would throw the satchels into the river and let the current carry them away.

Early on, the sewer workers had an opportunity to use this alibi during a dangerous encounter with a Gestapo officer as they attempted to descend into the tunnel from the street. The man approached them in a questioning manner, and Socha and Wroblewski quickly tossed their satchels into the water as planned, after which they argued with the man for distracting them and causing them to lose their supply of cement in the river. Their confrontational approach was effective, because the Gestapo officer soon waved them along. Of course, we went without food that day because our daily ration of bread and other supplies was floating down the Peltew.

On most days, Socha and Wroblewski would bring something else to go along with the food, whatever they could comfortably carry in the satchels they wore slung over their shoulders so that their hands might be free for crawling. When we were sick with dysentery, for example, and the cold water from the fountain seemed to aggravate our stomachs, my father requested some rubbing alcohol and a tin can of sardines; he improvised a Sterno stove by lighting the alcohol and warming the water in the tin can. In this way, my father was able to soothe our stomachs and still make sure we received the water we needed to survive. The sewer workers brought these things and anything else they could obtain and carry. They would also deliver news from the Ju-Lag, which my father and the others would discuss in whispers throughout the day. Socha and Wroblewski would not stay long, only long enough to assess our situation and to rest for a few moments before making the return crawl through the narrow pipe. They would also collect their payment, which my father handed to them daily. Socha himself suggested this arrangement. He did not want my father to give him a large sum all at once, because no one knew how long we would have to hide and because Socha did not want to put my father in the position of wondering whether or not the sewer workers would return to complete the job. What if something happened to Socha on his way to or from this hiding place? What if our sewer workers were discovered? It was better, Socha said, for my father to pay them each day and in this way to keep their association on a very professional level, with mutual trust.

Very quickly, the man who had orchestrated much of our escape and who attempted to coordinate much of our confinement revealed himself to be a man of dishonor. This did not surprise my father, he later said. And it did not surprise me. I was an observant child, and I could tell from the beginning that this Weiss was not a good person. He was mean-spirited and deceitful. He had left his wife and daughter in our basement barracks when they had been too scared to descend into the sewer. And now it turned out that he would not pay his full share of the money to Socha after all. Neither would his friends. There were other men who were meant to pay as well—strangers to us, but not necessarily to Weiss—and they would also neglect their debt. They simply did not have it to give. What little they had was gone in the first few days, and after that the burden fell almost entirely on my father. This placed my father in a dilemma. He was worried that if he told Socha about the default of the other men, it might upset our situation in any number of ways. He thought it would be better if he continued paying Socha the full amount and making up the difference from his own pocket. In this way, Socha would not have cause to think that the group he had chosen was in any way duplicitous. Certainly, my father resented the way this obligation had shifted to him, but he did not think it was in our interest to challenge the others or to call their delinquency to Socha's attention. And so he paid.

One by one, I began to take notice of many of our new associates. We tended to sit in two groups, on either side of the small chamber. In our group there was usually myself, my brother, my father, my mother, and my uncle. Also, Jacob Berestycki, a tailor who was perhaps the most observant Jew among our group; Mundek Margulies (Korsarz the Pirate), a barber, who was a practical joker and a determined worker; and a young woman named Klara Keler, who had attached herself to my mother on our first night in the sewer and said, "You will be my mother." *Pani bedzie moja mama.* My mother did not argue. Klara had come to our expedition through Korsarz, and we liked them both. Already, we could see they were of good, strong character. If Klara wanted to cling to my mother for security, my mother did not mind. Her arms were full with me and Pawel, but there was room in her heart for another.

In the other group there was Weiss, who continued to see himself as the leader of our underground society. With him was his mother, old Mrs. Weiss, whom we all called "Babcia," and a young woman named Halina Wind. *Babcia* was a good woman with an awful son. At the time, we all thought of her as elderly, but it was our situation that made her seem so aged, so frail.

Halina Wind was another story. She was a difficult character in those first weeks, when she was aligned with Weiss. She came into the sewer with him when his own wife would not, and she moved about in our small hiding place as if she were married to the man in charge. There was *something* between them—what, I could not be sure. When Socha and Wroblewski arrived with our daily bread, it was Halina who collected the rations and handed them out to the rest of us. She did this at Weiss's pleasure, of course. She carried herself like a queen feeding her royal subjects, my father always said, and invariably she gave the biggest portions to Weiss and his mother and his cronies.

Also in Weiss's group were Shmiel Weinberg and his wife, Genia, and the brothers Chaskiel and Itzek Orenbach. This was the disagreeable faction of our group. These were the men who were always criticizing Socha's ability to make good on his promise to look after us. They did not like the food he was bringing for us. The bread was stale, they said. The portions were meager. They did not like the living conditions, as if Socha himself were responsible for the filth of the sewer. They did not like my father, or Kuba, or Berestycki, or Korsarz, and they argued against any decisions or opinions they offered. Always, this disagreeable group huddled in the far corner of our small chamber, whispering some new strategy or other. Weinberg was probably the most vocal of this group, after Weiss. He was the loudest complainer. And he liked to criticize! So did the Orenbachs, only not so loudly. Together, the four of them were such a negative, disruptive influence on our lives that it was no wonder we could not get along.

In time we learned that during the German occupation, Shmiel and Genia Weinberg had placed their young daughter with an Aryan woman, in much the same way my parents had sought to make arrangements for me to be taken in by that nice teacher. This was a heartbreaking thing to discover about someone you had already decided you did not like; it put them in a different light. At least, it put Genia Weinberg in a different, more compassionate light. Shmiel Weinberg was too difficult and unpleasant to consider with any compassion. And here was another reason for compassion: Weinbergova was already a few months pregnant with another child when we descended into the sewer on the night of the final liquidation. She had not told anyone. I do not know if she even told her husband. Absolutely, Weiss and the other men would have discouraged her from seeking sanctuary in the sewer if they had known her condition. And Socha would never have allowed it. Of course, no one had any way of knowing how long we would be forced to hide underground, but everyone had to know such conditions would be unhealthy for a pregnant woman and her unborn child.

It took a long time for anyone in our group to notice Weinbergova's condition. She always wore a big black coat, and when she was sitting she covered herself with this coat, like a blanket. Also, it was very dark in this second chamber beneath the Mari Sniezna church, so it was difficult to make a close inspection of anyone. This was a good and welcome thing when it came to protecting one another's privacy—when we had to step into the shadows in the corner of the room to relieve ourselves, for example—but it also made it possible for Weinbergova to conceal her condition from the rest of the group for a while longer.

There was also a man named Dr. Weiss in our party. He was no relation to the bullying Weiss. In fact, I do not know that he was connected in any way to anyone else in our group. He was a lone character. He may have made an appeal to Socha when our group was being winnowed to its present number, after which Socha determined he would be included among us. We all liked Dr. Weiss well enough. He was helpful. He took his turn to fetch the water without protest. He accepted his daily ration of bread and water with gratitude. He gave what money he had as his share of payment, for as long as he had it to give. I do not think I exchanged two words with this man during the entire time we shared our underground place, but I never heard a word against him.

Finally, there were two other groups—three young men, who may or may not have had some prior connection to Weiss, and two young women, who like Dr. Weiss had probably made their separate appeal to Socha when we were a group of seventy and they were desperate to be included among our smaller party. I never learned the names of these young men and women, nor did I ever attach their faces to the hushed voices in our dark chamber. They did not stay in our company long enough for me and my family to get to know them. They were in the background, just.

Clearly, we were a disparate group. Some of us were connected to one another, and some of us were not. Some of these connections ran deep, as they did among my family and my uncle Kuba, and some were newly formed and on the surface. Weiss and his fellows, I do not think they cared so much for one another. They were out for themselves. And certainly they did not care for us. Weiss himself would not even remain with his own wife and daughter, so how could we expect him to place anyone else's interests alongside his own?

My father did not like that Weiss had put himself in charge of accepting the food delivery from Socha and Wroblewski, and he especially did not like the uneven distribution of the food at the hands of Halina Wind, but here again he did not say anything. Despite the trust and true friendship he seemed to be developing with Socha, at this early stage my father was careful to keep the dissension among our group away from our protectors. He did not want to trouble Socha with our own petty distractions, when there was so much already to occupy Socha's full attention. He did not even share with Socha my mother's concerns that Weiss was rifling through our few things whenever my father took his turn retrieving the water. I realize now that probably my mother's suspicions were born more of reason than of evidence. She had the feeling that Weiss was always wondering where my father kept his money. Instead of being grateful to my father for contributing most of our daily payment to Socha and the others, Weiss appeared to resent my father's resources. He thought it placed our family in Socha's favor.

My mother said she could hear Weiss collaborating with his buddies, trying to imagine where Ignacy Chiger kept his money and his jewelry. I do not think she ever discovered him looking through my father's pockets in search of valuables, but she heard him scheming. She could see the way the power of our group seemed to tilt between Weiss and my father. As it had been aboveground, whenever my father was absent from our group, Weiss claimed even more control. Whenever my father was present, there was a kind of stalemate between them. And when Socha was among us, Weiss was as quiet as a mouse.

And so our two groups stayed on either side of our small, dark chamber, without much interaction. In his journal, my father wrote diplomatically that some of our underground comrades were rebelliously inclined and not fit for coexistence, even as we managed to fitfully coexist. This tension troubled my father, as it must have troubled some of the others, like Berestycki and Korsarz and my uncle Kuba. Probably it troubled Socha as well, as he was made aware of it.

All these troubles were to change one afternoon, about two or three weeks into our confinement. My brother was still suffering with dysentery. He was very ill, very uncomfortable, very unhappy. He was not yet four years old, so it was only natural that a child of this age would sometimes cry beneath such a sickness. At other times, Pawel knew to cry silent tears, but here he could not help himself. He was not so terribly loud, and he was not so terribly persistent, but nevertheless he was crying, crying, crying. As it continued, Pawel's crying made Weiss and the others very agitated, very angry. Weiss especially. He worried we would be discovered by the sounds of Pawel's crying. His buddies encouraged Weiss in this agitation. Even Genia Weinberg, who was normally quiet and reserved, took the opportunity to criticize my mother for taking two small children into such a desperate, hopeless place.

On this day, it happened to be my father's turn to retrieve the water. I do not recall who went with him on this trip, but I do not think it was one of Weiss's buddies. Probably it was Berestycki or Korsarz, or maybe Dr. Weiss, the stand-alone member of our group. Weiss was receiving too much support from his side of our small chamber for me to believe his ranks had been thinned by the water run, and with my father gone he seemed emboldened. Every few minutes, he would tell my mother to keep Pawel quiet. "Shut up, already!" he would say. "Enough!"

At first, Weiss threatened to choke little Pawel if he did not keep quiet. He said this in an angry whisper from his side of the chamber. My mother ignored this and continued to comfort my brother. Finally, Weiss stood and walked in a stooped-over fashion to where our group was sitting. My mother noticed with horror what he was holding as he crossed to our side of the chamber. When he reached Pawel, Weiss put the gun to Pawel's little head and said in a menacing voice, "If you do not keep quiet, I will shoot you!"

We were all frozen in terror over this exchange. Those of us on our side of the chamber could not believe that such a thing was transpiring. Even those in Weiss's corner were horrified at this turn. I do not think any of us had seen this gun before. It had been well hidden, like my father's money and other valuables. Socha and Wroblewski carried guns with them, and these we could see clearly on their visits, but no one in our party had ever indicated that they too had a gun, and now one was being held to the youngest of our group. The rest of us were stunned into silence. Pawel, too, which of course was the intention of Weiss's bullying tactic. Poor Pawel was now too frightened to cry. He was still sick, but now he was also terrified, and my mother collected him in her arms and turned her back to Weiss. She collected me in her arms as well. She could not abide that our fortunes were now intertwined with the fortunes of such a horrible man. She considered him with the same mixture of hatred and revulsion that she had developed for the rats.

After a tense few moments, Weiss returned with his gun to his side of our small chamber. Nobody spoke for the longest time. There were no whispered congratulations for Weiss upon his return to his buddies. There was just silence. My mother rocked Pawel and me in her lap, whispering, *"Cicho, cicho, cicho."* Ssshhh,

ssshhh, ssshhh. Pawel was shaking a little bit, and she was trying to comfort us the way she used to do in our apartment at Kopernika 12, when our world was so much different from what it was at just this moment.

An hour or so later, my father returned with the water. We could hear him coming long before he finally appeared through the tunnel opening that spilled into our chamber. He could tell right away that something had happened among our group. Probably my mother gave him a look. He handed out the water and came over to where we were sitting. He huddled close with my mother, and she whispered to him what had happened. It was dark, so I could not see his face, but I imagined it was red with anger. I imagined he had never been so angry in his life, that this man should take a gun to poor Pawel's head and threaten to shoot him for the simple crime of crying in pain and sickness. All this time, I had been waiting for my father to come back through the tunnel. He would fix this problem, I knew. He would take care of Weiss. My father put his hand on Pawel's head, stroked his hair, and thought about what to do next.

It must have taken an enormous amount of restraint, but my father did not say anything to Weiss for the rest of the day. He did not confront him or challenge him in any way. At least, I did not see him do any such thing, and for years afterward he would say his emotions were exploding in such a way that he did not want the confrontation to escalate. He wanted to choose his response carefully. And so for the moment what he chose to do was nothing.

When Socha came the next day, still my father said nothing. Socha and Wroblewski handed over the satchel with our bread to Halina, and Halina broke off some big pieces for her group before delivering the leftover portion to our side of the chamber. The sewer workers inquired about this and that, and several of the men answered them in turn. Until it came time for my father to deliver our payment, it was as if nothing had happened. Here was the response he had decided to make: he wrapped a note around the bundle of cash he had prepared for Socha. On it, he hastily wrote the details of what had happened the day before. He told about Weiss threatening Pawel with the gun.

Socha collected the money without inspecting the bundle and disappeared with Wroblewski into the narrow pipe. When they left, there remained the same thick tension among our group that had taken hold the day before, when Weiss drew his gun. Then, about an hour later, we heard again the *slosh, slosh, slosh* of boots approaching us through the mud and water. For the longest time, we heard this noise. A few of the men began to panic, because we were not expecting another visit from our sewer workers. Once again, we started to think we were about to be discovered. No one could think what to do, how to respond, and then Socha and Wroblewski arrived in our chamber for the second time that day, this time with their guns drawn. They headed directly for Weiss.

Socha demanded that Weiss turn over his weapon. Then he turned to Weiss's comrades and demanded they turn over any weapons they might have been hiding. I think he collected another two or three guns. Then Socha pulled Weiss close and said, "I am saving only Chiger and his family. You are here by a lucky accident. If I see that even one hair has fallen from their heads, you will be killed."

He said this calmly, but his voice was thick with disgust. His message was clear.

Socha collected the other guns and made to leave, but not before consulting with my father in the corner. During this consultation,

I believe he gave my father one of the confiscated guns, to keep for our protection, but I never saw a gun among my father's possessions, and he never wrote about it in his journal. In any case, from that moment on, the dynamic in our chamber was changed. Weiss was quiet after this incident. He and his friends were still disagreeable, but they were no longer in charge. They still complained, but they no longer had a real platform for complaining. Nobody listened to them. And Halina Wind was no longer the queen.

My father called our group a collection of fortunates among the unfortunates, but of course we were not so very fortunate. Indeed, we had the bad fortune of beginning our underground odyssey during the rainy season in eastern Poland, and in 1943 there were heavy rains throughout the month of June. This made for treacherous conditions in the sewer, as the pipes filled with the water from several storms.

The conditions in our own chamber remained much the same as they had been upon our arrival. Unsuitable, but little changed. Our small hiding space was dark and dank and disgusting, although I imagine most small chambers connected to the sewer system were also dark and dank and disgusting. Yet from time to time, the men would talk longingly about the first hiding place they had prepared, back before we had descended into the sewer from the ghetto bunker. They remembered that it had been swept clean and that there had been a little bit more room to stand and to move. The women had never seen that first hiding place, so they had no basis for comparison, but they agreed anything would have been better than this small chamber beneath the church of Our Lady of the Snow.

For several days, they expressed their displeasure over our surroundings to Socha when he arrived with our daily bread, and finally Socha reported that Kowalow had discovered a new place for us to hide, a short distance downriver from our present position. It was too dangerous, they determined, for us to double back to that initial hiding place, but this alternative location might be an improvement. This was welcome news to everyone in our party, and almost immediately the men set about inspecting and preparing the new place. Socha and Wroblewski delivered supplies to help make this new place more habitable. My father took one of the first shifts, and he spent hours and hours cleaning and building a comfortable place for us to sit, removing the mud and silt, and when he returned to our small chamber he was exhausted. He was pleased with the progress he and the others were making, but it was a tiring effort.

Upon my father's return, it was determined that it was his turn to retrieve the water for our group. He dutifully prepared to go, along with Korsarz and Chaskiel Orenbach, until my uncle Kuba very graciously offered to take his turn for him. In fact, Kuba insisted, and after first refusing, my father finally agreed to let Kuba go in his place.

This was already the third or fourth week of June, the middle of the rainy season, and we were in constant danger of the rainwater flooding our underground hiding place through the sewer pipes and of the Peltew overflowing. Because of this, Kowalow had developed a new route for our group to travel in order to get to our freshwater supply. This way was more complicated, the sewer workers said, but the pipes were pitched and elbowed in such a way that there was less chance of the overflow water overcoming them inside, so for several days now the men had been traveling this new route. There was still some danger of flooding, but not so much as before.

It was along this new route that Uncle Kuba and the others set off, while my father stayed back and gathered his strength for the next day's errands. But it was not to be a restful time. As he was filling his kettle from the dripping fountain, poor Kuba was engulfed by a torrent of water and carried off in its flow. This was how forceful the current of rushing rainwater could be, that it could carry a grown man through a length of pipe and toss him to the rising river below. According to the report from Berestycki, the men did not see this rush of water coming at them. Already, there was water in the pipe as they crawled, and they were displacing so much more of it with their three bodies, but the current was not so fast until the pipe quickly filled and the water pushed Kuba to his death. The other men were approaching from an elbow in the pipes when this happened and so were spared Kuba's fate.

I cannot say who was more devastated by the news when Berestycki and Chaskiel Orenbach returned to our small chamber a short time later, me or my father. Certainly, my father felt guilty that Kuba had gone on this mission instead of him. Also, he loved Kuba, who had been married to his sister. He was our one surviving link to my father's family. I liked him, too. He was funny and kind and generous. And in an environment where my father could not be sure which men he could trust, it was good to have a trusted soul like Kuba among us. From time to time over the years, my father even questioned whether Kuba's death was an accident. This was how underhanded he felt Weiss's group could be. He trusted Berestycki, but he did not dismiss the prospect that Chaskiel Orenbach might have participated in some way in Kuba's drowning. My father could never prove this, but he always suspected that Weiss and the other men were somehow responsible, and underneath this suspicion was the responsibility he placed on himself, for allowing Kuba to take his turn retrieving the water.

My grief was of a different sort. Mine was over what Kuba's death represented, as much as for the loss of Kuba himself. Kuba's death filled me once again with sadness over what had happened to my cousin Inka, his daughter. It put the picture in my mind once again of my grandmother waving to me as she and Inka were being carted away. It represented the fate of my entire family. And it signaled that probably this was what would happen to all of us. In turn, we would all be swallowed up by the water or we would succumb to the dysentery or we would meet some other terrible fate. We were trapped here, I realized, and the only escape was death. I was not being fatalistic in my thinking so much as realistic, and even at seven years old I could see we were in a terrible situation. Kuba's death made me realize this more than anything, but of course I could not say anything to my parents or to anyone else. I could not cry about it. I could only place these thoughts as part of my inside life, alongside the other things I kept to myself and struggled to understand on my own. To talk about them might have been too upsetting for the others to hear. I could talk about these things with Melek, my imaginary friend. I could say, "Melek, I am scared." I could speak these words, in a tiny whisper. I could imagine Melek would stroke my hair and take my hand and tell me everything would be okay. He could tell me these things, but I was not so sure I could believe him.

Socha was also upset to hear the news about Kuba when he and Wroblewski arrived the next day with our bread. The sewer workers had liked Kuba. He was a good man. He was a part of our family, the family Socha was meaning to save. Together, we discussed how this was Kuba's fate, to drown in the Peltew, because already he had fallen into the river on two other occasions when my father was able to rescue him. Now, at last, he could not, and so we became a group of twenty.

I was not the only one to react to Kuba's death with such foreboding. Soon after, the two young women who remained unknown to me and my family asked Socha to escort them from the sewer. They were beaten down by our living conditions and now terrified that they would meet the same fate as Kuba. They felt claustrophobic, they said, and would take their chances aboveground; so Socha and Wroblewski led them to a manhole where they could escape undetected and hopefully make their way to the outskirts of the city. Socha made arrangements for the two young women to seek refuge with an Aryan family in his acquaintance, but the women were captured and killed by the Nazis almost as soon as they left the sewer.

This did not deter the group of three young men from pursuing the same course. They, too, asked Socha and Wroblewski to lead them from our chamber to the streets above, only their plan was to escape into the forest and meet up with the resistance movement. They could not last another day in our stinking underground prison, they said, but they were also immediately captured and killed.

Socha delivered the news of what happened to our former companions with great despair, because he did not like to see his efforts coming apart in this way. We were a group of desperate Jews, banded together, and despite the tensions and differences among us, we were all connected to one another in a kind of shared hope.

However, we were now a group of fifteen, and my family could only hope that these tragedies might in some way still the protests of the remaining malcontents in our group—Weiss, Weinberg, and the two Orenbachs. They no longer had any real power in our underground community, but they continued with their complaining, and even after learning of the fates of these others, they quietly discussed an escape of their own. However, they did not dare ask Socha to escort them from our chamber, because they knew he did not trust them. Probably Socha would have shot them before allowing them to escape to the city streets, where they could give up our location and identify our kindly sewer workers as conspirators and traitors.

Very quickly, I developed a sharp sense of hearing. When we first made camp in this underground chamber, I could not understand the whispering from the adults in the other group on the far side of our room. Now, though, after only a few weeks, I could hear Weiss and the men talking about fresh berries. The berries became a fantasy to them, to breathe the fresh air and eat the fresh berries that would now be in season. They talked about it all the time, but only among themselves and never in such a way that they appeared ready to go off in search of fresh berries. It was a fantasy, an ideal.

And then, one morning we woke up and they were gone—Weiss, Weinberg, and Itzek Orenbach. The storm of leaving continued. The men had plotted their escape in secret. For some reason, Chaskiel Orenbach decided to stay behind. Maybe he liked his chances better under the protection of our sewer workers. But the other three slipped away while the rest of us were sleeping, never to be heard from again. For a second time, Weiss left behind his loved ones—his mother, Babcia, and the young woman Halina.

Weinberg left behind his wife, Genia, who was pregnant with his child, probably unbeknownst to him. Itzek Orenbach left behind his brother, Chaskiel.

It was unclear whether Babcia and Weinbergova and the others had known beforehand. Probably Chaskiel Orenbach had known, while the others had not. My father worried how to tell Socha, because he knew the sewer workers would be concerned for our secret. He imagined a scenario where Socha and Wroblewski would have to hunt down Weiss and the others before they could reach the authorities and report our location. But we did not even have a chance to tell Socha of their disappearance, because when he and Wroblewski arrived later that day with our delivery, they also carried the news that the three men had been shot and killed immediately upon leaving the sewer, so they never had a chance to give away our circumstance.

This was the good news, we all supposed. The bad news was that we now numbered only twelve, and whatever strength and resolve we might have had going into this ordeal was now substantially diminished.

Six

Six

~⤳

ESCAPE, AGAIN

W e had only a few days to return to some kind of normalcy after the departure of our disgruntled cohorts and the death of my uncle Kuba before the next calamity found our group. Of course, to suggest that there was anything normal about our day-to-day existence is to understate our experience, but such things are relative. By normalcy here I mean a routine, because it was routine that allowed us to believe we were civilized human beings. It was inside our routines that we found the strength to continue.

The next calamity came during the second week of July 1943, almost six weeks after our arrival to the small chamber beneath the Mari Sniezna church, and it put a swift end to our confinement there. My father had just returned from retrieving our freshwater, and his boots were especially wet. This was what happened when you crawled through several kilometers of sewer pipes. All over, you got wet. And in the fetid wastewater of the sewer, you got so filthy wet that you did not want to think what the water contained. My father always emptied his boots upon his return to our chamber. This, too, was part of his routine, only sometimes the routine held an unwelcome surprise. My father once lost a valuable gem in this way. He often taped his valuable jewels between his toes, and on this occasion the tape had come loose and the gem siid into the river as he poured the water from his boots. It was a particular disaster for my family because this was a multicarat gem worth a great deal of money. According to my father, it was so valuable that it could have paid our underground living expenses for many months. But on this day, there were no gems for my father to worry about. His boots were simply soaked through. This was his primary worry.

It was still the latter part of the rainy season, and there remained an excess of water in the pipes, through which the men had to crawl to reach the main canal and the dripping fountain that was the source of our freshwater. Socha and Wroblewski, too, had to crawl and slog through an additional amount of water during this period. It was not as dangerous as it had been when the rushing floodwater claimed the life of my uncle, but it was a soggy nuisance just the same. My father knew that if he did not find some way to dry his wet boots, he would develop blisters and other ailments, which of course he could not treat properly in our primitive underground conditions. Plus, his boots were foul and uncomfortable so he hung them to dry on the iron ladder that was bolted into the wall above our chamber and which led to the manhole opening to the street. Very often, we would use the rungs of this ladder to dry our few things when they became too wet to wear, so this occasion was no different. At least, it started out no different. My father simply tied his boots to the ladder by the laces and hoped the little bit of fresh air from the manhole opening might help them to dry a bit faster than if he left them on the muddy floor with the rest of our things.

My father's drying boots were nearly our undoing, because another sewer worker, from a group other than Socha's, made an unscheduled inspection of our manhole that very day. There had been another small uprising on the streets of the ghetto, and it was believed that the Jewish perpetrators had escaped into the sewer system. The Gestapo had hastily organized a search, in which all sewer workers were to take part. We could hear the noise from the street as this sewer worker lifted the heavy manhole cover and peered inside. It was a terrifying noise because we knew what it could mean. We hugged one another close at the far, dark side of our chamber, fearful of being discovered. It was as if we had stopped breathing, that is how still and silent we became. There were only twelve of us now, so it was easier for us to huddle in silence than it might have been if we were in full number, but we dared not make a sound!

Little Pawel, he was so scared. He was trying to be brave, but he understood what was happening. He had been hiding for so much of his young life that he knew what it meant to be discovered. It was dark, but in the flash of light made by the opening of the manhole I could see my brother's eyes, open wide in terror. I wanted to collect him in my arms and tell him everything was going to be okay. I was also scared, but at the same time I was curious. I did not think we would be discovered. I did not think this man wanted to actually descend into our chamber to make a more careful inspection. After all, who would choose to walk about in the filth and waste of the sewer? Even a sewer worker does not wish to spend any more time in the sewer than absolutely necessary. Also, I knew enough about the darkness to realize that even though we could see the sewer worker by the light of the open manhole, he could not necessarily see us. His eyes could only stare into the blackness, unable to discern our shapes among the shadows.

It had been almost six weeks since we had escaped into the sewer, and in that time we had lived in fear of such a moment, and here it was upon us. As I suspected, the sewer inspector could not see us as he peered through the opening, and he at first had no reason to suspect any unofficial activity in this part of the sewer. But then he saw my father's boots. It must have made for a peculiar picture, to see a man's wet boots hanging by their laces from an iron ladder, so he climbed down for a better look. Still, he could not see us. He carried a lantern and pointed it toward our small chamber, but it did not give off a significant amount of light. All he could see were a mass of shadows, and soon he was satisfied that this particular area was clear. He must have thought there was a logical or long-ago explanation for the boots, so he made to leave.

Just then, just as the sewer worker was climbing back up the ladder to the street, the strangest, most inexplicable thing happened: someone in our group lit a match. It was Dr. Weiss, the kindly lone character who was of no relation to Weiss our tormentor. A match! The rest of us could not believe it. To light a cigarette! Of all things! At such a time as this! All the men smoked. It was something to do to pass the time. Socha and Wroblewski brought them cigarettes along with our other more necessary provisions. And since all the men were smokers, all the men carried matches, and Dr. Weiss chose this moment to strike one. Probably he was lighting a cigarette to calm his nerves. Probably he was panicked. Probably he did it without thinking about it, as a reflex.

The noise of the match sizzled against the stillness of our underground chamber like a firecracker. The flash of brilliant light briefly illuminated our entire group, before quieting to a more subtle flame that still left us visible, exposed. Dr. Weiss realized the foolishness of his action the moment he fired the match, but it was too late. It was only a split second before he blew it out, but it was enough to give us away.

Immediately, the sewer inspector raced up the ladder to the street. He shouted, "Jews! Jews! There are Jews in here!"

We could hear the commotion and frenzy this pronouncement caused. We could hear the voices and footsteps of the other officers, preparing to organize a search and descend into our small chamber to capture us. Why this sewer worker did not take the ladder down to our chamber instead of up to the street was both a mystery and a godsend. Certainly we would have been captured if he had come down. But instead this man retreated up the ladder, which gave us the opportunity we needed to escape. Of course, we realized later, this man was not a soldier. He was not Gestapo or SS. He was merely a sewer worker—and so, not trained for confrontation.

We grabbed whatever we could. Pawel was holding a blanket. My mother was holding Pawel. I was holding one of the household items—a small pot, I think. My father was soon holding me. The others also collected their few things, and we headed for the forty-centimeter pipe that led from our chamber. One by one, we slipped inside. Korsarz went first to lead the way. Old Mrs. Weiss, Babcia, was next, and then the rest of us followed. My family was in the rear of our group, just behind Genia Weinberg. This was significant, because after a short while of crawling, Weinbergova had some difficulty squeezing through a bend in the forty-centimeter pipe that led to the main canal. This pipe had been the way in, but the women and children had not left our small chamber for nearly six weeks, and in that time Genia had apparently grown. No one in our party knew she was pregnant as yet, but now her condition was apparent. Now, without her heavy black coat for cover, she was clearly pregnant. And stuck. My mother pushed her from behind, and in this way Genia managed to slither through.

No one discussed Genia's condition, as I recall, although such discussion might have taken place beyond my hearing—and, at seven, beyond my comprehension as well. It was simply understood by the other adults that Weinbergova was with child. There would be time for discussion later. Or, perhaps, we would be captured and there would be no need for discussion.

My mother too had her own difficulty slipping through the narrow pipe. Her legs and feet had become swollen by the dampness of our underground chamber. She had been complaining about this swelling for some time. Among our many supplies, Socha had brought her several pairs of men's shoes, because her own shoes no longer fit, and she was now wearing a pair of boots that were otherwise too big for her. Somehow one of her boots became stuck and she could not move. She tried to free her foot from the boot, but it was so difficult to move inside the pipe that she could not reach down to untie the laces. She struggled and struggled with this, and as she struggled the pipe began to fill with water. Somehow, in the struggling, my mother also turned her ankle in such a way that she could not walk properly for several weeks, but this was the least of our worries just then. There were so many of us trapped inside this pipe behind my mother that the little bit of water that had been there in the beginning was now being displaced, so the water level kept rising, and as the normal flow of water was slowed by our bodies, we worried we would be drowned.

It was just like what happened to my uncle Kuba, only here the water that could have drowned us managed to save us instead, because when it reached a certain level the pressure became so great that my mother was finally able to clear her boot from its mooring and in this way continue forward. The water pushed her free.

Yet the water would continue to threaten us. Once we safely left the narrow pipe, we reached once more the slippery ledge along the Peltew. Here we attempted to move a little bit faster, to find a new place to hide from the German officers we knew would be coming, but the floodwater was a constant danger. My mother slipped once more on her bad ankle as she carried Pawel and tried to keep his little head above the rising water. Even my father had difficulty carrying me in his arms, held high so I would not be swallowed up by the river.

By some new miracle, Socha and Wroblewski managed to find us. At least it seemed a miracle, although in truth they discovered us by some cleverness and forward thinking. They knew from the commotion on the street what had happened, and they could guess in which direction we would flee, so they tried to intercept us. It was a logical course: we could leave only by the single forty-centimeter pipe that opened into our chamber, and this pipe in turn led only to another pipe, and then another. Eventually, they knew, we would snake our way back to the river, where they hoped to meet us. However it happened, the light of the sewer workers' lantern up ahead was a welcome sight indeed. We could tell it was their lantern because of the way they swung it back and forth. They had told us they would swing the lantern in this way so we would not be alarmed when we saw them approaching.

Together, we continued through the tunnel until we were beneath the riverbed, where we stopped to consider our next move.

Socha reported that the search of our abandoned chamber had concluded and that the other sewer workers had already taken to teasing the inspector who had come upon us for seeing ghosts. That was how the sighting was described, as an apparition. The sewer worker's colleagues were saying that maybe this man was drunk, maybe he was seeing things. Certainly, a careful inspection of our chamber would have revealed our recent presence there, but apparently no such inspection was made, and we were therefore free to resume our uncertain lives in the sewer in a new location.

Socha led our group to a small room that looked more like a cave than a chamber. This was where Socha and Wroblewski left us—temporarily, they said, while they waited for word from Kowalow on a more permanent location—but we could not stay in this place for very long. There was hardly enough height for even me to stand straight, and it was so damp, so dirty, so horribly cold. A ripping wind sliced through us as we counted the hours until Socha returned. At some point, the men grew tired of waiting and encouraged us to follow them back toward the main canal, because they could not remain one moment longer in this terrible hovel. We did not like going against Socha's directions, but we felt we had no choice.

Here again, we met up with Socha and Wroblewski a short time later. It was inevitable that our paths would cross: there were only so many twists and turns you could make in the sewer if you meant to keep close to the main canal. It was at this moment that Dr. Weiss asked the sewer workers to escort him safely to the streets above. Now that he was out of our initial chamber, Dr. Weiss said he could not imagine returning to such a difficult internment. Our few hours in that abysmal cave confirmed this for him. He said he had some Aryan friends who would give him shelter. He said he had been thinking about abandoning the sewer for some time. No one was worried about Dr. Weiss giving away our location to the authorities, as they had been with Itzek Orenbach, Shmiel Weinberg, and the other Weiss. That group had been devious and scheming. This Dr. Weiss was a good and decent man, and apart from the silly mistake of lighting his cigarette at such an inopportune moment, he had never once jeopardized our group; and because of this, Socha agreed to lead him from the sewer after he had relocated the rest of us to the new hiding place Kowalow had selected.

Our next hiding place was no improvement over the cavelike hovel we had just abandoned. In some ways it was worse. It was colder, if such a thing was possible. The winds were fiercer, louder. There was no place to sit. The ceiling was lower still, and there were more rats than we could even consider. Indeed, the sea of rats would not even part for us as we crossed the small area. Ironically, we learned that this was not the place Kowalow had intended for us. Kowalow, who knew the sewer like his own name, had described for Socha the place he had in mind, but Socha made a wrong turn and so we did not have any choice but to stay here for the night.

This was where we made our good-byes to Dr. Weiss. Remarkably, this was the last my family ever heard of him. Unlike the other refugees from our group who were immediately shot and killed upon leaving the sewer, Dr. Weiss was not a reported casualty, and the efforts my father made after the war to locate him did not turn up anything. It was as if he had vanished, like the wisp of smoke from the burned-out match he foolishly struck while we were trying to hide. In any case, now we were a group of eleven—a big change from the commotion and tumult of the night of the final liquidation, when we numbered over seventy, and a complete transformation from the mistrust and tension that characterized our group when we numbered twenty-one.

As we strained to find sleep and replenish our energy after the ordeal of the day, we counted ourselves lucky yet again for escaping the sewer inspection beneath the Mari Sniezna church. My father stayed up the entire night trying to keep the rats from our huddled-together bodies with a candle. He found that they did not like the flame, but there was only one flame and there were many, many hundreds of rats. Everywhere you looked, there were rats. It was, everyone agreed, the most miserable night we had passed underground since leaving the Ju-Lag. I do not think anyone slept, not even me or Pawel.

The next day, when Socha arrived, he was deeply sorry. We had not yet had a chance to tell him how miserable we all were, but he knew he had taken a wrong turn and veered from Kowalow's directions, and for this he apologized. When he saw for himself the dreadful conditions and the depths of our misery, he was sorrier still, and he immediately led us to our intended tunnel. The way was especially treacherous in the beginning because we had to grasp a steel bar and hoist ourselves up while water spilled down on us from a seventy-centimeter pipe above, but once we got past this difficulty, the going was fairly simple. One of the men remarked that it was a good thing this new place was so difficult to get to, because it meant it would also be difficult for the Germans to find. We would be safe there. There was a good, hopeful feeling among our group, despite the horrible night we had just passed. In fact, there was such a good feeling that as we walked I started to whistle. I was so happy to be standing upright and walking like a human being to a new, better place that I could not help it. For all these weeks, I'd had no reason to be happy, and now here I was, whistling.

My father and I walked hand in hand along the Peltew. We were both barefoot. I believe we were the only two people in our group in this condition. There had been no time, of course, for my father to reclaim his boots before we had to leave our chamber in such a hurry. Socha would bring him a new pair, but not until we were settled in this new place. How I came to be barefoot, I can no longer recall, but I do remember stepping on what I thought was a hat pin as we walked. I did not say anything to anybody, and I did not break stride, but it was very painful. I quickly removed the pin without losing my place in our parade of underground exiles, and as I walked a little bit of blood began to drip from my foot. My father noticed this, probably because it was not such a little bit as I imagined. He knew that it could not be good to dip an open cut into the foul wastewater of the sewer. So he lifted me onto his shoulders, and still I continued whistling. I was so happy. Even the stick of a hat pin could not dampen my happiness. My father was happy, too. Certainly, we had nothing to be happy about, but as I whistled, my father told me later, I gave everyone energy and hope.

We walked along the river for several minutes. I was whistling the entire time. Finally, we arrived at a shelter that was a little bigger than the chamber we had just left behind. The walls were wet and covered with mold and cobwebs. A layer of mud covered the ground. Rats covered every surface. The men did not like this place because they could see how much work there would be to make it habitable. It was still, after all, a small tunnel along one of the tributaries of the city sewer system, but Kowalow had determined that this was the place where we would be safest of all.

Socha smiled at the disinterest of the men and turned to my

mother. "Chigerova," he said, "it does not matter, the opinion of the men. What matters is the opinion of the women."

At this, my mother turned and held out her arms, as if to marvel at our new surroundings. "It is like a palace," she said. "Here we can stay."

And so we stayed. For over a year we stayed. In a place we would all come to call the Palace. A palace for the hen and her two chicks.

Seven

THE PALACE

I was always grateful that my mother was able to see the possi- bilities of this chamber we called the Palace. She was the only one among our group to recognize the space for what it could be. I was also grateful to Dr. Weiss for impulsively lighting that match and giving our group away, because it forced us to abandon that dismal hiding place beneath the Mari Sniezna church. It was a blessing disguised at first as adversity.

The men were right to view this new chamber as merely an- other dark, damp hovel, but my mother could see beyond the mud and the cobwebs and the rats. She had a great vision that came from only reasonable expectations. She could see that this hiding place would be more suitable than any other we could expect to find in the sewer. It had a higher ceiling—not quite two meters—so the grown-ups did not have to walk stooped over all the time. They still had to stoop over, but not so much. The shorter ones could stretch almost to their full height. Also, the chamber had an L shape, which meant there was a smaller room to the side of the large main room, and this could be used for privacy. She was smart to see that we could be comfortable here for an extended period.

Of course, we did not know how long we would be here, in what was essentially a storm basin beneath the Bernardynski church, located underground somewhere between the Bernardynski and Halicki squares. We could pray that our stay would be mercifully short, but we had to plan for it to be hopelessly long. No one could predict. My father had been keeping up on news from outside. This was what we called the rest of the world—outside, *na zewnatiz*. Socha would bring reports on outside developments, and then in the evening we would discuss these reports. There was nothing to do but discuss. Soon, Socha began bringing the daily newspapers, in Polish and German, and my father and the others pored over every word. We talked about the war. We talked about the hoped-for Russian liberation, which already seemed our best chance for surviving this ordeal. We talked about the camps. Mostly we talked about what our lives might be like when we returned to the outside. This last was always discussed as a certain eventuality. It was never *if* we returned to the outside. It was always *when*. In this there was probably the most important aspect of our survival: hope. And it was not just my parents who remained hopeful; it was our entire group. Without the negative influence of Weiss and his cronies, without the constant fear of being discovered that began to abate after nearly two months underground, we were now trying to be positive about our circumstance. Chaskiel Orenbach was still a disagreeable, offputting personality, but there were enough of us taking an optimistic view to drown his pessimism.

Another key aspect of our survival, as I wrote earlier, was the presence of routine. Socha was quick to recognize this on our behalf. As soon as we were settled in this new place, he set about dividing the daily tasks we would need to accomplish in order to keep our group safe and whole. Socha and Wroblewski began making their deliveries at a certain time each morning, usually between nine o'clock and ten o'clock, and this meant we could build our day around their visits. This was useful to us and helped us to know when to have our breakfast, when to have our supper, when to have our dinner. It gave us a necessary sense of structure, something we had not had before, and it allowed our bodies to return to their accustomed rhythms. Now there was an order to our days.

When we were hiding under the Mari Sniezna church, the sewer workers came to us whenever they could sneak away from their assignments or whenever they felt they could do so without being detected, but here in the Palace they made an effort to keep to the schedule. Socha also made a schedule for the men, telling us who would go to retrieve the water, who would collect the supplies he and Wroblewski would leave to improve our new living space, who would do this or that. He made a schedule for the women, telling who would help with the cooking, who would help with the cleaning. Always, he would tell us what to do and when to do it. Everybody had a job, except me and Pawel. Probably Babcia, too, did not have any defined duties. She was a very good woman, but she was getting sicker and sicker. The dampness, the bacteria, the cold, the unsanitary conditions . . . it made her appear so very old. She was not such an old woman by today's standards, but by our circumstance she was made tentative and fragile. She would help when she was strong enough, and at other times she would sit and rest.

My mother used to say she had a special ache in her heart for the suffering of old Mrs. Weiss. The poor woman could not have been proud of her son, who bullied his way around our group in our first weeks underground, who abandoned her here, who had earlier abandoned his wife and daughter. Most of the time, Babcia was lying down. It was difficult for all the adults to stand, but for Babcia it was especially difficult. Always, my mother took care of Babcia. She bathed her. She held her hand. Babcia blessed my mother. She said, "Every day I say a prayer that you and your family will survive." My mother cherished this prayer. She believed that it helped keep us alive.

My mother's primary responsibility, Socha said, was to take care of her two chicks, and in many ways she took on this same role with the other women in our party. She was like a mother to us all. She was like a mother to poor Babcia, a woman who was probably old enough to be my grandmother. She was like a mother to Klara Keler, a young woman who had lost her own mother during the liquidation and now looked to my mother for strength and comfort. She was like a mother to Genia Weinberg, who carried the weight of her secret pregnancy alongside the memory of the child she had left behind and the cowardly husband who had abandoned her. She was even like a mother to Halina Wind, a young woman who carried herself as if she did not need any carrying. It was my mother's nature to look after others, and now, according to Socha, it was also her job.

In this way, Socha was like the puppeteer of our group. He recognized our individual strengths and characteristics and put them to use for the common good. This was the most important thing, he always said, the good of the group. He wrote everything down for us so we would not forget our roles, and by our first week in the Palace you could not recognize the group we now were from the group we had only recently been. We were like our own little functioning society, and our trusted sewer workers were our benevolent rulers. I use the word *benevolent* because despite the exchange of money it really seemed a kindness, what these men were doing for us. They were devoted to our safekeeping. Every day, they were putting themselves and their families at great risk, and the money was not so great that the equation was not also balanced with compassion. In Socha's case, there was also the matter of redemption. The money alone could not justify the chance he was taking.

I use the word *ruler* because Socha and Wroblewski were very much in charge of every aspect of our lives. We survived at their pleasure. We looked to them to arbitrate our petty disputes, to ease our concerns, to cure our ills. It was as if by their very freedom they held every authority. Leopold Socha, our guardian angel, and his sewer worker colleagues would determine our shared fate.

We no longer saw Jerzy Kowalow, but he too was busy on our behalf. Every time Socha and Wroblewski came to the Palace to meet with us, Kowalow was standing watch on the streets above, ready to signal his colleagues in some manner at any sign of trouble. He was just as vulnerable, just as exposed, as the two men who actually crawled through the pipes each day to bring us bread and supplies, and just as invaluable. Usually, he signaled the others by tapping on the pipes in some kind of code, but sometimes more direct intervention was required. On one occasion, Kowalow noticed a German officer watching the sewer entrance Socha and Wroblewski were intending to use. Kowalow proceeded to place scraps of wood through the manhole opening, as if he were following orders to do so. Then he returned to the sewer through another entrance to warn his colleagues to exit the sewer by some other opening to avoid suspicion.

Without Kowalow, we would never have come across this place we now called the Palace. Without Kowalow, we would never have located the source of our freshwater. Indeed, Kowalow located a new source of freshwater for our group to reach from the Palace, and the men reported that it was somewhat farther than the journey had been from the old hiding place, but at the same time the journey was easier—the pipes were not so narrow, there were not so many sharp turns, and the way was not so arduous. Now we were not limited to three-quarters of a cup of water each day; the water was more plentiful because the source was easier to reach and the men could make more than one trip and they could carry more than one kettle. They would crawl to an area beneath the Fountain of Neptune, just below Glowny Rynek, the main marketplace in the city. At first they would have to mark their way as they crawled, to ensure that they returned by the same route, but after a few days they knew the way by memory. The long daily trips for water would be the most difficult chore after our new hiding place had been thoroughly cleaned and established, but it was one the men accepted gladly. Sometimes Klara Keler would accompany one of the men on this long trek, though the women usually stayed behind and saw to the cooking and cleaning.

The cleaning consisted of removing the mud from the walls and trying to remove some of the mud that was piled at our feet. Also, it involved organizing the area that would serve as our kitchen and putting our pots and pans and our one Primus stove into good working order. And it included the scrubbing and drying of several old planks of wood, which Socha and Wroblewski had discovered in a chamber beneath the Nazi headquarters. Socha escorted my father and a few others to this place, and together they rummaged through the left-behind wood. There was too much to carry back, so the men made additional trips to complete the hauling. The wood they brought back was so wet that the men could not do a good job of drying it before we had to at last put the planks to use. We placed them on stones, in two rows of four boards each, and in this way they served as benches during the day. At night, we pushed the planks together and used them as beds for sleeping. This was important because the "beds" provided the adults with the only opportunity they would have in our chamber to stretch to their full height.

The remarkable thing about these boards was that they were so damp when the men collected them, and within weeks they were completely dry. Indeed, everything was damp upon our arrival. The walls were dripping with moisture. But as we sat on these boards, and as we lay on them, the heat from our bodies dried the wood. Indeed, the heat from our bodies soon dried everything— the walls, the floor, the air around. In the beginning, we could even see the vapor from our own breath form little drops of moisture, but soon the air itself was dry as well, and in this way we were like a living science experiment, confirming that so many bodies in such a small space could not help but have this effect on our self-contained environment.

We knew the difference between day and night only by our routines, by the timing of our sewer workers' daily visits. We had two carbide lamps, which we used to light our small space, but for long stretches, when our work for the day was done, we would remain in darkness. For most of the day, we would sit on our improvised benches. Pawel and I would engage each other in games of imagination. Or he would play with the rats. We lost our fear of these underground creatures and grew used to them over time, as my father had predicted. Pawel in particular was fascinated by the rats, and there were three or four of them in his acquaintance he called by name. I tried to learn their names and their personalities as well, but I did not have the patience of my little brother in this regard. I could not tell one rat from the other.

The adults in our group had a harder time adjusting to the rats than the children. The rats were not interested in us. They were interested only in our food. Infection was probably a worry, but who had time to think about such things? The worry was all around—the contaminated air, the wastewater, the close quarters. To Pawel and me, they became like family pets. To the adults, they were more like tolerable pests. A great swarm of tolerable pests. Several times, Pawel and I would attempt to count the rats in our view, as a way to pass the time, and always we would lose the count and have to start over. During the night, they would crawl over us as we slept, and we also got used to this in time. Sometimes I would wake up and one of the rats would be licking my ear or staring at me as if waiting to play. I could never tell if this was one of Pawel's friends or just another from the group, so I always smiled back at the rat before gently shaking it away. Somehow I felt we had intruded on their space and that we were meant to get along.

Very quickly, our group became like a family. Socha was our true leader—a benevolent ruler, to be sure, but also an inspired leader. It was a wonderful thing, the way our spirits lifted each morning when he arrived with our delivery. Previously, we had been a divided group, with divided loyalties and agendas, but now Socha put himself in charge of almost every aspect of our lives. I do not think any of the men in our group wanted to take on a leadership role for themselves; however, as a practical matter, when the sewer workers were not among us, it appeared that my father was now in charge, and my mother by extension became a kind of figurehead for the women. Already, my father was responsible for paying our fee for protection and safekeeping, but he also seemed in charge of other matters. The others came to value his opinion and to look to him for guidance. He was the most attuned to events in the outside world and to a possible timetable for our liberation. And he was among the most resourceful of our group and one of the hardest workers.

It was my father, for example, who fashioned a way to store our food and keep it from the hungry rats. He made a small shelf where he thought we could place some of our perishables. This worked for a time, until the rats discovered the bread on the shelf and managed to reach it by crawling along the stone walls. After this, my father had the idea to place crushed glass along the surface of the shelf, like a minefield protecting our scraps of bread, and in so doing, he hoped it would be difficult for the rats to cross the shards. The glass came from some bottles that had been discarded in the sewer. This too worked for a time, until the rats discovered a way to shimmy beneath the shelves by gripping the edges with their outstretched claws and moving upside down until they could find a toehold in the stone wall and lift themselves to the surface above without stepping on the broken glass. They were so clever! So persistent! On one occasion, I watched with my brother and father in disbelief as a pair of rats attempted to transport an egg without breaking it. One rat lay on its back with the egg on its belly while the other rat pulled its partner along by the tail. Such ingenuity!

The rats were always getting into our food, so my father devised a storage system for the potatoes, coffee substitute, and sugar

Socha and Wroblewski would now bring us with our daily bread. We stored these items in tins, in the hollow beneath our makeshift benches. We also stored our bread in this way, but the rats would somehow manage to get into the bread. Always, we would eat the stale bread first and in this way keep the freshest bread on hand. If it was kept too long, it would grow moldy from the dampness. Also, we wanted to keep an extra supply of bread in store in case our sewer workers could not make a delivery to us for a period of time, although usually it was a race with the rats to see who could get to the bread first. It was not until my father fashioned a kind of bread box that he could hang from the ceiling that we were able to keep the rats from our bread—a welcome innovation as far as our group was concerned. Pawel and I were especially pleased with this contraption because we enjoyed watching the rats attempt to reach the bread box. This was our entertainment.

On most days, then, our routine went like this: we awoke from our sleeping boards in the morning and rearranged the planks to make our improvised benches. We did this hurriedly, as if we had someplace else to be. We were determined to be civilized, to lead a productive existence in our underground home. Jacob Berestycki, our lone observant Jew, used this time to say his morning prayers. Somehow, he had his tefillin in the sewer. His tallith, too. I had never seen these items before, and I did not know their purpose or their meaning. I had been to synagogue only a few times before the Russian occupation, and I was so young that it never registered to me what the men were wearing. I imagine Berestycki carried the phylacteries with him as we fled the ghetto on the night of the final liquidation. Every day he wrapped his arm with the leather straps and placed the box against his forehead and began to chant. This was very meaningful to him, and it was meaningful to us as well, for this was the reason we were here, after all, because we were Jewish. He prayed throughout the day, and from time to time one or more of the other adults would join him. I remember the Palace as such a spacious area, but in truth it was a small room, so we offered Berestycki the respect and solemnity he required to complete his prayers, and this was how we participated. This was how we were Jewish.

We sat quietly in small groups as Berestycki said his prayers, and then we took our turns washing in the basin that we had positioned at the far corner of our chamber for just this purpose. Socha and Wroblewski would occasionally bring us small buckets of rainwater that we could use for washing. Sometimes we collected the runoff water from the street above, and once we determined that it had not mixed with the wastewater, we used this water as well. The rainwater was not suitable for drinking or cooking, but it was okay for washing. From time to time, if there was enough water, we would brush our teeth, using our fingers and some salt. Once each week, usually before supper, we would take a proper sponge bath using water that had been warmed on our Primus stove, and I remember feeling so refreshed and revived after I was clean. This was when I would change into the fresh underclothes that Socha's wife, Wanda, would boil and clean for us, also once each week, and for a moment I could fool myself into believing I was like every other girl in Lvov, scrubbed clean from a warm bath, wearing fresh clothes. It felt so good! I could close my eyes and pretend I was someplace other than this mud-filled chamber, surrounded by vermin and raw sewage. I could close my eyes and imagine I was in a field of flowers.

For breakfast, we would have the coffee substitute and sugar and a small piece of bread. After breakfast, we would straighten our compartment and wait for Socha and Wroblewski to arrive. This would become the highlight of our day. The longer our confinement, the more we looked forward to these visits. In the beginning, the sewer workers would not stay more than a few minutes after making their deliveries, but once we were in the Palace, once our living conditions were more tolerable, they began to stay longer and longer. It became more like a visit than a delivery. Initially, our benefactors said they were taking the time to rest before making the return trip through the pipes, but they kept extending these rests until they were an hour and longer. Eventually, these visits would continue for hours, until Socha and Wroblewski would have to leave and we would return to our plain existence.

Soon they started to bring sandwiches with them, which they ate with us. Always, Socha would share his sandwich with me and Pawel. This was a fine treat. Wroblewski would share his sandwich with Klara and Halina. And as we ate, everyone would talk. It was during these talks that we learned of Socha's dubious background. It had never occurred to my parents that our safekeeping was in the hands of a reformed thief, but they came to admire Socha all the more for the way he had managed to turn his life around. Even the story about how he robbed our family's antiques store did not upset my parents, because they saw this as another time, another life, another Socha.

I can still remember my first taste of pork, which I had never eaten until our imprisonment in the sewer. We were not terribly religious, but at the same time I had never eaten pork, so when Socha offered me and Pawel one-half of his pork sandwich one day, it was at once exotic and forbidden. Pawel and I did not question that we should eat the pork. My parents did not question that we should eat the pork. Even Berestycki did not question it. And so we ate, and it was delicious—so sweet, so juicy. I tried to make it last a long, long time. I was taking a very big bite of bread and a very small bite of the pork, and I continued in this way for a long while, until well after Socha had finished his half of the sandwich.

Finally, Socha said, "What is wrong, little one? You are not hungry? You are taking such small bites. You do not like the pork?"

"Oh, I like it," I said. "And I am so hungry. But I do not want to finish just yet."

For dinner, we had only soup, which Weinbergova prepared for us each day. Cooking was her principal duty, and she did it without complaint. We had our one small Primus stove, which Genia used to heat the coffee in the morning and the soup in the afternoon. Socha brought us a full supply of benzene, which we used to boil the water. Every day it was the same soup. Sometimes Genia would mix in potatoes or barley or onions, if the sewer workers had been able to bring us the necessary provisions. Sometimes there was buckwheat and kasha, sometimes beans. Whatever she could use to chase the monotony of our meals, she put into the soup.

One day we discovered our miserable companion Chaskiel Orenbach eating his soup in a particular way. First he sipped the liquid with his spoon. After this he mashed the beans or onions that Genia had included into a kind of paste, which he then ate separately. In this way, he had made a two-course meal from a simple bowl of soup. Everyone thought this was a good idea, and soon we were all eating our soup in this way.

It was a difficult assignment, to feed so many people in such primitive conditions, but Genia Weinberg was quite capable. Of all the young women in our party, she was probably the most serious, the most harsh. She was quick to judge and often very critical of my parents for bringing two small children into this place. I do not recall seeing her smile more than once or twice during our entire time together, though this was probably because there were a lot of things weighing on her. There was the daughter she had left behind, the husband who had abandoned her, the baby she now carried in an open secret. We did not talk about this baby. Of course, it is possible that this matter was discussed beyond my hearing, and it is also possible that at seven years old I did not entirely understand the true nature of pregnancy and childbirth, but looking back, I believe it was as if the adults had pushed this truth aside and hoped it would not find us in this place. Weinbergova still wore her heavy black coat—probably to keep warm and to conceal her condition, both. Still, Socha and Wroblewski did not know she was pregnant, and my father and the others worried how to tell them, how they would react.

Weinbergova's heavy black coat was not so unusual among our group. All of the adults wore heavy coats. Despite the fact that it was summer, it was frightfully cold in our underground environment. The air temperature was considerably cooler than the summer air aboveground, but the wet stone walls also contributed to the chill, and there was often a heavy wind you could hear through the pipes and feel in your bones. I wore my precious green sweater and huddled for warmth alongside my mother or father or brother, so I did not mind the cold so much. I remember talking to my imaginary friend, Melek, about this one day. I said, "The others, they are so cold. How come you are not so cold?"

He said, "I am as cold as you."

It was a very philosophical response, yes?

Weinbergova's closest underground friend was Halina Wind, who went from being a queen beneath the Mari Sniezna church to a princess here in the Palace. She was always brushing her hair. I do not know if she brought her own brush when we disappeared into the sewer or if she asked Socha or Wroblewski to collect one for her, but I have a clear picture in my mind of this young woman sitting and brushing her hair. All the time, brushing. Such a beautiful girl! Such beautiful hair! And it did not seem to bother her in the least that there were hundreds of tiny lice hiding in her long, flowing hair. She completed her strokes each day on one side, her strokes each day on the other side, as if she had just come from a salon and her hair was fine and clean.

The lice were a big problem. Every day, sometimes twice a day, my mother would inspect me and Pawel with a special comb Socha had brought for just this purpose. The grown-ups would take turns inspecting each other, although there was not much we could do to thwart these creatures. We could only know that they were there. The lice were so big, and so many, you could actually see them. Even in the dim light of our carbide lantern you could see them. And once we knew they were there, we had to scratch. It was psychological. Just knowing they were there, we had to scratch. I am scratching now as I write this, just thinking about it. But you can get used to anything, and eventually we got used to the lice as well. My mother discovered that the lice liked to hide in the folds of our shirt and coat collars, and when she found them she would brush them off and we would pretend that we were free of lice for the time being, and the next day they would be back.

Mundek Margulies—Korsarz—had been a barber in Lvov before the war, and he began cutting everyone's hair once we were established in the Palace. This was one of his special jobs, and he did it with good cheer. It was Socha's idea to have the Pirate cut everyone's hair, once he learned of Korsarz's skills in this area, and

Korsarz happily agreed. Everyone thought it would be a good way to lift our spirits and to keep us from looking and feeling like cavemen. We were civilized, after all. Korsarz was the perfect man for this job. He was always cheerful and smiling, a happy, boisterous presence in our dim surroundings. Socha brought him special tools and a small hand mirror for just this purpose. The men had full beards by the time we fled our hiding place beneath the Mari Sniezna church, and our hair had grown long. My mother asked Korsarz to cut our hair very short, to help with the lice problem, but the lice still found places to hide. The others also cut their hair very short, the men and the women. At least, my mother and Klara and Babcia had their hair cut short. Weinbergova left her hair long. She wore it in a braid. With all those lice festering inside it, she tied it up each day in a braid. And Halina, she was too vain to cut her hair. She just kept brushing it and brushing it, as if the lice weren't there.

Korsarz was the joker of our group. He used to wear a Greek sailor's cap on his head, turned backward. This was why we called him the Pirate. He was always singing songs, always telling jokes, usually in Yiddish. "Whatever it is," he used to say, "it is funnier in Yiddish." Eventually, I learned Yiddish and understood what he meant. He was probably the most easygoing member of our group. He was willing to work hard, he was adventurous, and he was fearless. Once, when Klara Keler expressed a particular sadness over the fate of her sister who had been taken to the Janowska camp, Korsarz offered to go outside to find her. They had developed a bit of a romance, Klara and Korsarz. Even so, this was an astonishing gesture. It was courageous, and probably also foolish, but this was what Korsarz wanted to do for Klara. He told Socha about it, of course. Socha and Wroblewski even helped him make

a safe exit from the sewer, and somehow Korsarz made it to the
Janowska camp and managed to walk the grounds without being
detected. For two or three days, he was gone from our group. We
worried he had been captured. But then he returned with the news
that Klara's sister was alive and well in the camp and that he had
informed her that Klara was also alive and well in the sewer. This
was a great comfort to Klara.

In addition to the news about Klara's sister, Korsarz brought
back a song he had learned at the Janowska camp from one of the
prisoners. He was anxious to teach it to our group, and we were
happy for the distraction. It was a silly song about a merchant from
Shanghai, selling porcelain cups and porcelain chamber pots. I can
still remember the words to this song:

> *Jestem Chinczyk Formanjuki,*
> *Kita Jajec, skosne oki,*
> *Porcelane do sprzedania mam.*
> *Filiżanki fajansowe,*
> *I nocniki kolorowe,*
> *To ja wszystko tobie mila dam.*

For years afterward, whenever we would meet, Korsarz and I
would sing this song. It became our special form of greeting—a
happy reminder of a tearful time.

My father came to regard Korsarz as the most helpful, most
resourceful, most reliable member of our group, and he probably
viewed Halina Wind as the opposite. Halina did not work. She
was not helpful. She went from being a difficult character who
stole the biggest pieces of our daily bread for herself and her
friends to a more benign character who still did not contribute to

our welfare. She did not play with me and Pawel, as Klara and Korsarz did. She did not help with the heavy lifting and the retrieval of freshwater, like the men. But she was a good person, and my family came to like her. She began to care for us, we could see, once Weiss and the others left. And she proved to be my father's favorite intellectual companion, because she was the only other educated member of our party. Chaskiel Orenbach was educated, but he was not schooled in general knowledge, so to keep their minds sharp, my father and Halina engaged in a constant game of Intelligentsia, a word game that was a cross between Boggle and Scrabble. My mother sometimes played as well, but my father and Halina were the main combatants. Someone would suggest a long word—for example, "Constantinople"—and from this word you had to create as many smaller words as possible, using only these letters. When our daily chores were complete, when we were sitting on our benches, our knees touching, there would be a good-natured back-and-forth between my father and Halina, arguing over the results of this game, or over some development in the war, or over the merits of some work of literature they had each read.

Klara Keler was very different from the other two young women. She was not as classically beautiful as Halina or Genia, but I liked her much better. To me, she was prettier, because she was nicer. She took the time to play with me and Pawel. She was warm and genuine, and she made an effort to be helpful. Sometimes she took it upon herself to empty our chamber pot. This was usually a job for the men, but Klara did not mind. We had one pot for all of us. Socha brought it to us. It was big, like a cistern, with a handle so you could carry it, and we would leave it in the dark corner of the Palace, where we could use the shadows for privacy.

And every day, one of the men or sometimes Klara would have to carry this chamber pot and empty it into the Peltew.

I liked Klara a great deal. She was like a big sister to me. She was devoted to my mother and therefore to the rest of my family. She was always hugging me and Pawel, always telling us stories. Stories about birds, stories about children, stories about flowers. My mother was our favorite storyteller, but Klara did a fine job of it as well. Some of Klara's stories were about the children we could hear playing in the small park by the Bernardynski church above the Palace. Some of her stories were about Baba Yaga, the witch I remembered from my time in the countryside. Some of her stories she pretended to take from the newspaper. She would open the paper and pretend to read a fantastic tale of a little girl who rescued her entire village.

I did not recognize the romance between Klara and Korsarz, but I could see that they were close. Certainly, for Korsarz to put himself at risk like that, to leave the sewer for an inspection of the Janowska camp only to bring back news of Klara's sister, was an indication of deep affection. Deep affection, courage, and foolishness, all mixed together. But this kind of affection was not limited to Klara and Korsarz. Over time, there was such a strong bond among our entire group that probably any one of us would have made such a sacrifice for any one of the others.

I should say, *most* any one of us would have made such a sacrifice, because probably there was one exception. Chaskiel Orenbach remained disinclined to such affection, such selflessness. He was the most difficult puzzle. He was still disagreeable, even without his brother and Weiss and Shmiel Weinberg for support. He was against every plan, every objective, every initiative. Do not misunderstand: Chaskiel did his part, he contributed, but he never did anything willingly. Even when there was nothing to argue about, he argued. Even the way he ate his soup was like an argument—first the liquid, then the beans and onions, not all together like everyone else. We all tried it this way and liked it, but with Chaskiel it was like an argument between the broth and the vegetables. Maybe he was not always this way. Maybe it was the Germans who had given him this sour disposition. Maybe it was the war and what his family was made to suffer. Or maybe there had been some particular hardship or setback that we did not know anything about. Who can say how such circumstances can change a man?

It was always interesting to me that Chaskiel stayed behind with our group while his brother and his cronies sought a better fate aboveground. Even at seven years old, I was intrigued by this. Was it that Chaskiel wanted to disengage from those others? Or did he simply believe that his chances for survival were better here in the sewer than they were on the outside? I never had the nerve to ask him. He was not the sort of man who appeared open to such questions, especially from a child. And so, instead, I wondered.

In his unpublished memoir, my father wrote that our group was such an intriguing collection of personalities, from Socha and the other sewer workers all the way down to little Pawel. We came together as in a menagerie, he said. In another life, at another time, we might never have associated with one another, but here we had been thrown together by fate and circumstance and the simple fact that we were all Jewish, all desperate to survive. And in this way we became a family.

There was another essential aspect of our survival, in addition to our sense of hope and our sense of order and routine: a sense of humor. My father had a great sense of humor. My mother, too. We were always laughing at this or that occurence, like the time my father was nearly hanged by the ghetto commander Grzymek and was admonished for leaving the gallows without his clothes. There was nothing to do but laugh, and very often this was how we made sense of the madness all around. We tried to find the humor in the simple accomplishment of remaining alive.

Once, I was sitting on the chamber pot, off in the shadows of the Palace, listening to the grown-ups argue about something or other. Always, the grown-ups were arguing, in a good-natured sort of way. Sometimes they seemed to argue just to hear themselves talk, to take up one side merely to contradict the other. I was a big philosopher when I sat on the chamber pot. I liked to sit and think and listen. The others would sit and go efficiently about their business, but I would remain on the chamber pot for the longest time, sitting and thinking and still somehow participating in the conversation in the main part of the Palace. I did not like to be left out, I suppose. Pawel used to have my mother help him when he had to go to the bathroom, but I was old enough that I could go by myself, and this privilege made me feel like a grown-up.

There was only the illusion of privacy. The adults and I were not so far away from each other, only three or four meters. Whatever the discussion was, I would put in my two cents, and on this one occasion it seemed the adults were bickering without letup. I was only seven, but I had heard enough, so from my philosophical seat on the chamber pot I said loudly enough for the others to hear, "You can never agree on anything. It is no wonder the Germans want to kill us all!"

It was a brazen thing to say, and darkly funny, especially coming from the lips of a child. It took the grown-ups by surprise, and right away they stopped their arguing and considered the precocious child in their midst, off in the shadows on the chamber pot. It even took me by surprise, that I should be so dismissive, so sarcastic, so bold in putting my elders in their place. To make a joke from our endlessly dire predicament, it was a very sophisticated thing. My father told me later that even the sour Chaskiel Orenbach was shocked into a smile over my remark. It was only a slight smile, this was true, and if you blinked, you might have missed it; but it was a smile just the same.

There was another time when I turned my sense of humor into mischief. The victim was Chaskiel Orenbach, and here again I was able to coax a smile from this cheerless man, only this time it took a while longer. Orenbach and Korsarz were quarreling over some small matter or other. It was nothing unusual for these two to quarrel, only it happened on a day that Korsarz was meant to cut everyone's hair. Orenbach would not let the Pirate anywhere near him with a sharp pair of scissors, so I volunteered to cut Chaskiel's hair instead, and he warily agreed.

I put on a small show for my parents and the other adults. No one in our group was particularly fond of Chaskiel, except perhaps for Genia Weinberg, who also had a sour disposition. I knew that my audience would play along with me and hold back their laughter, and sure enough they did.

I said to Chaskiel, "You point with your finger where you would like me to cut."

He did as I asked, but I did not exactly follow his instructions. I let him hold the mirror only in the front, and in the back I kept guiding his finger farther up his neck toward the top of his head, cutting steps into his hair as we went along. The others were watching and trying to keep from laughing. Weinbergova, too, was trying not to smile. Chaskiel did not suspect that I was sabotaging his haircut. Who would suspect a child of such a thing? But that is just what I was doing. Each time he moved his finger a little bit higher, I followed with cuts that made a series of steps at the back of his head.

As I was working the scissors, I was singing a popular Russian folk song. The chorus was, *"Schavischa, schavischa."* Higher and higher. The others could see this was the punch line to the bad haircut I was giving Orenbach. As I inched higher and higher on his head, as he moved his finger higher and higher, I sang the words *higher and higher* in accompaniment.

Finally, when I was nearly finished with my mischief, the others could not hold their amusement any longer. They burst into laughter. Weinbergova, too. Poor Chaskiel's hair was cut into several tiers, like a wedding cake. It looked ridiculous! And so funny! We were all howling—quietly howling, I should note, because of course we could not make so much noise as to be heard aboveground, and probably the effort to stifle our laughter made us laugh even more. I felt bad for Chaskiel, that he was the object of such derision, but not so bad that I regretted what I had just done.

It took a moment for Chaskiel Orenbach to realize that he had been made a fool by a little girl, and when he finally did he thrust the mirror into the air behind his head to see for himself what I had done. Oh, he was so angry! If he could have stormed off and stamped his feet, he would have certainly done so, but there was no place to go and he could not stand to stamp his feet. The others were all laughing and telling him to relax, that his hair would grow back, that it was just a joke, but he did not think it was funny.

For days he would not talk to me. The others quietly congratulated me for putting on such a show, for putting Chaskiel in his place, but Chaskiel himself was not amused. This put me in a difficult position each night because when we were sleeping my place was between my father and Chaskiel. I hated to be so close to that man, but what could I do? These were the arrangements Socha had made for us. I had to lean close to my father and pretend Chaskiel was not there. And now with Chaskiel still so angry at me, I leaned closer still.

After a few days, Chaskiel softened. I caught him one afternoon holding the mirror to the back of his head, inspecting the damage I had done, and he at last allowed himself the smallest of smiles. He saw me looking at him, and he shook his fist at me as in a playful threat. He said, "Krysha!"

Probably this was the first time he spoke my name, and I counted it as a great accomplishment that he did so with apparent good cheer. It told me that beneath the cold exterior of Chaskiel Orenbach's difficult personality there was a little bit of warmth, and this was an enormous comfort at the time. I was already hardened to the ways of human nature, but I did not need to be so hardened among our closest companions.

Socha went to elaborate lengths to help build for us an underground home. Very quickly, he began bringing ordinary household items for us to go along with our essential supplies. He drew the money from our daily payment to procure these items, so my family considered these purchases a generosity, because whatever the sewer workers did not spend for our upkeep they were entitled to keep for themselves.

Whatever we required, whatever we requested, Socha would endeavor to bring for us. Newspapers, books, paper and pencils, utensils . . . Sabbath candles, even. Every Friday, he would bring a set of candles, and my mother would light them and say the blessings before our evening meal. Socha admired this, he said, that we would keep to our rituals and customs even in such feral conditions. He admired Berestycki with his daily prayers and his tallith and tefillin. He admired that we fasted on Yom Kippur, which came around on our calendar soon enough. He and Wroblewski even celebrated Rosh Hashanah with us, with a special meal prepared by Weinbergova from our meager provisions, because Socha said he wanted to experience what it was to be Jewish, and we could see that this was as meaningful to him as it was to us.

Sometimes Socha would bring us items before we could even ask for them. He knew my father was trying to teach me to read and write, to make productive use of our time underground, so one day he arrived with a book to help me with my letters. Already, he had brought a writing tablet and some pencils for my lessons. The book was about a girl named Ala. On each page there was a different scene with a story for each letter of the alphabet. On the first page there was a picture of the girl and her cat. It said, "Ala has a cat." *Ala ma kota*. And that was for the letter "A."

He was so pleased to be able to bring me this book, and each day he would ask me to sit with him and read so he could check on my progress. We would read by the light of the carbide lamp. This was another big improvement to our daily lives. We had always had the lamp, but we had used it sparingly. Now, every few days Socha would bring us an additional supply of carbide, which came in the form of a grayish white powder. When the powder was finished, we would dump it into a pile at the edge of the Palace. Because we had carbide in abundance, we started to leave the lantern glowing for longer and longer each day. This in turn meant there was more time for reading, more time for studying, more time for social pursuits that we could not take up in darkness. We still passed many long hours in darkness, only not so many as before.

One of our primary activities in the early days of our confinement in the Palace was getting to know our new friends Socha and Wroblewski. Up until now, their visits had been brief, and there had always been some detail of our hiding to discuss. Over time, however, we drew each other into conversation, and in this way we learned a little bit more about the man who had taken us into his protection. In this way, we learned about Socha's wife, Wanda, a resourceful woman who had never associated with Jewish people. This was what Socha told us. He said with some embarrassment that his wife came from a family of anti-Semites, yet she contributed to our safekeeping in a variety of ways. At first, she did so reluctantly. Later, she recognized her husband's deep connection to our group and helped more willingly. We learned, for example, that it was Wanda who shopped for most of our food and other supplies, buying in small quantities from different merchants so as not to arouse suspicion. Also, after our housekeeping was well established, Socha would take our laundry home to Wanda, who boiled our clothing in hot water to eliminate the lice and then cleaned and folded our few things.

Often, Wanda would complain that Socha was spending so much time and effort on our behalf. "Go to your Jews!" she would say to him whenever they argued. *Idz do twoich zydow!* Sometimes she would threaten to report us to the SS or to the Gestapo, and at these times Socha would threaten her in return. He told her that she would be captured and killed by the authorities, while he would be able to escape into the sewer and go into hiding. He tried to present his argument in practical terms. Once, he held a gun to her head to demonstrate his point. He said, "If you tell about this, this will be your fate." He loved his wife, and he did not mean her harm, but he meant to demonstrate that the Germans would not tolerate her role in our hiding.

Socha himself told us this story. He was very upset by this. He did not like how it made his wife seem, how it made him seem, but he told it just the same. He wanted us to know, my father thought, what was at stake for him and his family by helping us.

We learned about Socha's young daughter, Stefcia, whom Socha worshipped. She was about ten years old at the time, and I believe it was his fondness for Stefcia that drew Socha to my mother and us children. He spent so much time with me and Pawel because we reminded him of Stefcia, because he imagined how his own child might endure such an ordeal. His heart broke for us because it would have broken for her. This was why he shared his sandwiches with us, why he made those second trips to return with our medicines and remedies, why he took such special care. Once, when it was winter, just after the first snow, Socha brought me a snowball. It was such a perfect snowball. Perfectly round, perfectly smooth. For little Pawel, he brought one as well, and we played with our snowballs until they melted. He knew what it was for a child to miss the first snowfall of the season. He knew the joy such a small gift could bring. And he knew these things because he knew what they would have meant to his Stefcia.

Socha believed that the help he extended to us was his greatest mission in life. In the depths of his soul, which he revealed to us during our long conversations, he felt he was called by God to this assignment as an opportunity to repent for his sins. He went to church regularly, more and more as his relationship with us continued. He had been raised as a practicing Catholic, but he had stopped going to church a young man. When he married Wanda, he returned to the church, and now, perhaps inspired by Berestycki's daily ritual and my mother's observance of the Sabbath, he attended church even more frequently. When he went, he told us, he prayed for his underground family. He lit candles as an expression of thanksgiving that we were still alive. He recited the Lord's Prayer, and at the end he would add, "Forgive us our sins, O Lord, for we are rescuing the innocent, the abandoned, and the threatened."

Socha's deepening commitment to our plight was going on while he was still collecting money in exchange for our protection. However, the modest means of the other men were soon exhausted, and my father was the only one left with the ability to contribute to our daily payment of 500 zlotys. Following the departure of Weiss and his cronies, there had been some very small contributions from Korsarz and Orenbach, but these dwindled to nothing after only a few weeks. Among the others, there was not even a single grosz, other than the 20-zloty bill that Halina Wind kept hidden safely away, which my father would not accept.

From time to time, I overheard discussions between my mother and father about the high rate of payment, which had been agreed to when it appeared the war would end soon and that there would be others to share the burden. My father took a practical view. He said he did not mind making the entire payment as long as he had the money. He said the money was of no use to us otherwise. He despaired about the valuable gem that had slipped from his boot, which could have supported us for several weeks.

At last he allowed that his money and resources had about run out. He had given away his valuable gold watch and all his other possessions, and he was down to almost his last zloty. This was a great and looming crisis for our group, but my father did not want to trouble the others with this concern. He kept it between him and my mother, just. I discovered it only because my ears were very much attuned to their secrets.

Finally, my father went to Socha with his dilemma. He did this quietly, away from the others, probably in the bend of our L-shaped chamber. Previously, he and Socha had discussed this eventuality in general terms. Socha had always said that our most difficult time would be when we ran out of money. He had an expression for running out of money that my father often repeated: "When you can no longer pay for the last cutlet."

My father did not want to consider that we were down to our last cutlet, so he presented Socha with a whispered proposition. He told him about our visit from my father's uncle on the last night of the August action, more than a year earlier. He told him about the secret fortune hidden somewhere in the cellar of an apartment building. He told him the address and a description of the hiding place.

My father said, "My pockets are empty, but there is money and jewelry outside."

"What if I cannot find this fortune?" Socha asked.

"You will find it," my father assured him. "You must."

The next morning, Socha and Wroblewski arrived with an extra few satchels. In these they carried the coins and jewels and silverware and other fine things they had recovered from the inheritance passed to my father by his uncle on the night he was killed. My father was so happy to see these things when Socha handed them over to him. He did not even bother to count the money or to make an inventory. He simply handed the satchels back to Socha and said, "You take it. The money, the jewelry, everything. It is of no use to us here. This is our payment in full."

Socha would not accept this. He suggested instead that my father keep the valuables and that he continue to parcel them out to the sewer workers at the rate of 500 zlotys per day, as before. My father did not understand Socha's refusal at first, but then he came up with an explanation. He decided that Socha did not want my father and the others to feel indebted to them and that he did not want to encourage his sewer worker colleagues into thinking they had been fully paid and in this way entertain the notion of quitting the job. Whatever Socha's thinking, this is what my father did, until after another few weeks this fortune ran out as well. This was when Socha finally revealed his true character. He took my father aside one day and gave him some money. He told my father that he was to return the money to him at the end of each visit, at the agreed-upon rate, and that he did not want Wroblewski and Kowalow to know of this arrangement.

My father was astonished by this turn. It appeared that Socha was returning the money he had already collected and preparing to redistribute his share to Wroblewski and Kowalow, in exchange for their continued cooperation. It was as if Socha himself were now paying for our protection. It was a subtle charade. The reason for this, we learned later, was that the three sewer workers were in some disagreement over our continued care. Socha wanted to keep coming to look after us for as long as it was necessary; he was committed to us, no matter what. Wroblewski, with his daily visits, had also developed a close bond with our group. He was uncertain what our fate should be, but without his share of our daily fee, he could not justify the risk to himself and his family. Kowalow, who by design had no contact with us once we reached the sewer, took a hard view. He wanted to disassociate himself from our group and abandon us to the sewer. Socha told us this after the war. Kowalow allowed that it would be cruel simply to leave us to starve to death and suggested that Socha and Wroblewski put strychnine into our food, which would cause us to asphyxiate.

This was how Socha came to this plan, to quietly deceive his colleagues while continuing to enlist their cooperation. My father was briefly concerned about his complicity in such an arrangement, until Socha pointed out to him that the only one being harmed by the deception was Socha himself. At this, my father could not argue. He could only sigh in relief that we were not down to our last cutlet just yet.

Of course, this deception could not last. Wroblewski and Kowalow figured out what was going on. Wanda Socha also discovered that their savings were dwindling under this arrangement. However it happened, there came a time when we had to consider leaving the sewer. We had no other resources, no other recourse. Socha and Wroblewski arrived one morning and told us they could not continue with our safekeeping. Socha had a heavy heart, we could tell. Wroblewski was also saddened by this development, but there was nothing they could do about it, he said. The men offered to see us safely outside, to a part of the city where we would have a good chance of fleeing into the countryside.

My mother would not go. She said, "We will die here if that is what it comes to, but we are not going outside with the children." *My zostajemy tu nawet jak mamy umrzec tu razem.*

My father, what could he do but agree with my mother?

The others were conflicted. They knew what happened to the other members of our group when they left the certainty of the sewer for the uncertainty of the streets. They did not want to split from my family. They had come to rely on my father for his resourcefulness, just as they had come to rely on my mother for her care and concern. They were the leaders of our group, among the men and the women. And yet, without Socha and Wroblewski to bring us our food and other supplies, we would surely perish in our underground chamber. We would become meals for the rats we had spent so long trying to keep from our store of food.

In the end, it was decided that we would not go. Already, my mother had so decided for our family, and now the others were in agreement. We would take our chances in the sewer on our own. It was thought that possibly Korsarz and some of the other men could occasionally venture outside in search of food and return safely to our small chamber. He had done so before, and he could do so again, and in this way we could possibly survive until the Russians occupied the city once more.

Socha and Wroblewski made their final good-byes. It was another tearful time, among many tearful times. We could not begrudge our sewer workers their decision. They had their own families to think about, their own lives. They could not live their lives for us any longer.

I remember feeling very sad when Socha left us for what we thought would be the final time. He had been a stranger to us, and now he was like a part of our family. I thought back to that kindly Aryan schoolteacher who visited our last apartment in the ghetto, who wanted to take me in and raise me as her own daughter. I would not go with her, but I would have gone with Socha. Absolutely, I would have gone with him. It was never discussed as far as I knew, but if it had come to that, it would not have felt as though I were being separated from my family.

It was not like me to think in such dark, gloomy terms, even after everything we had been made to endure, but just then I did not think I would ever see Leopold Socha again. I could not say for certain whether it was day or night outside, but in our small chamber in the storm basin beneath the Bernardynski church, it was our darkest hour.

Happily, our dark hour turned bright the following morning. We rose as usual and removed our sleeping boards and set about preparations for yet another day in the Palace. Berestycki began his morning prayers. Weinbergova boiled water for our coffee. Nobody talked, because we were still intimidated by this change in our fortunes, but then we heard the familiar *slosh, slosh, slosh* of the sewer workers as they crawled through the pipe that spilled into our chamber. We were not expecting Socha and Wroblewski, but who else could it be? For several minutes we heard this noise of approach, but we would not let ourselves become too excited. We were wary because it was possible that, on this first day of our independent existence, we were about to be discovered. It would have been an unfortunate coincidence, but it was certainly possible.

At last, Socha's head appeared in the opening, and our hearts soared as one.

"Poldju!" my father said with some excitement, using the familiar derivative of Socha's name. "Where is Stefek?"

"It is only me today," Socha replied.

"And tomorrow?" my father said.

"Tomorrow we will see," Socha said.

"Kowalow?" my father said.

"Tomorrow we will see," Socha said.

This was the last time we spoke as a group about the money and the sewer workers' decision to continue protecting us. Whatever happened among our sewer workers remained unspoken. It is possible that Socha and my father had a private conversation about the change to our arrangement, but I never learned about it. It was only important that Socha was back to look after us.

In this way, we resumed our plain existence in our underground chamber. The next day, Socha returned with Wroblewski, and there were once again warm greetings all around. Kowalow was once again on the lookout, and once again each day was much the same as the day before, only now and then there was some variation to our routine. There was the time, soon after our money had run out, when Socha and Wroblewski looted a German-run clothing store on our behalf. This was not such an ethical dilemma for Socha, our reformed Catholic and reformed thief, because the Germans had already taken everything from us and he considered it a kind of justice. How he came upon this opportunity, I never knew, but one morning he reported to our chamber and announced that he and Wroblewski had deposited dozens of tailored men's shirts in a nearby manhole. He told the men how to get to this place. We had been underground for several months by this point, and our clothing was ragged and torn. Socha thought it might improve our spirits if we had some new clothes. Berestycki had been a tailor in Lodz, and I remember how he admired the quality of these shirts. For the next few days, we made an incongruous picture, men and women and children prowling our underground hideaway in fine men's shirts, until these items too became ragged and torn.

In addition to the clothes, the sewer workers managed to steal a number of other items from this store, fabrics mostly, which they fenced on the black market and converted into money to buy our daily supply of bread and other necessities. Here again, there was no ethical dilemma, only opportunity. It was a way for the Germans to underwrite our cost of living. This was as it should be, Socha said. This was only fair.

There was the time our sewer workers came upon another windfall—a truckload of potatoes. It was winter, and there had been talk throughout Eastern Europe of a potato shortage. My father had read about it in the papers. This was of some concern to us because potatoes were a cheap staple of our diet. Socha, too, was concerned. The more money he and his colleagues had to pay for our upkeep, the less they would have left over for themselves, and already Kowalow and Wroblewski were not happy that there was no longer any money. When Socha came upon this truckload of potatoes, he thought he could get them down to the Palace and save himself and Wroblewski the trouble of carting the small bags of potatoes they brought on a regular basis, as well as the money from not having to buy any potatoes for several weeks or more.

He was alone at the time, and he located a manhole where he thought it would be dry underneath, and he set about dropping these potatoes to the sewer below. They were bundled in sacks, about two pounds each. After a while, a group of Germans came by and asked Socha what he was doing. They were Germans in authority, probably SS or Gestapo. Socha answered their concerns with authority of his own. One of the Germans stopped him and said, "Why are you throwing potatoes into the sewer?"

Socha said, "They are spoiled. I have been instructed to dispose of them."

There was enough authority in Socha's voice that the Germans left him alone to continue dumping the potatoes into the sewer.

When he was finished, Socha closed the manhole and made note of the location. With Kowalow's help, he drew a map for my father and the other men, describing how to get to this place underground, and the next day my father went with Orenbach, Berestycki, and Korsarz to collect the potatoes. There were too many to carry on one trip, so back and forth they went, back and forth, until all the potatoes were carried to the Palace. Such a mountain of potatoes! Maybe fifty or sixty pounds! We stored them in the space between our two benches and hoped we could eat our way through them before our friends the rats.

There was the time little Pawel slipped on a stone and hurt his leg so badly that it appeared certainly fractured. We did not have any plaster for a cast or any way to make a proper splint, so there was not much my worried parents could do for him. Socha could not attempt to procure such supplies or fill any prescriptions for pain medication without attracting attention, so Pawel could only sit still for several weeks until the bone could heal. My father would carry him to the chamber pot whenever he had to go. Luckily, Pawel was young and in otherwise good health, and the bone healed quickly.

There was the time when a small fire enveloped our close space and nearly accomplished what the Germans could not. Weinbergova was cooking our daily soup when suddenly the Primus stove tipped over and a fire erupted. And it was not just a small kitchen fire, but an open, roaring flame. The benzene used to light the stove had spilled, so the fire spread. It happened in an instant, and soon it was like a raging fireball, which was especially dangerous in our tiny chamber. There was nowhere for the group of us to go. We would have been incinerated or suffocated were it not for the swift action of our group. Immediately, Korsarz and my father threw blankets on the flames and tried to extinguish the fire. Their efforts were not terribly successful, for one of the blankets took the flame and caught fire itself. Then, one of the men determined that our store of used carbide powder would be a good way to smother the fire. All along, we had been emptying the used powder in a pile at the far end of our chamber, and the men scooped this up and threw it on the flames. This proved effective. At the same time, my mother and Klara covered the small opening that led to the street, thinking only to prevent the smoke from escaping and giving away our location, but this action had the unanticipated effect of closing off a source of oxygen to this chamber and making it difficult for the fire to breathe. Both courses of action, taken together, allowed us to put out the fire, but not before we experienced some difficulty breathing ourselves. Our hair and eyelashes were all singed from the flames, our faces blackened from the ash and soot, our routines momentarily upset by the chaos we experienced until the fire was under control.

When Socha and Wroblewski arrived the next day, they could not believe what had happened. They commended us for our heroics and our cleverness in extinguishing the flame, only there had not seemed much of either on display during the ten or fifteen minutes it took for the fire to be stilled. Really, it was more like a series of desperate measures that happened to do the job before we were done in by the flames.

There was the time, almost seven months into our confinement, when we celebrated Christmas with Socha and Wroblewski. Socha had been talking about this for some months. He felt that since he had celebrated our Jewish New Year with us, we should in turn celebrate his holiday with him. I cannot imagine how Socha and Wroblewski managed to separate from their families on such an important holiday, but they passed most of Christmas morning and much of the afternoon in our company. They brought vodka and sandwiches and a festive mood. My father was worried that Socha and Wroblewski would drink too much and become talkative once they returned to the outside and give away our location. My father did not drink, but on this occasion he pretended to do so. He kept filling his glass and spilling the vodka into the mud, and in this way he hoped there would be less vodka for our sewer workers to consume. We learned later that Socha was also worried about Wroblewski. Always, when the two men retired at the end of each day and Wroblewski suggested they stop for a drink before heading home, Socha worried. He trusted his colleagues implicitly to keep their secret, but he did not trust them under the influence of alcohol. He did not trust himself under the influence of alcohol, either, and so determined not to drink beyond a social glass or two as long as we were in his care.

There were birthday and anniversary celebrations, too, but of course there was no real cause for celebration, merely gratification that we had survived another milestone under the brutal Nazi regime, in such inhospitable conditions. Socha in particular made a grand show for my mother's birthday. He very much admired my mother, the way she cared for us two chicks, the way she cared for Babcia and the other women in our group, the way she shouldered our hardships with grace and composure. Once again he brought vodka, and once again my father pretended to drink more than his share, to keep as much alcohol from the lips of our visitors as possible.

For these special occasions, my father would prepare a performance of some kind; he wrote plays and satires and new lyrics to popular songs. He was very clever in this way. His satires were commentaries about the individuals in our group, and we used to laugh so hard at how we appeared in one another's eyes. His songs were clever pieces of wordplay that often poked fun at our own characters and at our struggles at the hands of the Germans. We were not so desperate, he believed, that we could not laugh at our situation. Halina was also clever with words, and she contributed some poems and satires of her own.

The L of our chamber would be offstage, and this was where we would go to prepare our scenes. There was not a lot for us to be excited about in the monotony of our underground work, so we came to enjoy the preparations as performances. There would be a part for everyone who wanted to participate, only not everyone wanted to participate. Genia Weinberg and Chaskiel Orenbach, as I recall, would not take part. They considered it a waste of time to stage these little plays for Socha and Wroblewski, but doing so was how we reminded ourselves that we were still a civilized group, that we could be creative and productive, that we were human beings after all. We came to look forward to these performances—the sewer workers, too. I would look up from practicing my letters and see my father busy scribbling in the 1938 pocket diary Socha had brought him for just this purpose and know that a new satire was soon coming.

These aberrations from routine were life itself. Indeed, the most dramatic of these came in the form of a birth and two deaths. The birth, of course, was the inevitable result of Weinbergova's secret pregnancy, which was not such a secret as our time underground continued. Still, Socha did not know of her condition until the very end. We had put off telling him for so long that it was now thought best to wait for the last possible moment. Finally, my mother and father took Socha aside to explain the matter. At first, my parents reported, Socha was shocked. He thought back to the difficulties of the past months and wondered how a pregnant woman could endure such hardships. Then he wondered how a baby could be safely delivered in such unsanitary conditions, and after that there was the greater worry about how to care for the baby and keep its certain cries from being heard aboveground. Surely the activity of a healthy baby over a prolonged period would lead to our discovery. This was a big dilemma, everyone agreed, but no one could offer a good solution to any of the problems the pregnancy presented. Finally, Socha threw up his hands and said, "We will have to think about what to do."

But Weinbergova could not wait for Socha to develop a plan. She went into labor shortly after this encounter. Genia was moved into the private corner of our chamber. I remained with Pawel and a few of the others in the main part of the chamber. I did not know exactly what was happening, only that something was happening. I was nearly eight years old, but despite the maturity and wisdom that had been forced upon me by our circumstance, I was still innocent of such things as childbirth. I would piece together the particulars later. My father acted as midwife. My mother and some of the other women frantically boiled water. There was a good deal of rummaging through our few things for a suitable blanket or piece of cloth. This, too, I remember. There was the low moaning of Weinbergova. This I remember most of all, and as I listened to Genia's moaning, I felt so terribly frightened for her. I did not know what could cause such pain, such anguish. I could not even imagine. She must have been so afraid!

Regarding the details of Genia Weinberg's delivery, I can only share what my parents shared with me afterward. After the birth, my father cut the umbilical cord with a pair of rusty scissors. The baby, I learned later, was a boy. Babcia collected the newborn from my father and tended to him while my mother prepared a mixture of warm sugar water to get the child to nurse. After a while, the baby was placed alongside Genia's oustretched body on one of the planks we used for sleeping. My mother said Genia appeared to agonize over her natural maternal instincts to protect and nurture this child and our unnatural circumstance that cast this infant as a threat to our survival. No one knew whether to welcome this child or to fear his arrival, not even Weinbergova.

It was an anxious time in our part of the chamber. Even Pawel was nervous. He did not understand the commotion all around. He did not understand the sound of the baby crying. "This is a baby, Krysha?" he asked me at one point.

I could not think how to answer.

Meanwhile, outside, Socha was just as anxious. He had spent the time since learning of Weinbergova's condition trying to find a home for the baby that was about to be born to our underground family. He did not know that Weinbergova was now in labor, and we did not know he was making these inquiries on the child's behalf. Socha knew only that the baby was coming, probably soon, and he went to church after church, trying to find a group of nuns that would care for a newborn child without asking any questions. Finally he located such a church, such a group of nuns, and he could not wait to return to our chamber the following morning to deliver this welcome news.

Weinbergova passed an uncertain few hours with her newborn baby pressed to her side, not knowing what Socha had arranged. She only knew that with each cry her baby threatened to give us all away and that the baby's chances of survival in our damp, dark hovel would not be good. My mother sat with them and watched as

Genia moved closer and closer to the child. Genia kept covering the baby's face with a rag, and at first it seemed this was merely to quiet the sound of his whimpering, but then it became clear that she was attempting to suffocate the baby and put an end to the uncertainty. My mother gently pushed the rag away from the infant's face, and then a few moments later, at the next sound of whimpering, Genia returned with the rag and my mother gently pushed it aside again. All of this happened without any words passing between the two women. Their eyes did all of the talking. Back and forth they went like this, as everyone else drifted off to sleep. It had been a long, eventful night. My mother stayed up with Genia for as long as she could, stroking her hair, pushing her hands from the baby's face, but eventually she too drifted off, and it was at this moment Genia determined to smother her newborn baby, to sacrifice the one, whose chances were slim, for the good of the others, whose chances were only a little bit better than slim.

My mother always felt guilty that she had fallen asleep at such a critical time. She was crestfallen when she awoke and realized what Weinbergova had done. We were all upset about this, but my mother most of all. She thought that if she had stayed awake, the baby might have been spared. Perhaps this was so, but my mother was not to blame. No one was to blame. Also, at just that moment, no one in our group could say that Weinbergova's decision was not for the best. Our underground chamber was no environment for an infant. His constant cries would have placed us in danger. Because of this, it was possible to look on this sad development as an act of great courage on the part of Genia Weinberg, only it did not appear so a little bit later that morning, when Socha arrived in our chamber with what he had thought would be his welcome news.

Such a tragic moment! Such a cruel irony! For Weinbergova to learn that her baby might have been spared after all! That Socha had made arrangements for the baby to be raised by nuns, to have a chance at a full and happy life! It was the situation she had chosen for her young daughter, when Weinbergova had an opportunity to place her with an Aryan family to escape the liquidation, and it was the situation she would have chosen for her infant son, if only she had known that such a situation was possible.

Poor Genia Weinberg was inconsolable, and she would remain so for the next while. For the next few days, she kept to the elbow of the L in relative privacy. She would not speak. She would not eat. She was weakened from the childbirth, so this contributed to her distant mood, but she was also broken by what she now regarded as the unnecessary death of her infant child. Gradually, however, she returned to her routines. She resumed her responsibilities with the cooking. She joined us when we were sitting and talking. She was not the same, of course, but she was back once again to the business of surviving, to making the best of what was left for her.

The second death, sadly, was Babcia's. In the end, the horrible conditions in the sewer became too much for old Mrs. Weiss, and she died in her sleep one night. She was asthmatic, and the dampness of the underground air was not helping her condition. Her breathing was becoming worse and worse. We could hear her wheezing all night long. Each day, it was a little more difficult for her to move. My mother had to help her when it was her turn for a bath. My mother checked her each day for lice, after she was through checking us children. My mother was at her side at the very end, holding her hand, and in the morning the men wrapped Babcia's body and waited for Socha and Wroblewski to arrive and determine what they should do next.

Socha was very superstitious. He did not want to be in our small chamber with a dead body. He told us what to do and then he left. Wroblewski, too. He was not so superstitious, but he would not stay without Socha.

Berestycki said the prayers. I can still picture him in his flowing tallith, chanting the mourner's Kaddish. Some of the other adults said a few words of remembrance. We all shed a few tears. Next, the men pushed Babcia's body into the narrow pipe opening, and through the pipe to where it opened by the main canal. In this way they carried her to the Peltew. There they said another few prayers and buried her body in the river. Then the men returned to the Palace and to the rest of their lives. There was no traditional period of mourning for old Mrs. Weiss, just as there had been no traditional period of mourning for Weinbergova's baby or my uncle Kuba or the others of our group who had been shot and killed upon leaving the sewer. We did not sit shiva. Every day for us was shiva, so we said our few prayers and shared our few thoughts and continued on.

For the longest time, we had been a group of eleven. For the briefest time, we were a group of twelve. Now we were ten, and I began to worry that this was the start of some new heartbreaking pattern, that one by one we would take turns leaving, that soon we would be just my immediate family, and that after that we would be no more.

Eight

THE PRISONER

These life and death developments led me to a period of despair unlike any I had known. I did not know to call it a depression, but that is most certainly what it was. My parents, too, did not know to give my new mood a name. All they knew was that I had become silent, sullen, sad. This was in such contrast with my usual cheerful personality that of course they worried. I became a different little girl.

I cannot say what precisely brought this change to my temperament. Perhaps it was the many long hours in hiding in our ghetto apartments. Perhaps it was the weight of all the time in the sewer, detached from a normal childhood existence. Perhaps it was the one-by-one death and departure of the others in our underground family. Perhaps it was the erosion of the very hope that had sustained us all along. Probably it was all these things taken together at once, all of a sudden.

I could be philosophical at times, but regarding my own circumstance or disposition I was not so introspective or insightful. I was not self-aware. All I could do when one of the adults asked what was troubling me was shrug my shoulders. Sometimes I could not manage even that. I could not put what I was feeling into words. I would not even try. For a week or more, I continued in this way. I would barely eat. My mother told me later it reminded her of the time when I was a stubborn little girl, refusing to eat for the nanny I did not like, but it was not the same thing to me. It was not anything I could control. I was not trying to be stubborn. I simply did not feel like eating. I did not participate in our evening social hour, but it was not because I was being difficult. I only had nothing to say.

My father wrote about my depression in his memoir. He wrote how I appeared lost to him and my mother, how the life seemed to disappear from my eyes and from my soul. After so long underground, so long in darkness, so long in uncertainty, I was alive but at the same time lifeless. I was breathing, but that was all.

Whenever I could, I would listen to the playful cries of the children in the square above our underground hiding place. This was where my mind would wander. In the afternoons, I could hear the children most of all, particularly on Sundays, before and after church. Such joy! Such innocence! I longed to be among such children once more, to play their games, share their jokes, sing their songs, breathe their fresh air, smell their flowers. This last became a small obsession. Whenever I did manage to utter a few words, it would be about the flowers. I wanted to talk only about the flowers and how much I wanted to hold a fresh bouquet in my hands.

It was Socha who finally rescued me from my melancholy. For days and days, I had not eaten my share of Socha's sandwich when he offered it to me. I had not smiled in greeting when he and Wroblewski appeared through the opening to our chamber. I had not read to Socha to show him my progress in this area, because I was not making any progress between his visits. For many days, I had not done a single thing eagerly, and only a few things reluctantly. Yet despite the transparent change to my personality, Socha did not seek to intervene. Probably he did not think this was his place, to take an active role in such a delicate matter with someone else's child. He was like a second father to me, after everything he had done, yet I was not his daughter.

My mother was desperate. She worried that my temperament had been forever changed, that her Krysha would never be returned to her, and one day she spoke with Socha about her concern. This was when Socha did a remarkable thing. He took me into a quiet corner of our underground chamber. He held my hand. He said, "Krysha, you have to eat."

I said, "But I am not hungry."

He said, "You have to speak. Your parents are worried about you. Your underground family is worried about you."

I said, "But I have nothing to say."

He said, "Let us see about that."

Socha led me by the hand to the narrow pipe that opened into our chamber. He indicated for me to climb inside. It had been about a year, and I had never once left the Palace. The men had all taken turns leaving and returning. Every day, they would come and go as if heading back and forth to work. Klara had left from time to time. My mother had crawled through this pipe several times to complete some chore or other. But I had not moved from the small room even once, and here Socha was waiting for me to crawl away from my family. My parents had not said anything about this, and Socha did not say where we were going. He only said, "Come. Let me show you something."

And so I went. We crawled in silence for several kilometers until we came finally to a hatch and then to another iron ladder built into the stone wall. We climbed the ladder to an opening leading to the street. Here I could see the sunlight peering through the sewer grate. It was the first bit of sunshine I had seen in over a year. I lifted my face to it, to soak in its warmth. I could not believe it, that I was feeling this little bit of sunshine. A part of me had believed the sun had set so long ago.

I listened to the children playing outside, just beyond the sewer grate. Their voices seemed so much closer than they had when I could hear them in the Palace. It was as if I were outside with them, running and playing and laughing. It was as if the other children were near enough to touch. For a moment, I tried to be happy.

Socha said, "You have to be strong, little one. In just a few days, you will be up there playing with the other children. You will smell the same flowers."

And in this way I became whole once again. Because Socha had willed it so.

I was no sooner returned from my brief depression than a disaster nearly put an end to us all. It was once again the height of the rainy season, as it had been a year earlier when the cascading waters claimed my uncle Kuba as he was trapped in one of the narrow pipes. Now it was spring, and as the snow began to melt, there was a torrential rain. It was inevitable that we would experience a storm during this time of year, but it was an especially unfortunate time for such a heavy storm. We heard the clap of thunder from our underground chamber. We heard the rushing water from the hard rain and the snowmelt as it crashed into the sewer. It was such a sudden downpour, such a sudden overflow, that the sewer could not accommodate all the water at once.

Very quickly, there was a flash flood that caused the Peltew to spill over its banks, to go along with the backup from the streets above. Our small underground chamber was attacked from above and below by torrents of water. The volume of water from the Bernardynski and Halicki squares had no place to go but down, the rising tides from the river had no place to go but up, and we were caught in the treacherous middle. Within moments the Palace began to fill. We had talked in theory about just such a prospect with Socha and Wroblewski, who knew from experience how dangerous the rushing waters could be during rainy season, but despite these warnings we had believed we were relatively safe and dry in our perch beneath the Bernardynski church. That is, we believed we were safe until we realized we were not, and we went from sloshing in water at our feet and ankles to wading in water waist-deep and higher in the time it took to panic. Soon, the rising water reached Pawel's chin, and soon after that to mine. My parents had to lift us up to allow us to breathe the wet air, and still the water kept rising. We were certain we would all drown.

The adults in our group stretched to their full height—on tiptoe, some of them, to keep their faces above water. There was a second pipe that fed into our chamber, to go along with the one just above the ground that we used as our primary entrance and exit, and it was through this second pipe, high along the opposite wall, that most of the water fell. During the frenzy of trying to keep his head above water, my father managed to take off his shirt and attempt to divert the water with it from the high pipe to the low pipe across the room. The other men thought to divert the flow with blankets and shovels and other crude tools. But there was no way to stop the flood. The men succeeded only in exhausting themselves and exerting a few extra breaths they probably did not have to spare. The water kept coming and coming, the level kept rising and rising, and we had only a short moment to consider our certain demise.

Pawel and I, we were plainly terrified. I do not think I had ever heard my little brother scream as loudly as he did during this unfolding moment. There was no reason to quiet our voices—we could not be heard above the roar of the rushing water. We would be dead before we would be discovered. Me, I did not scream so much as shriek. As we opened our mouths we were swallowing up the rushing water. I thought that we would surely drown, that we were drowning already.

Somehow, I managed to grab Jacob Berestycki's coat. I was pulling and pulling at it, like a lifeline. I said, "Pray, Jacob, pray!" *Jakob, modl sie!* Over and over, I said this. I thought since he prayed every day, he would be closest to God. If our prayers would be heard, it would be through Jacob Berestycki.

By yet another miracle, the water level started to subside. We had stretched ourselves to ceiling height in our small chamber. There had been barely enough air to breathe between the top of the water and the bottom of our low ceiling, and as we grabbed what we all believed would be our few final breaths and our final few glances at one another, the water began to drain. Whatever pipes had been momentarily clogged feeding in and out of our chamber were now cleared. Whatever prayers Berestycki managed to utter on our behalf, they had made it through, and very quickly we were left only with piles and piles of mud to clean from our small chamber. Everything we owned had floated away. Pots, pans, spoons, tins of food, and other supplies . . . all of it, gone. The planks of woods and other items that had been too heavy to float away had managed to drop to the mud at our feet once the water receded.

But we were alive. This was the most important thing. This was the only thing. Our tools and supplies could be replaced as needed, but we could not so easily replace one another, so we allowed ourselves the small sigh of survivors after an especially harrowing ordeal. It had been such a brief but powerful display of the might of the Peltew, the might of the elements. It was unbelievable, really; we had been living here along the rank shores of the river for over a year, and in all that time we had never truly considered the danger of these rushing waters. Yes, we had lost my uncle Kuba to these rushing waters, and still we did not feel in jeopardy, until now.

The next morning, Socha and Wroblewski came to our underground chamber expecting to find only our corpses. Before climbing down into the sewer, in fact, Socha stopped at his church to light a candle of remembrance for each of us, such was his certainty that we had perished. He believed some of us would have undoubtedly been swallowed up by the currents, and some of us would remain in the Palace even in death, as silent and still as we had been in life. But there we were, all ten of us, living and breathing still. It was the most astonishing thing, and Socha came to regard it as an act of divine providence. We could not help but agree, because surely there had been a guiding hand to see us safely to the other side of our ordeal.

For the rest of our time in the sewer, I was deathly afraid of rain. For the rest of my life, this fear has continued, but here is where it began. I had only recently been freed from the grip of a fleeting depression, and now I was gripped in fear over the sound of even the slightest rain dripping into our chamber. Whenever it started to rain, however slightly, I would say to my mother, "It will be a big rain, Mama?" *Bedzie ulewa, Mama?* Long after the war, this was what I would say to my mother whenever the rain started to fall. "It will be a big rain?" Even into adulthood, I would become tense and nervous at the sound of a heavy rain. It would take me back to that time in the Palace when all appeared lost. It did not matter that we had managed to escape the floodwaters with only a story to tell. It mattered that I was made to consider our demise in the first place.

All this time, my father had been charting the progress of the Soviets. It was our best hope, he said, that the same Russian army that had once so oppressed us would now be our saviors. Every day, my father would huddle with Socha and study a map of Poland. Together they would read between the lines of propaganda in the daily newspapers and try to gauge the progress of the war. They would read the German newspapers, the Russian newspapers, the Polish newspapers. In between, they would discover the truth of the war. Every day, it was changing. One day, the Germans were advancing. The next day, the Germans were retreating. One day, the Russians would enjoy a success on the front. The next day, there would be a setback. As the Russians moved west, my father was pushing papers here and there, studying the situation. He would point to places on the map and say, "They are not here, they are not here." Always, he had to know what was going on. He was like a general, fighting to win the war on his pieces of paper.

I listened in and allowed myself to become excited at these developments, but it was not always a positive turn. Kowalow noted with concern one morning that Wehrmacht officials were preparing a land mine operation on the streets around the Bernardynski church. The houses there had been abandoned and taken up by German officials, who of course wanted to see their homes protected from Russian tanks. Also, the Germans kept a headquarters office in this square and so were taking pains to protect the high-ranking officials who worked there as well. As part of this initiative, German soldiers began tearing up the streets and placing active mines just below the surface. This was a potential disaster for our party below, and Kowalow signaled Socha and Wroblewski to return to the surface to discuss the matter.

It was the middle of June 1944, and the German defense lines were beginning to collapse. This land mine operation was a last desperate measure to maintain control of Lvov. Wehrmacht personnel were digging trenches along the city streets. There was such a noise that we could hear the hammering and the jackhammers below. We did not know what these noises might mean. At first we thought the Germans had discovered our location and were breaking through to capture us from the streets above, such was our narrow worldview from our underground chamber.

Thinking quickly, the three sewer workers approached the Wehrmacht officer who appeared to be in charge. Our friends were dressed in their working clothes and so had the authority to accompany their charade. Kowalow presented himself as an engineer for the city's sewer district. He told the officer that the sewers below were filled with pockets of explosive gases. Along every pipe, he said, there were also gas lines. He warned the officer that his soldiers were in grave danger by digging in this area without a map of these underground pipes. It was a suicide mission, he said, to lay mines in such proximity to these explosive gases. It was even dangerous just to dig, he said, because if one of those gas lines burst, the entire area would be threatened.

As Kowalow, Socha, and Wroblewski made their arguments above, we moved frantically to secure our position below. We did not know what was happening. We could only scramble to protect ourselves and so began to cover the opening to our chamber with dirt and mud and silt. My father and some of the other men thought this would be a good strategy. We used some of the empty food storage tins to help move the dirt. It was a fool's mission, we realized later, but at the time we feared we were about to be discovered; so as the Germans were digging from above we were digging from below, trying to unearth enough dirt to conceal the opening into our Palace chamber.

Meanwhile, up above there was such authority and concern in Kowalow's voice that the Wehrmacht officer put an immediate halt to the mining. He was not happy about it, but he did not want to put his men at risk. He did not want to go against the recommendation of this man who presented himself as an engineer and who spoke so convincingly about the danger of the gas lines below. Our sewer workers, of course, were extremely happy about this and knew that we had diverted disaster once more.

Down below, our underground family breathed a happy sigh when the sounds of the digging suddenly stopped. We would have to wait for Socha's next visit to learn what had happened, but for the time being we knew that we had been spared.

A week or so later, we could hear the sounds of fighter planes flying overhead and the bombs being dropped on the streets of the city. This development corresponded to the accounts my father and Socha had been reading in the newspapers, but the events filled our chamber with a mixture of excitement and dread. We knew that the same bombs meant to liberate us might kill us first instead. An explosion on the street directly above our chamber would certainly compromise our sewer and the stone walls all around, and we would be crushed in the rubble.

It was an anxious time, and the curious thing was that it was a good anxiety thrown together with a bad anxiety. We began to believe our liberation was near, and this was a welcome development because we did not know how much longer we could survive in our primitive environment. It had been over a year since we had set up housekeeping in the Palace, and although we had made the best of our unfortunate circumstance, we recognized that we could not remain here forever. Our health was quickly deteriorating, especially among the adults. Pawel and I were mostly fine; after our initial bouts of dysentery and occasional other ailments, we had developed a kind of immunity to the germs and the bacteria and the malnutrition. We were a sturdy and resilient pair. However, the adults in our group were experiencing more and more aches and pains as our confinement continued. Already we had lost old Mrs. Weiss to these impossible living conditions. To live so long in such constant dampness, with so little oxygen, so little food, it was only a matter of time before others began to fail. My father noted in his memoir that some of the adults in our party were experiencing difficulty with their eyes because of the constant darkness. Others were experiencing joint pain and swelling. Others feared their spines would be permanently crooked from being constantly bent in a stooped-over position.

At night, when they thought everyone else was asleep, I could hear my father whispering privately to my mother that we were reaching the end of our endurance. This was his worry. He whispered this in Yiddish so Pawel and I could not overhear, but I had learned enough Yiddish by this point to understand his concern. I knew that what Korsarz said about the Yiddish language was not always so, because certainly there was nothing funny about my father's apprehension, even in such a joyful language as Yiddish.

Probably my father was right to be so concerned. We were reaching the end of our endurance. We could only hope that our will to live would outlast the Germans' hold on our city.

Our underground family received an unannounced visitor toward the end of June 1944, almost thirteen months into our confinement. Socha and Wroblewski arrived one day with a Ukrainian soldier, a young man who was the boyfriend of Socha's sister-in-law. His name was Tola, and he did not look like the sinister Ukrainians I had been accustomed to seeing on the streets of the ghetto before we escaped into the sewer. I guessed he was in his early twenties. His face at first seemed kind and handsome. He had light blond hair, and he was both skinny and strong. Of course, we were all dreadfully skinny, after so long without the proper nutrition, but Tola was naturally skinny. He appeared rail thin but also powerful.

We were so surprised to have a visitor at long last. I had not realized how hungry we were as a group to engage in conversation with someone new, to participate in a normal social exchange. To make a new acquaintance is a basic human interaction, and we had been without such an opportunity for so long.

For his part, Tola must have been shocked at our appearance. Socha and Wroblewski saw us every day and so did not notice how emaciated and haggard we had become. We must have looked like the starved prisoners in the concentration camps, and for all we knew, a young man like Tola was not so hungry to make our acquaintance. Our clothes were tattered and worn, our bodies beaten down by the unnatural conditions. To his credit, Tola did not remark about our unsightly condition. He simply made the appropriate greetings and attempted to adjust to his new surroundings.

Very quickly, we learned Tola's story. Like many Ukrainians, he had been fighting in the Russian army. Unfortunately, he was captured by the Germans and made a prisoner of war and forced by his captors to fight against his own countrymen. This was a famous German tactic, to turn their prisoners into traitors, and these were considered the lucky ones. The prisoners who did not join the German army were warehoused in camps that resembled the concentration camps, or they were simply killed.

Tola would not fight against the Russians. He wore the German uniform for a short time until he managed to escape. Somehow, when he was in hiding, he met Socha's sister-in-law and fell in love. Her name was Michalina. It was a dramatic romance, made even more dramatic because of the underlying danger and because Tola was a man without a country. The Germans would kill him for deserting, and the Russians would kill him for fighting for the other side. He had no place to turn. Klara and Halina were especially attracted to the romantic, forbidden elements of Tola's story. They thought it would be a grand adventure, to help two young lovers survive their tragic circumstance so they could one day be together.

It was Wanda Socha who suggested to her husband that he consider hiding Tola in the sewer along with his precious Jews. He was her sister's boyfriend, after all, and he at least deserved the same chance as a group of Jews who had been strangers to their family. It would be nothing, she thought, for us to add another hideaway to our group, and Socha had no choice but to agree.

Socha explained our situation to Tola. He described our Palace home, how we were living, and how we had built our own little society in our underground world. He made it sound as though it were not so terrible, because to him it was not so terrible. Socha explained that he himself chose to spend many long hours with us in this place. He described our various personalities and told about the hen and her two chicks and the plays we liked to perform. He assured Tola that we would welcome him into our group and care for him as one of our own.

Tola agreed that this would be a good place for him to hide until the Russians once again controlled the streets of Lvov and he could at last explain his situation to the authorities. Already the Russians had been moving farther and farther into the region, and it seemed from newspaper accounts that our persecution under the Germans would not last much longer. And so it was arranged. However, we did not know of these arrangements. Tola simply arrived in our midst without warning. We were shocked to see this stranger, certainly, but by this point we trusted Socha implicitly. If he told us to take this man into our company, we were only too happy to do so. And Tola made a fine first impression. He was agreeable and pleasant and grateful for the sanctuary we offered. Indeed, when he first crawled through the pipe into our chamber, it felt to all of us as though this Ukrainian soldier were a guest in our home.

But the spirit of welcome left us almost as soon as Tola arrived. He could not get used to our dungeonlike surroundings. He could not understand how we could live in such a filthy place. He could not stand the mud, the stench, the cold, the rats. "You are like animals here," he said. "And you have been here for thirteen months! I could not survive thirteen hours in this place."

However, Socha persuaded Tola to keep an open mind, and soon our sewer workers left to continue their rounds. Tola stayed behind, and we of course assumed he would become gradually accustomed to these surroundings as we had become gradually accustomed. But in this we were wrong. Tola could not last even one day. He could not rest. He became very agitated, almost claustrophobic. "How can you live here?" he kept saying. "It is impossible." Remember, this was a man who had survived for several weeks in a German POW camp, where the conditions were unspeakable. That, he could endure; this, he could not.

Tola became frantic and restless as his first day in our company wore on. Soon, he was telling us he had to leave, but my father did not think this was a good idea. He had not discussed this possibility with Socha, that Tola would not wish to remain in the sewer, but he did not think Socha wanted his prisoner of war wandering the pipes and tunnels of the sewer on his own. Certainly, he would be discovered if he tried to leave, just as the others had been discovered. For Tola's sake, and for our sakes as well, he would have to remain, at least until Socha and Wroblewski arrived the next morning. At that point, Socha could determine an appropriate course of action.

It was quietly decided that the men would take turns watching

Tola, in four-hour shifts, to make certain he would not flee and possibly give away our location. Several times, Tola rushed to the open pipe and attempted to crawl his way through, until one of the men grabbed him by the legs and pulled him back toward our chamber. When this happened, another of the men would join in the capture, because the young soldier was too strong for only one man to pin down. With each failed escape, Tola became more and more agitated, more and more difficult. He became like a madman.

There would be little sleep for any of us on this night, there was so much agitation and difficulty in our small chamber. It is a wonder to me that those long hours passed at all, such was the slow anguish of Tola's first night among our group, until finally Socha and Wroblewski arrived the next morning. Socha was startled to hear about the trouble his soldier had caused. My father explained the situation, and Tola did not dispute his account. Tola said he could not stay here, but Socha said he now had no choice. He said he could not risk allowing Tola to return to the outside, that he could no longer trust Tola to keep quiet about our location or about the sewer workers' conspiracy to conceal us. Tola assured Socha he would keep our secret, but Socha would not take the chance. He told the Ukrainian he had put our group in a predicament. At this, Tola's agitation returned in full force. He had tried to reason with his girlfriend's brother-in-law, but now he became hysterical. He flailed about our small chamber, yelling and screaming. We all feared his shouts would give us away. He quieted only when Socha drew his gun. "Shut up or I will shoot," Socha said.

At last, Tola was quiet.

Socha crossed to where my father was sitting and gave him his gun. "Chiger," he said, "you must watch this man. You cannot let him leave." Then he produced a length of rope, which he wound around Tola's hands to restrain him and restrict his movement. "This way, he cannot crawl," Socha explained.

Once again, Tola became a prisoner of war, only now he was being held by our underground sovereignty. Now the men in our group would be his guards, and they would resume their four-hour shifts behind the barrel of Socha's gun until we were liberated or until Socha came up with another plan. We meant this young soldier no harm, of course, but at the same time we could not allow him to threaten our survival.

And so began the unexpected final chapter of our time in the sewer. A new character who had not been a part of our story was now placed in a central role. I did not like that this man had come to stay with us. I did not like that the camaraderie of our group was now upset. After a year and more in our underground Palace, we had become comfortable with one another and established in our routines. Now, with Tola, we could not be as we had been before. I could not sit with my father and study my letters. We could not sit in the evening and perform one of my father's plays or satires. We could not be ourselves.

Even such a simple thing as going to the bathroom was disturbed by Tola's presence. Always, we had enjoyed only the illusion of privacy, but now with this stranger among us we could not relieve ourselves without feeling self-conscious. I do not think, for example, that any of us ever relieved ourselves when Socha and Wroblewski came to visit. We went only when we were alone. This was a curious thing, and yet we had developed such an intimacy among our group that this was how we maintained our civility. We developed our own bathroom routines, our own personalities, when we had to use the chamber pot. Some of us were quick. Some of us took our time. Me, I liked to sit and think. Sometimes I would sit so long that my mother would call out to me from the shadows to make sure I was okay. Now, however, we were all very quick to do our business, and when Tola needed to use the bathroom, we were all a little bit embarrassed. It was like a violation. Now even the illusion of privacy was no more.

Pawel, too, was disturbed by Tola's presence, only he did not care so much about having to use the bathroom. He cared about Tola's disposition, which grew more and more angry each hour he remained with us. Tola would kick at the rats that had become Pawel's friends. He was more sour and disagreeable than Weiss and his cronies had ever been, and we had not seen those men for nearly a year. Pawel could sense this soldier's foul demeanor and the bad temper he had brought with him into our small chamber. We had lived a long time in our self-contained little world, with our eccentricities and personalities, but somehow we had managed to get along. We had learned to coexist.

With this hostile stranger among us, a virtual prisoner, I realized for the first time that we were prisoners, too. I had not thought of our circumstance in just this way until just this moment. Tola, he could not go anywhere. His hands were tied and he was held at gunpoint, against his will. And the rest of us, we could not go anywhere, either. Our hands were not tied and we were not being held at gunpoint, but we were prisoners just the same. We, too, were being held against our will.

I did not think to share this observation with my father and the others. I did not think anyone would appreciate the observations of an eight-year-old girl. Instead, I kept quiet and silently prayed that things could go back to how they were. Whether I was praying that things could go back to how they were before the war, before the initial Soviet occupation, before the German occupation, before our time in the ghetto, before the final liquidation, before our confinement in the sewer, or before Tola's arrival had upset the fine balance of the life we had finally made, I could not say. I was not self-aware enough to know the full extent of my deepest thoughts, only that I, too, was restless, a prisoner of my own unfortunate circumstance.

Nine

❧

LIBERATION

One day in July, Socha arrived in our chamber with a report that the Russians had captured the city of Tarnopol, less than a hundred kilometers east of where we were sitting. We were overjoyed at this, because it meant the Germans were indeed retreating, confirming the accounts my father and the others had been reading in the newspapers. For over a year, we had been praying for this, dreaming about it, willing it so. We thought now it would be only a few days more before we, too, were liberated. Such was the momentum of the Russian army, and such was the strength of our fervent hope. But our happiness was short-lived, because only two days later Socha was back with a revised report. This time, it was revealed that the Germans had recaptured Tarnopol. It was a dispiriting turn. Furthermore, we learned that while the city had briefly been in Soviet hands, hundreds of Jews who had been in hiding came out from their shelters and started to celebrate. When the Germans regained control, these hundreds of Jews were swiftly exterminated.

To experience the joyful prospect of liberation and then to have it suddenly revoked struck us as particularly cruel at a time when we were particularly vulnerable to such cruelty. The turnabout reminded me of the cat-and-mouse games the ghetto commander Grzymek used to play with my father, telling him first he was free and then he was not free. The news played with our emotions, and already we were in a fragile state. The arrival of the prisoner Tola had upset the fine balance of our underground community, and our will to live was slowly leaking from our pores. Probably we saw ourselves through Tola's disbelieving eyes, and the picture that came back was one of weakness and desperation. What had once been our shared strength was now, to someone like Tola, merely stubbornness and leftover will. We had made the best of a bad situation, this was true, but more and more it seemed that the bad situation would prevail. And so to have this bulletin of such great elation be so quickly deflated with a bulletin of such great tragedy was especially damaging to our spirits.

Nobody could say whether it had been a strategy on the part of the Germans, to lull the Soviets into victory on the streets of Tarnopol and at the same time coax the Jews out of hiding. Or maybe the Germans had been truly defeated and then gathered their resources and resumed the fight. However it happened, whatever it meant, the way the Germans recaptured the city left us wary of any future positive reports. It was a difficult paradox: we could not trust the Russians to win this fight, and yet without a Russian victory we were doomed to an eternity in this underground place.

And then a strange thing happened. Jacob Berestycki arose early one morning and asked who among our group celebrated a birthday in July. It was an odd question, as if from nowhere. In addition to his religious beliefs, Berestycki believed in the power of dreams to help see into the future. However, he was also a pragmatist. He was all these things taken together, and on this night he experienced a dream that he felt would tell our fate. In his dream, he saw a vision of an elderly rabbi with a long white beard. The rabbi said, "In July, you will all be free."

We discussed this dream, over and over. We pressed Berestycki to share the details: who else was in the dream, what were they doing? We could not agree what it might mean, if it meant anything at all. Berestycki took it on its face, that we would be free in July. My father took it as an omen, that our liberation was indeed coming. Chaskiel Orenbach dismissed it as nonsense. Someone suggested that it was a dream of wish fulfillment, an indication only that Berestycki was hoping to be rescued sometime soon. Even Tola, our headstrong prisoner, had an opinion. Already he thought we were foolish, to live like animals in our underground chamber. Now he thought we were foolish on top of foolish, to give such careful thought to something as inconsequential as a dream.

I did not venture an opinion, but I liked that an elderly rabbi with a long white beard had something to say about our future. It did not matter that it was an elderly rabbi in Berestycki's imagination only. It was a rabbi, after all, and Berestycki was a grown man, after all. I liked that between the two of them someone had taken the time to consider our circumstance. It made me not feel so all alone.

Still, we could not understand what had prompted Berestycki

to inquire about our birthdays, because there was nothing in his dream to require this information. Berestycki himself could not say, only that it was the first thing on his mind when he awoke.

We planned to ask Socha what he thought the dream might mean when he arrived later that morning with our daily delivery, but the hours passed with no sign of our sewer workers. The next day, there was no sign of them again. Of course, this became the new topic of our group discussion, what had happened to Socha and Wroblewski. It was more important than Berestycki's dream, because it was not like Socha and Wroblewski to stay away from our chamber for two days in a row. Only once or twice in the year we had been in the sewer had Socha not come to us for such a long time. Something must have happened, we all agreed. Perhaps the Germans had announced a curfew to keep civilians off the streets and there had been no way for our sewer workers to pass undetected into the sewer. Perhaps they had been detained for some reason or other. There were any number of explanations for their absence, and none of them were good.

Another day passed without a visit from Socha and Wroblewski, and our mood darkened considerably. For a few days more, there would be enough to eat. And yet we despaired. As we sat in the evening, my father did not even bother to take out his map and solicit opinions about the war, because there was no new information to add to the last discussion and also because no one could offer a positive report. There was nothing to do but wait and wonder.

When the adults were quiet, I pressed my imaginary friend, Melek, for an explanation. "What do you think, Melek?" I said. "They have been killed?"

"It will be okay," he said. "They are coming."

For a fourth day, the sewer workers did not come, and our

thoughts turned to the worst. Had our friends been captured at long last? At the very end of the German occupation? After everything we had been through? There was no other explanation for their continued absence from our chamber. We would have mourned for them, except that to do so would have meant to accept their sorry fate; so instead we prayed. Here again I encouraged Berestycki to do the job for us, because I believed he was closest to God. I said, "Pray, Jacob, pray." There was the same urgency in my voice as there had been on the day of the great flood, such was my concern for my beloved Socha.

The following morning, July 23, Stefek Wroblewski appeared through our tunnel, as if by some final miracle. It was my mother's birthday, whether by a great coincidence or a divine hand that had somehow grabbed Berestycki's dream. We were overjoyed to see our friend, who told us of the fighting in the streets of Lvov. He had been anxious to escape the bombing, and so he sought refuge in the one place he knew the fighting would not find him, the sewer. *Our* sewer. It was like a second home to him, he said. He knew he would be safe with us, he said. And so he came.

Wroblewski had not been in contact with Socha, but he assured us that our friend was safe. Then he offered his account of the fighting. My father and the others tried to place this new information alongside what they already knew and made their own assumptions about the progress of the Russians and the retreat of the Germans. Later that day, with Stefek still in our company, Korsarz separated from our group in an effort to gather more information. He crawled through the pipes to an area of the sewer that would allow him to see and hear for himself the activity in the streets, and in this way he listened to a group of Russian soldiers assessing their circumstance. He pushed aside a manhole cover so he could see and hear clearly. He concluded that the Russians had indeed captured the city and returned to our group to report this happy discovery.

This was indeed good news, but we were cautious in our rejoicing. We knew what had happened in Tarnopol. Wroblewski, too, was wary of the situation. He decided to return to the streets, to hopefully locate Socha and Kowalow and see about our rescue, but he told us to remain in the Palace until he returned. We did not wish to be so reckless that our premature celebration would lead to our execution, so we agreed to wait.

Tola did not see the point of remaining in the sewer when it was clear to him that the Russians controlled the streets. He became enraged. The men were exhausted from keeping our prisoner silent and still. He kept shouting, "Let us go already! Enough!"

For another few days, there was no sign of our sewer workers. This meant that it had been nearly a week since we had seen Socha, and this was by far the longest stretch of time we had been without his company since we began our confinement. We were filled with worry, but at the same time we were filled with elation, that our liberation would be soon at hand. The two emotions were knitted as one. It was like a birthday gift to my mother, my father remarked, to receive such news on July 23. Now we had only to wait, to unwrap this present when our sewer workers told us it was safe to do so.

And so we waited. There had been no bread or other food deliveries for several days. We were getting by on our stores of coffee substitute and sugar, and these too were getting low. We could not remain in this place, in such a state of agitation, for such an indeterminate period; soon our patience would run out along with our resources. We were too excited to think about food, but in time, of course, we would need to eat.

At this point, we could hear the Russian voices overhead. Where there had once been the playful shouts and cries of children in the square by the church, there were now the stern commands of Russian officers. More and more, we became comfortable with the notion that the Russians were now in charge. More and more, we thought of venturing out into the city on our own, without the guidance of our sewer workers.

Still, we would wait for Socha and Wroblewski until we could not. We tried to keep to our routines. We woke each morning and established our sitting area. We washed. We watched as Berestycki said his morning prayers. We drank our few sips of coffee. The men took their turns guarding Tola, in the same four-hour shifts that had been established on the night of his arrival. Finally, in the early morning hours of July 27, my father took his turn with Tola while the rest of us tried to sleep. When my father completed his shift, he handed his gun to Korsarz. My father was tired and looking forward to a few hours of sleep before the rest of the day got under way. As he slept, we received the summons for which we had been waiting, praying, dreaming, hoping. . . .

Until the end of his long life, my father would say that this was his greatest regret, to have slept through the announcement that the tyranny against us had been lifted and that we were free to rejoin the world that had forsaken us so very long ago. For months and months, he had imagined this, and when it was at last upon us, he was fast asleep.

It was Socha who came for us, only he did not come to us through the usual opening. In fact, he did not come into our chamber at all. He came hollering through the sewer grate above our chamber.

"Chiger! Chiger!" Socha shouted. "You are going out! The time has come! Your freedom is at hand! Everybody out! You are free!" *Chiger! Chiger! Idźcie na gore, wychodzic—jestescie wolni!*

The words were too beautiful to be believed, but of course we believed them. We were not all awake, but the declaration found us through our sleep and we were awakened soon enough. We ran about our underground chamber in a fit of happiness. Korsarz was shaving while he was guarding Tola. My mother was already awake and beginning to prepare for the day. She shook my father to tell him of Socha's declaration, and he could not believe he had slept through such a moment.

In the commotion that followed, I cannot say for certain what happened next. Socha told us to leave everything behind and to come quickly, this I remember. He told us where to go. Korsarz led the way. For some reason, we could not exit through the manhole directly over our heads, so we crawled and crawled through the wet pipes. Through the forty-centimeter pipes. Through the seventy-centimeter pipes. The forties, as we called them, were not so difficult as they had been on the way in. We were all so much thinner than we had been a year earlier. Now we had no trouble slipping through these tight spaces.

Pawel and I crawled just behind Korsarz. My mother was at our heels. Behind us came Weinbergova, Klara, and Halina, followed by Tola, Berestycki, Orenbach, and finally my father. Never before had a group of eleven individuals crawled so quickly through these narrow pipes. It was not such a long way. Before we knew it, we had climbed a small ladder and had arrived at the manhole opening Socha had described.

We did not know it just yet, but we had reached a small court-yard behind a cluster of apartment buildings, where a large crowd had gathered. Korsarz climbed through first, and then we followed in order. When it was my turn, Socha reached a hand to lift me from the manhole opening, and with this hand he hoisted me toward him in a great hug. He twirled me about inside this hug, and I was dizzy with emotion. I had to close my eyes to the brightness of the day, and this of course combined with the twirling and contributed to my dizziness. I could hear clapping and shouts of congratulations, but I could not open my eyes. When I tried to do so, everything was colored in orange and red. It was like looking through a photographic negative. I could make out only vague shapes, so I closed my eyes and listened to the sounds of our new freedom and imagined what it might look like.

Next, Socha set me down and reached for Pawel, whom he also collected in a great hug. This I was told, because still I could not see. Little Pawel, he was so scared by all of the excitement and all of the people. He screamed in terror, and Socha held him close and covered him with hugs and kisses. When my mother climbed through next, Pawel raced to her and began tugging on her coat. He shouted, "I want to go back! I want to go back!" *Ja chce isc z powrotem!* He had been so long in the sewer that it had become his entire world. He did not understand all of this noise and commotion. He could not comprehend all of these people, or the open space of the courtyard, or the bright sunshine that seemed to me to wash everything in shades of red and orange. At one point, he let go of my mother's coat and attempted to climb back through the manhole opening, until Socha once again lifted him up and tried to comfort him.

Poor Pawel had been so young when we descended into the sewer. And he was still so young. For him, it was as if he had spent his entire life there. It was the only world he knew. This other world, this aboveground *outside* world, was strange and terrifying to him. It was a logical thing that he wanted to go back, but Socha was able to calm him down after a short time, after which Pawel did a remarkable thing. He raced to one of the Russian soldiers who had assembled to greet us and threw himself at the soldier's feet. He began kissing this soldier's muddy boots, as if in gratitude.

One by one, the members of our underground family climbed through the manhole opening. Each time, there would be applause and shouts and astonished cries. We must have looked pitiable, our clothes reduced to rags, our faces worn and hollow, our spines bent and nearly broken. But we were alive! We emerged like cavemen, like some band of primal animals, but we were alive! The people, they could not believe it.

Finally, my father's head appeared through the opening, and the shouts and cries seemed louder still. My eyes had not yet adjusted to the daylight, but I could tell this excitement was for my father. I heard people calling his name: "Chiger!" He had been well-known throughout the ghetto before the final liquidation, and probably Socha had told of his efforts in organizing our underground escape. Then Socha called out to my father as he stood to his full height for the first time in fourteen months and called him the captain of our shipwreck. The two men embraced, and there was once again applause and congratulations all around. I opened my eyes to this and could see their shadowy figures well enough.

Tola had been led away from this scene, probably by Wroblewski, so it was now only the ten of us in the open air of this courtyard. The ten of us, and Leopold Socha, our guardian angel. This was our underground family, and we were fairly surrounded

by dozens of Russian soldiers and neighborhood residents and local officials and other workers. We stood in the center of a makeshift circle, and Socha lifted his arms and indicated our group.
"These are my Jews!" he said proudly. "This is my work." *To sa
moi żydzi, i to jest moja praca!*

Slowly, the onlookers who had gathered to witness our resur-
rection began to disperse, but not before a few of them came to
speak to us, to hear firsthand some of the stories that Socha had
already shared with them and to share with us some of their own
observations. A woman who introduced herself as the superinten-
dent of one of the apartment buildings backing onto this courtyard told us that she had often detected the aroma of soup coming
up through the sewer grates, just over where we had been sitting.
Another woman remarked that during winter there seemed always
to be only the thinnest patch of snow near our manhole, as if it had
been melted away by the warmth from our bodies below or from
the constant flame of our Primus stove. Everywhere else, the snow
was piled thick and full, but here in this one spot it was thin and
soft.

Soon, the other people disappeared into their own lives, and it
was Socha and the ten of us once more. In this group, my parents
found each other, and then they found us children, and we clung to
one another as if the rest of this aboveground world had fallen
away.

One of the main reasons Socha had been so long in coming was
that he had been making sure that the Germans had indeed been
put down by the Russians and that it would be safe for us to walk
the streets once more. Another reason was that he wanted to have

everything organized for us once we left the sewer. He knew we no longer had any money. He knew we did not have a place to live or any proper clothes to wear, so he set about organizing our lives aboveground just as he had organized our lives underground. We learned this once the crowd of onlookers dispersed.

Socha had worked diligently over the previous few days preparing a new home for us. One of the buildings that backed onto this courtyard had been occupied by the Germans during the war, but now that the Russians were in control the building was empty. Socha had arranged for us to occupy the first floor of this building. He had gathered a full supply of furnishings for us as well. Chairs, tables, beds, and bedding . . . whatever he could think we might need. We had not thought of these things during our time underground because they were secondary to our survival, but Socha was clever enough to think of them on our behalf. Such was the depth of his commitment to us that he would make this extra effort even after our survival had been assured.

There were four rooms on the first floor of our building. Socha assigned my family to one room. Korsarz and Berestycki occupied the second room; Halina Wind and Klara Keler occupied the third room; and Chaskiel Orenbach and Genia Weinberg occupied the fourth room.

Almost immediately, some of the onlookers took pity on us and brought us food and other necessities. By the light of day, we must have looked frightening. Pawel and I especially became the objects of great concern. Our cheeks were pale, our arms and legs as thin as reeds. The hollows beneath our eyes were as deep and empty as a corpse's. Our feet were wrapped in rags and newspapers, since we had no shoes. Even our hair, which we had taken great pains to brush and keep clean, appeared matted and unkempt, like a bird's nest under siege. To the other adults in our party, who had become accustomed to our appearance, we were only Krysha and Pawelek, the indomitable children of Ignacy and Paulina, but to these strangers we were an unbelievable sight. One kind lady brought us a jar of honey, which Pawel and I devoured like hungry bear cubs. This woman was astounded that two small children could live in such desperate circumstances for such a long period of time and that we appeared before her as a pair of wild waifs. The very least she could do, she said, was to bring this jar of honey.

Others brought bread and barley. Others, fruit and sandwiches. Whatever people brought, we accepted it gladly. Truly, we were overwhelmed by the kindness of these good people, almost all of them Aryans who had been brainwashed by the Germans into believing that Jews were the lowest form of life. And yet here they were, trying to help. Two of my father's friends from his athletic club came by with whiskey and kielbasa, which the adults consumed eagerly. Of course, we were careful not to eat or drink too much too quickly, because our stomachs had been inactive for so long. Indeed, these treats and delicacies were a welcome kindness, but we longed for the simple diet we had left behind. We had been so long without a visit from Socha and Wroblewski that we had barely eaten any of the basic staples over the past several days. We had not had any bread. Our soup had no ingredients but boiled water and maybe some onions. For fourteen months we had been undernourished, but for the past week we had been starved, so we longed for just a bite of bread, a sip of coffee, a drink of water.

The next day, my father returned to the sewer with Socha and Wroblewski to gather some of our left-behind provisions. If you had told my father he would be returning so soon to his underground prison, he would not have believed it. But there was a good amount of food in the Palace, which we now urgently needed. There were other items that could be of use to us aboveground as well, such as pots and pans and the carbide lanterns that had for so long been our only source of light. So my father revisited our underground home, to rummage through our few things, to see what food might be salvageable. It was a desperate measure, but we were certainly desperate. And we would remain so for some time.

Ten

❦

WHAT HAPPENED NEXT

The story of our endurance did not end in that courtyard on July 27, 1944, just as it cannot end here in these pages. Already, I am the last survivor of my underground family, but our story continues in the retelling. It continues in our legacy and in the lives we leave behind.

My firsthand memories of the beginning days and weeks of our new life aboveground are mostly a blur, but they are complemented by the handed-down memories of my parents and others. I do recall the initial exhilaration of first freedom that found us immediately following our liberation. Such a wave of excitement! Such relief! And underneath and all around was such a grand happiness as cannot fully be described or understood. The memories reach beyond simple emotion: I can still picture the eerie, unfamiliar light as my eyes struggled to adjust to the outside world. For days, I could see only through the orange red film that colored my first steps aboveground. It made me so dizzy! I can still remember the luxury of my first night in a proper bed, which despite our otherwise drab furnishings was like staying in a world-class hotel. And I vividly remember holding a bouquet of fresh flowers for the first time in the longest while and burying my nose in the scent and thinking our troubles were over.

In this I was premature, and it was only a few days more before I realized that we had merely traded one set of troubles for another. I did not recognize this right away, but soon enough. My parents probably realized it the moment we reached daylight. They were optimists, which explained how they were able to grab the smallest piece of hope and pull our family along by its thread, but they were also realists. They knew we would now have to think about things like finding a place to sleep and something to eat. They knew the many kindnesses of these strangers would soon fall away. They knew we would continue to struggle, only now it would be a different struggle. Now it would be a struggle to live under a regime that had already marked us as an enemy.

The primary benefit to our time in the sewer was that we struggled together. Now our underground family had simply decamped to new quarters, and we continued as one. We were once again under Soviet rule, a hardship we now accepted as a better alternative only to the killing rule of the Germans. We were free only by comparison to how we lived in the sewer, but of course we were not so free after all. The Russian government was suspicious of all Jews who had managed to survive the Nazi regime, so we were closely monitored. Also, the Soviets still recognized my father as bourgeois, which was as much of a crime after German rule as it had been before, even though we now lived like peasants. We had no money, no prospects. Friends and family members who might have been in a position to help us become reestablished had either fled or been killed. Our circumstances were almost as desperate as they had been in the ghetto, only now they did not seem so desperate because of everything that had happened in between.

Sometimes, shop owners would take pity on us as we passed by their windows and offer us a piece of fruit or some other sweet, which we accepted gratefully. At other times, we would find food in the street and considered ourselves lucky for the discovery. Of course, my mother did not like it when we ate food from the street, but we were so hungry. What could she do? We were very nearly homeless by the standards of today, and certainly impoverished by the standards of 1944 Lvov, which was now called Lviv.

Sometimes we would be visited by the Russian soldiers who had gathered in the courtyard the day Socha led us out of the sewer. Usually it was the soldier who had received Pawel's emotional outburst and another one or two of his friends. He was so moved, this one soldier, so touched by Pawel's outpouring, that he felt a strong and immediate connection to our family, so he came to sit with us and to share his food. Pawel always liked it when these young men came because it felt to him that he was the one being visited. It felt to him as though they were his friends.

On one of these visits, Pawel's soldier caught my father's attention. Most likely this was the first time my father had been at home during such a visit, because usually he was out looking for work or for food. This time, though, my father crossed the room to shake the soldier's hand, and as he did the soldier said, *"Am 'hu."* It was the first time I heard this word. It is a Hebrew word, difficult to translate. It is almost like a signal, passed from one Jew to another, a powerful acknowledgment that you are part of the same nation.

After the war, we heard this word all the time. It followed us all the way to Israel almost thirteen years later, where people would still catch one another's attention and speak this powerful word: *Am 'hu*. In this word was a shared look, a shared past, a shared identity. In this word was a hope for our future. And this was where I heard it for the first time, in our small, sparsely furnished room adjacent to the courtyard where I walked in daylight for the first time in nearly a year and a half, spoken by a kindly Russian soldier who was only now admitting to my family that he, too, was Jewish.

By the end of our first week of freedom, my father found a job at the health club where he used to work, only he did not earn a salary. He was paid with vouchers that he could exchange only for food, which he would forsake for himself and take home for my mother and us children instead. If there was any left, my father would offer it to Klara or Halina or Genia before taking any for himself. The others found work here and there, and what they had in plenty they, too, shared with the group. There was still a surplus of potatoes, which my father had managed to collect from the Palace among our few other provisions, so my mother made latkes for Pawel and me to sell on the streets. Also, we discovered a container of empty shoe polish canisters in an abandoned store, and these we filled with shoe polish and sold as well. We did not consider this begging. Rather, it was a way to make something out of nothing in order to survive. We found that the more miserable and disheveled our appearance, the more latkes and shoe polish we managed to sell, only this was not a strategy, it was our reality.

We were still hungry, but I would not accept my mother's share of our food. In the sewer, she would not take her small bite of bread or her few sips of water. She would give them instead to me and Pawel. But it was not enough to really share, and we were so desperately hungry that I did not think to quarrel with her about this. I was merely grateful for the nourishment. Now, I was a little more mature than I had been in the sewer, a little less selfish. Now, there was a little bit more, and still my mother would not eat. Now she would continue to give her portion to me and Pawel, and I started to worry about her health. She was so thin! I had become a very nervous person, and this caused me great anxiety, that my mother would not eat. I decided I would not accept her portions. I said, "If you do not eat, I will not eat." And in this way I forced her to eat.

We could not afford new clothes, so we collected thankfully the few simple items that were donated to us by kindly families and made the best of whatever we had worn throughout our time in the sewer. It was a wonder to me what my mother and the other women could do with a little bit of cleaning and sewing. We looked almost presentable in the rags that had survived our underground ordeal. I thought back to those crisp, clean shirts Socha had stolen for us some months earlier and longed for the feel of new clothes on my back. Until then, I continued to wear with great pride my precious green sweater, which my mother lovingly cleaned and repaired. Proper shoes, however, we could not afford, and I walked barefoot or in homemade shoes fashioned from rags and newspapers. Even this I did not mind at first. I did not even notice the pitying stares of the others as my family passed on the street. That is, I did not notice until those stares were coming from the other children. Suddenly, I was embarrassed by our situation. In the beginning, the other children teased me for living in the sewer with the rats and the waste and the filth, and I shrank in the face of their taunts. I may have been strong enough to stand up to the subhuman elements of the sewer, but I was not so strong that I could shoulder the jeers of the very children I longed to befriend.

My mother registered me for the first grade in August 1944, only a few weeks after our liberation, and at first the woman who helped her fill out the paperwork could not understand that we were Jewish. She had been under the impression that all Jews living in Lvov had been exterminated, and here was this woman and her eight-year-old daughter filling in the space marked "Jewish" on the official form. The school registrar was so surprised that she would not at first allow me to enroll, until my mother appealed this decision to the school principal. Here it was decided that I could indeed attend school but that it would probably be better for my mother not to advertise that we were Jewish. I would be registered as Jewish, but we would not talk about it. Such was the lingering nature of anti-Semitism in the hearts of the Aryan population that remained in the city. Such was the awareness of the other children, that they were able to guess at my past and ignore me in kind. And such were the depths of our misery and misfortune that my mother chose to follow this woman's advice and bury our Jewish heritage in this one regard. It was difficult for her to accept, that after somehow surviving the tyranny of Nazi Germany, we still could not live openly and proudly as Jews. Yet she had no choice but to accept it, because this, too, was our reality.

A part of me was terribly excited to be attending a proper school at long last, but at the same time there was another part that dreaded the isolation I felt each day. I was so lonely! The other children knew I was different. One day, a girl asked in a mean way why I was not writing from right to left, instead of from left to right. I did not know what she meant by this. I did not know how to speak or write Hebrew at that time and so did not recognize this as a kind of taunt until my mother explained it to me. This was typical of how I was treated by the other children. I was a curiosity to some and an irritation to others. I managed to make one or two friends, but for the most part I kept to myself during the school day. In this way, I was in hiding, still.

I remember feeling so ashamed of my makeshift boots that I raced to school ahead of the other children and tucked my feet beneath my desk. It was difficult enough to be known among the other schoolchildren as the girl who lived in the sewer. This was embarrassing. It was difficult enough to be marked as Jewish and made to feel somehow inferior to the other children. This was upsetting. I did not want to compound the teasing by allowing anyone to see what I was wearing. When I finally did receive a pair of proper boots, I was so proud. Now I took my time going to school. Now I walked up the aisle to my desk as if I were a model on a runway, and when I sat down I left my feet in the aisles where everyone could see I was appropriately shod.

Very quickly, the others in our underground family began to realize they might have an easier time in their hometowns, and one by one they announced plans to seek a better life elsewhere. Jacob Berestycki, for example, had only moved east to Lvov during the first Soviet occupation to escape the Germans. Now he returned to his native Lodz, where he hoped to find family and better opportunities. There he remet and married a childhood friend. Together they had two children, a girl and a boy, and eventually settled in Paris.

Berestycki was the first to leave, but the others would follow. If the putrid Peltew was the current that ran through our time in the sewer, then it can be said that many tributaries flowed from that river. Our group was carried away by these currents to all corners of the globe. We did not stay so terribly long together once Socha placed us in these four rooms in the abandoned building overlooking the courtyard, probably only a few weeks. We would never again know such an intimate bond outside of our own families, but it was inevitable that we would go our separate ways.

We did not all separate, of course. Klara Keler and Korsarz the Pirate, Mundek Margulies, were married soon after the liberation and moved to the Polish town of Gliwice. I liked that they were together and would now be a family. This did not surprise my parents, who of course knew that a romance had sparked between Klara and Korsarz during our time underground, but it was a complete surprise to me and Pawel. We did not know of such things as romance. We knew only the love of family, and in this one respect I was overjoyed that two people who had become so dear to me would now be husband and wife. It was like something out of a storybook, I thought. They also had two children, also a girl and a boy, and eventually settled in London.

There was another romance to emerge from our underground group: Chaskiel Orenbach and Genia Weinberg were married soon after the liberation and moved to Lodz as well. After a short time, they settled in Germany, where they had a daughter. No one would have guessed that these two would find each other in this way or that they would make a life and a home surrounded by the very people who had persecuted us. They were both difficult personalities, but together they had been through a lot. Genia lost her husband and two small children, including the one she carried secretly and had to smother in our underground chamber. Chaskiel lost his brother and the rest of his family as well. They suffered on the common ground of our Palace chamber.

Halina Wind, we did not see so much after the war. She moved first to Gliwice in the company of a friend, and after that we fell out of touch. It was not until several years later that we learned she had moved to the United States, where she lived a long and healthy life. She married and had two children, also a girl and a boy.

Tola, who had been a reluctant member of our group for the last days of our confinement, would return to the Russian army, but he was soon killed.

Our guardian angel sewer workers were also carried away by the aftercurrents of postwar Europe. We finally met Jerzy Kowalow a day or two after our liberation. He had worked so long and at such risk on our behalf, yet during all this time we could not even say what he looked like. My father had met him only once, during his initial descent into the sewer when he first encountered Socha, but now he was anxious to remake his acquaintance and to thank Kowalow personally for his role in our safekeeping.

Socha and Wroblewski would remain our good and trusted friends, although in the case of the latter that friendship was briefly threatened by charges of treason. It was discovered soon after liberation that Wroblewski had belonged to an anti-Communist group, a punishable offense under Russian rule. It did not matter that Wroblewski had not associated with this group for several years, only that he had at one time. Socha, too, belonged to a similar organization, but only Wroblewski had been arrested and charged.

A group of us went to the Russian prosecutor to argue Wroblewski's case: my parents, Pawel, myself, Korsarz, Klara, and Halina. We thought if we spoke highly of Wroblewski's bravery in helping to hide us from the dreaded Nazis, the prosecutor might look favorably on Wroblewski's case. We thought that we could help with his safekeeping, for once. My father also contacted a journalist friend who worked for a Russian newspaper, *Ogoniok*. The man's name was Bielajew, and he agreed to print the story of our life in the sewer and the sewer workers' role in our survival. These two initiatives contributed at least in some small way to Wroblewski's release.

Meanwhile, Leopold Socha and his family quietly fled to the Polish city of Przemys. He believed that the suspicions that were now following Wroblewski would soon find him as well. We were sad to see him go, but soon my father recognized that we too could not stay in Lviv. Already, my father had been visited by Russian officials on a few occasions, and it was becoming apparent that he was some kind of target. They were very organized, the Russians, very efficient. Certainly they realized that my father had his own business before the war. Always, because of this, my father was worried he would be sent to Siberia. One night in February 1945 he heard from some friends that there was a Russian official looking to arrest him, so he came home and said, "We have to run."

We did not question this. We gathered our few things and took a carriage to the train station, where we boarded a cattle car for Poland. There were other people in this car, dozens as I recall, and we were pressed so close together that I could hear the breathing of the strangers closest to me as we moved slowly through the night. Some of the people had permission from the Russian government to leave, and others, like us, were looking to leave without permission. Before the train left the station, we could hear a Russian official calling my father's name: "Chiger! Chiger!" This confirmed that we had been right to leave. Of course, my father did not answer, hoping that we could pass anonymously among all these other people, and soon the train started to move.

It took us three weeks to make a journey into Poland that now takes forty-five minutes. The way was difficult because many of the bridges and tunnels had not been repaired since the war. On what was now the Russian side of the border, there had been considerable damage. The conditions were also difficult because it was winter and because there were so many of us traveling in such a confined space. It was as if we were in the sewer once more. It was terribly cold, this I remember most of all. I had a coat, my beloved green sweater, and my proper boots. We did not know the journey would take so long. We had only a few tins of sardines, and soon we had eaten our way through them. From time to time, the train would stop and we would get out and stretch our legs. My father used this time to go out in search of additional food. Some of the people made fires in this cattle car, which we used to warm ourselves and to do some simple cooking. My father would take snow and warm it in the empty sardine tins, just as he had done to purify our drinking water in the sewer. In so many ways, this was like the sewer all over again, yet it was because of our experience in the sewer that we were able to endure such as this. The other people were so cold, so hungry, so desperate, but the four of us were okay. We thought, This is not so bad.

Finally, we arrived in Przemys, which was not far from the border, on the Polish side. It had not been our plan to get off the train in Przemys, but the journey had been difficult. We were at last safe in Poland, and it was said that the rail passage would be a little bit better now that we were in Poland, where the bridges and tunnels that had been damaged by the bombing were mostly repaired. But we knew that Socha had settled here and thought we could visit with him as we considered our next move, which is what we did. We ended up staying with Socha and his family for a week or so, and it was during this time that Wanda Socha finally warmed to us and began to look past the fact that we were Jewish. She had been helpful to us during our time in the sewer only because Socha had insisted on it, but here in Przemys she showed a genuine kindness. She became fond of my family. She liked that my father took time to help her daughter, Stefcia, with her homework. Just as he had done with me in the sewer, he worked patiently with Stefcia, teaching her math, Latin, history. Wanda Socha looked on and could see that my father was a good person, that we were all good people, wanting the same things in life: to live freely among friends and family.

We were happy to be reunited with Socha in such an intimate way. Now we were refugees together. He talked to my father constantly about his plans for the future, about the redemption he owed to his role as our protector, about his faith. He valued my father's advice. And he adored me and my brother, now as before. This much had not changed, only now he was more a beloved uncle than a benevolent authority figure. And his admiration for my mother and the stoic way she cared for her baby chicks had only deepened in the months since our liberation.

It was a glorious time, to be together again under such pleasant terms, under one roof. Jewish, Catholic . . . it did not matter. We were two families living as one, and it was with heavy hearts that we continued on to Krakow, where my father was determined to rebuild our lives. We arrived there on March 18, 1945, ready to make a new start. My father even changed our family name from Chiger to Chyrowski, thinking if his name sounded more Polish, he would have a better chance of finding a job. When we arrived in Krakow, we had only an address given to us by my mother's uncle. At this address there was only one room, with maybe twenty people sleeping on the floor. It was as if all the refugees from the eastern part of Poland had this same address. It was the opposite of the exodus that took place during the first part of the war, when Polish Jews immigrated east, choosing the oppression of Communist Russia over the tyranny of Nazi Germany. Now we moved west, choosing the uncertain freedom of what remained of Poland over the continued Soviet oppression in our former Polish territory.

It was in Krakow that we learned Socha and his family had left Przemys to join Klara and Korsarz in the town of Gliwice, where Socha hoped to establish a tavern. It had been a lifelong dream, Socha wrote to my father, to operate a small tavern. He was excited to finally have this opportunity, an opportunity provided in no small measure by our time in the sewer, because Socha used his savings from my father's payments to establish his business. We were all so pleased that our dear friend and benefactor would be able to leave behind the misdeeds of his past and live a meaningful life in a quiet town, and to know that we had contributed to his redemption just as he had contributed so mightily to our salvation. We talked of Socha and his family often, and whenever we did it was with great warmth and gratitude that our paths had crossed so fortuitously at such a desperate time. We wrote back to Socha that we would visit at the earliest opportunity, to toast the success of his new tavern, to celebrate with Klara and Korsarz this exciting new chapter in the life of our extended underground family.

And then, on May 13, 1945, less than two months after we said our last good-bye, we received a telegram from Korsarz with the devastating news that Socha had been killed the day before in a tragic accident. He was riding bicycles with his daughter, Stefcia, when a Russian army truck approached recklessly along the streets of Gliwice. Socha was struck and killed by the truck, but somehow Stefcia was spared. According to the police report, Socha's body fell over a manhole opening, and his blood could be seen dripping into the sewer below.

I was standing with my mother when she read this telegram and she sank to the floor in sorrow. At first she could not say what she had just read, so I looked at the telegram myself. I saw only enough to know that something terrible had happened to our Socha, and I too began to cry. The news was like a punch in the stomach. This is a cliché, I realize, but this was how it felt, and this alone was worse than the pain I felt over all the other tragedies I had been made to experience. Uncle Kuba, Babcia, my grandparents, my cousins, my aunts, my uncles . . . their tragic deaths did not add up to the pain of this one loss. To be forced from our apartment and sent to live in a series of smaller and smaller dwellings and eventually to the ghetto barracks and to the sewer below . . . these tragedies did not add up to the pain of this one loss. To be stripped of our family dignity, our family fortune, our family heritage . . . these tragedies too did not add up to the pain of this one loss.

To lose someone so dear in a time of relative peace, on the cusp of relative prosperity and happiness, it was a particular agony. I thought back to that day toward the end of our time in the sewer when Socha took me by the hand to find that small sliver of daylight, to ease me from the depths of depression. I closed my eyes and pictured his big, bright smile. I heard his voice. I felt the positive energy he brought with him into our Palace chamber each day when he arrived with food and provisions and news of the war. I considered all of this and held fast to my mother. Together, we were crying, crying, crying. Little Pawel, I do not think he knew exactly what had happened, but he began to cry as well, as did my father when he arrived home and learned the sad news.

We went immediately to Gliwice, and as soon as we arrived we went to the place where Socha had fallen. The street had been cleaned of his blood, but Korsarz indicated where it had been dripping into the sewer below. This was a meaningful symbol to our underground family, as we stood in silence and remembered the great bravery and humanity this man had demonstrated over our long confinement.

Such an irony! Such a sadness! I was still a mere child, and so too young to weep for Wanda Socha and her daughter. Now, as an adult, my heart breaks for poor Stefcia, to have witnessed her father's frightful death at such close range. She was only twelve years old! It breaks too for poor Wanda, to lose her husband when he was finally at peace with himself and excited about his prospects. But back then I thought only of what my family had lost. What *I* had lost.

Our guardian angel.

Our Socha.

In his memoir, my father wrote that on Leopold Socha's tombstone it should be inscribed, "He who saves one life saves the entire world." *Kto ratuje jedno zycie—ratuje caly swiat.* Such was the strength and character of our beloved Socha. Indeed, every year on the anniversary of his death, I light a *Yahrtzeit* candle in his memory and I consider these words as I prepare to chant the mourner's Kaddish. I think of Socha and the life he lived before he met us, the lives he saved with his protection, the lives we all managed to build for ourselves after the war . . . and in this way I honor his memory.

As for the life my family built after the war, it continued for the next twelve years in Krakow, where my father eventually found work in an office, where my mother reunited with her sister, where Pawel and I resumed our childhoods, and where soon we were no longer worrying constantly that we would be tortured or terrorized by some Nazi or Soviet official. Soon we were almost back to normal, although life could never be the same as it was for us at Kopernika 12, when Lvov was a thriving city filled with such hope and purpose. Still, we had come through an unimaginable hardship and so could not complain. This became like a theme for my family, that we should not complain or advertise our suffering, that whatever difficulty we were encountering was nothing compared with the difficulties just past or the difficulties of others.

When it was just the four of us, we spoke often about our time in the sewer, but we hardly spoke of it at all when we were with friends and family. There would be a story in the newspaper that might call to mind an event in the ghetto, or there would be a smell that would take us back to how we used to live, or a taste of soup that reminded us of the soup Weinbergova used to cook for us, or a resemblance between some stranger on the street and one of our underground family members. Together we would consider this connection, and together we would remember. It was a time we might have chosen to forget, but it was a part of us after all, and it was not as if every memory were unpleasant. There were happy memories, too. The songs and satires my father used to write. The jokes Korsarz used to tell. The warmth and security we would feel whenever Socha came to nourish us with food or news from the outside. In truth, we never laughed as hard as we did during the comic moments that found us during our time underground, probably because the contrast between joy and sorrow was so great that we seized every small piece of happiness and coaxed it to appear larger still, and so we were eager to laugh over these same moments again and again in memory.

In 1957, we left Poland for Israel, where my father believed he could improve our circumstance. We went first to Gliwice to say good-bye to Wanda Socha, to see if perhaps there was anything we could do for her. She was grateful for our visit, but of course she did not need anything. To demonstrate this point, she took us to her kitchen and pointed to a large coal stove in the corner. It was an old stove, and it looked as though it had not been used for many years. She opened the heavy iron door and pointed inside. She said, "Do not worry about me. I have everything I need here. Until the end of my life, I will have enough."

My father looked inside and saw bundles of neatly stacked zloty notes and a good deal of the fine jewelry and silverware he had paid to Socha for saving our lives. Whatever our guardian angel had spent to buy our food and provisions, whatever he had spent from his own pockets to pay Kowalow and Wroblewski so they would not know that our money had run out, whatever he had spent on his small tavern before he was so cruelly taken from us, there was still a small fortune left over. And my father did not begrudge Wanda Socha this small fortune. At one time it was all he had in the world, but now it would be used to care for the wife and daughter of his beloved Poldju. And that was as it should be, he said. Indeed, my father told me later that he was grateful to learn the money was still there, that it had amounted to something after all.

In Israel, nobody talked about the war. Nobody talked about the Holocaust. Whatever we experienced, however we had come to this place, it was in the past and not to be discussed. Such was the attitude of the Jews we met in our adopted homeland, and in many ways it echoed the attitude we had developed at home; however, here we numbered in the tens of thousands. Everywhere you looked, there was a survivor of one kind or another. Around every corner there came a tale to match our own. On the bus or in a public square, if you happened to see a number burned into the forearm of a man or woman, marking him or her as a concentration camp survivor, you dared not mention it. You looked away in embarrassment. It took me a long time to get used to this and to weigh it against my own experience. Already, we did not talk about our time in the sewer except among ourselves. Already, we had put the years of the German occupation behind us. Yes, it was a miracle that we survived, but everybody had the same miracle. Nobody survived easily. To be here among us, still, meant to have suffered along the way.

I was a young woman when we arrived in Israel, and the "inside" emotional life I began keeping to myself during the first Soviet occupation had deepened over the years. There could be months now when my family would not speak a word of our time in the sewer. It was buried beneath the surface of our lives, like the sewer itself. I struggled to understand this, and as I did I began to realize that everybody carried a heavy bag behind them. All around, there were Jews who had survived by some separate constellation of miracles. All around was the heavy baggage of a time of great upheaval.

It would not be fair to suggest that our bag was heavier than most. It was just ours, that is all, and I would carry it proudly, going forward.

Krystyna Chiger survived the Holocaust by hiding with her family in the sewers of Lvov, Poland, for fourteen months. A retired dentist, she lives on Long Island.

Daniel Paisner has collaborated on many books, including the *New York Times* bestselling *Last Man Down: A Firefighter's Story of Survival and Escape from the World Trade Center.*